CW00741425

NOTTINGHAMSHIRE – UNUSUAL & QUIRKY

NOTTINGHAMSHIRE
Unusual & Quirky

Andrew Beardmore

HALSGROVE

First published in Great Britain in 2015

British Library Cataloguing-in-Publication Data
A CIP record for this title is available from the British Library

ISBN 978 0 85704 266 8

HALSGROVE
Halsgrove House,
Ryelands Business Park,
Bagley Road, Wellington, Somerset TA21 9PZ
Tel: 01823 653777 Fax: 01823 216796
email: sales@halsgrove.com
website: www.halsgrove.com

Printed and bound in China by Everbest Printing Co Ltd

Nottinghamshire – Unusual and Quirky

Welcome to *Nottinghamshire – Unusual and Quirky*. This is the second book in a new series that calls to mind that classic series of travel books called *The King's England*, written in the 1930s by Stapleford-born Arthur Mee, since each volume in Mee's series was suffixed with "*There have been many books on <insert county>, but never one like this…*" Well the very same tag line could be applied to this book, as some of its elements are certainly unique. Having said that, the book still has plenty to offer in terms of conventional reference, but it delivers this in a lateral and humorous format never seen before.

Essentially, then, the book is comprised of two main sections which are called *Conventional Nottinghamshire* and *Quirky Nottinghamshire*. The *Conventional Nottinghamshire* section kicks off with some county maps along with key facts and figures relating to the county – such as county town, population, highest point, key industries and famous sons and daughters. The facts are then followed by a history of the Nottinghamshire *area* from the Stone Age to the 11th century – by which time Nottinghamshire, along with most of England's counties had been officially formed – after which the last one thousand years of county history is covered, bringing us up-to-date and into the 21st century. Nevertheless, in keeping with the title of the book, the *Nottinghamshire County History* also has a number of small, but appropriately historical "Quirk Alerts" interspersed, too; like an anecdote called "George's Grill" showing up in prehistoric times, along with an 18th century nod to *Game of Thrones* and a lateral 19th century reference to *Vampire Diaries*!

So, thus far into the book we have covered the facts, figures, maps and history of Nottinghamshire. However, it is at this point that the *Conventional* section ends and the *Quirky* section begins … and it is here that we realistically begin to earn the "*… but never one like this …*" tag line. For although the *Quirky Nottinghamshire* section delivers some "seen it before" place-name origins and historic trivia, it does so via several twists. For starters, it doesn't cover place-name etymology like most traditional reference books do, and it certainly doesn't focus on the more well-known county places, either – although don't assume they'll all be missed out; that rather depends, as we'll see shortly.

As for the reason for this apparent "stick a pin in a map" approach, this is because the history and trivia snippets in this section of the book are driven by a quirky poem, called a Shire-Ode. Told in rhyming verse, the Shire-Ode portrays the eccentric nature of imaginary inhabitants of Nottinghamshire. But as an extra twist, the poem contains dozens of place-names found within the historic county, each subtly (and some not so subtly) woven into the tale – and it is these place-names upon which the *Quirky Nottinghamshire* section focuses. Firstly, the places have their location pin-pointed via a map of Nottinghamshire. A series of chapters then follow in (largely) alphabetical order for each place featured in the Shire-Ode – and it is here that the strangest and most interesting facts and features about each place are explored, with facts including place-name status, population, earliest recording, place-name derivation, and famous sons and daughters, and feature topics ranging from both straight and unusual history to some quite bizarre happenings … plus a lot more in between, too! As a result, you get a random almanac of places that would never ordinarily appear together – along with photographs taken to prove that these bizarrely-named places really do exist!

So, feel free to commence your obscure Nottinghamshire fact-digging; to read about some very famous people and their Nottinghamshire exploits, to read about ancient battles and, quite frankly, some ridiculous legends, too … but to hopefully have a little chuckle along the way. For example, find out which Nottinghamshire village is home to the Black Pig Dancers, which one has a gravestone commemorating a certain Harry Potter, and which village managed to somehow swap sides of the Trent in the late 16th century without rebuilding a single stone! Or discover which Nottingham suburb is home to the most burgled road in Britain and which one is the location of "the hardest pub in Britain". Alternatively, learn which village hall is haunted by an inebriated butler, and which other is haunted by Roman soldiers, an Elizabethan lady, a little boy playing a piano, and an evil bishop! Or what about finding out who lives in a place called Friezeland, which village was named after a famous early 20th century battle, or which place-name means "nook of land frequented by eagles". Then historically, there's the Nottinghamshire village that is strongly linked to the Pilgrim Fathers, another which was chosen to represent Britain as the "Festival Village" of 1951, and another that saw the chance capture of the serial killer known as the Black Panther in 1975. Or if it's bizarre that you want, find out which village sells T-shirts with an upside-down deer on them, which town is home to the Flying Bedstead and which village's wise men tried to drown an eel in a pond, keep a cuckoo captive in a hedge and put cows on thatched roofs to keep them topped up on straw!

Alternatively, check out the quirky Shire-Ode, called *Arnold's Daughter*, that drives the idiosyncratic *Quirky Nottinghamshire* section and learn how the daughter in question (Kimberley) causes poor Arnold untold stress! And if you'd like to hear *Arnold's Daughter* in song format, then go to this website: www.andybeardmore.com.

Anyway, that's the introduction completed. As you have probably gathered by now, this book is indeed "unusual and quirky"… so it's time to prime the quirkometer and pull up a pew at St Strangeways – oh, and did I mention a lethal Roman curse, an eight foot trumpet, a pub chair that increases fertility, Gretna Green-style marriages delivered by the Reverend Sweetapple, an oven made of gravestones…

Contents

Nottinghamshire Facts and Figures 8
Nottinghamshire Maps 8

Conventional Nottinghamshire: A County History 9
Prehistory 9
Romans, Anglo-Saxons and Vikings 12
From the Normans to the Wars of the Roses 20
From the Dissolution to the English Civil War 31
From the Restoration to the Industrial Revolution 37
From the Late Victorians to Present Day 44
Some Quirky Nottinghamshire Stats 50

Quirk Alerts
George's Grill 9
Budby Burrow 10
Lashes to Ashes 14
He Who Mustn't Be Conveyed 15
An Evens Chance 17
Score Draw 18
Pancakes and Chauvinism 19
Snot Funny! 19
The Bell of a Thousand Years 21
Ye Olde Legends of Inebriatelem! 23
To Dye For 24
A Blinding Sentence 24
Key Monk Business 30
Evil Exit 31
Three Wives and Twenty Five Little Whalleys 32
Out of the Frame 33
Out of Order 34
Seventh Heaven 35
The Final Hurdle 36
Eakring Rude and Eakring Crude 37
Vamping Diaries 37
The A-peel of Elopement 38
The Swan With Two Necks, The Bull and Mouth, and a Beautiful Savage! 39
All Men Must Die! 40
The Font of No Knowledge 42
In Loving Memory 42
Ann Burton, Aged 248 42
Rail Wars 43
The Forest Hackers 43
The Loot of Boot 44
Blyth and Blidworth's Blessed Blend 47
Seismic 93 48
Double Diamond 51

Quirky Nottinghamshire 52
Introducing the Shire-Ode 52
Nottinghamshire Shire-Ode: Arnold's Daughter 52
Location Map for Arnold's Daughter 54
Place-Name Table for Arnold's Daughter 54

Arnold's Daughter – A Nottingham Shire-Ode Almanac 55
Arnold 55
Awsworth 58
Threes Up: Askham, Beckingham and Bevercotes 60
Bole 62
Boughton 64
Bulwell 65
Bunny 68
Chilwell 71
Coates 73
Colston Bassett 74
Threes Up: Commonside, Kersall and Little Green 77
Colwick 78
Cromwell 81
Dunham-on-Trent 83
Eaton 85
Edingley 86
Elton 87
Everton 89
Friezeland 91
Gotham 92
Grove 95
Hayton 96
Headon 97
Holme 98
Hucknall 100
Idle 103
Kimberley 106
Kirton 109
Lenton 111
Threes Up: Ruffs, Spion Kop and Stanley 115
Mansfield 116
Maun 120
Meadows 122
Misson 124
Norton 127
Nuthall 128
Old Basford 130
Oldcotes 133
Plumtree 135
Rainworth 137
Ryton 139
Scofton 141
Scrooby 143
Sherwood Forest 146
Thorney 149
Thrumpton 150
Trent 152
Trowell 156
Upton 158

Bibliography 160

Nottinghamshire Facts and Figures

County Status: Ceremonial county and (smaller) non-metropolitan county (i.e. minus Nottingham)
County Town: Pre-1959: Nottingham Post-1959: West Bridgford
County Pop'n: 1,086,500
County Pop'n. Rank: 15th out of 48
Cities: Nottingham
Largest City: Nottingham
City Pop'n: 305,700
City Pop'n Rank: 12th English; 14nd UK
City Status: Unitary Authority
National Park: None
Other Areas: Sherwood Forest
County Area: 2,160km^2/830 sq. mi
County Area Rank: 24th out of 48
Highest Point: Newtonwood Lane (205m/669ft)
Longest River: Trent (298km/185 miles) *
Idle (42km/26 miles) **

* Passes through Notts **Entirely within Notts

Football Clubs: Nottingham Forest (Championship), Notts County (League 1), Mansfield Town (League 2), Eastwood Town (NPL Division 1 South), Worksop Town (Northern Counties East League Premier Division), Hucknall Town (Central Midlands South), Retford United (Northern Counties East League Premier Division)
Rugby Union: Nottingham RFC (RFU Champ), Newark RFC, Paviors RFC (Both Midlands 1 East)
Industries (Present): Brewing, Credit Reference, Energy, Engineering, Finance, Gaming, Insecticides, Pharmaceutical & Biotechnology, Services, Tobacco, Tourism
Industries (Past): Bicycles, Brewing, Coal Mining, Cotton, Lace, Malting, Pharmaceuticals, Soap, Tobacco, Wool
Born in Notts: Rebecca Adlington, Keith Alexander, Viv Anderson, Richard Bacon, Jamie Baulch, Richard Beckinsale, John Bird, John Blow, Richard Bonington, Jesse Boot, William Booth, Stuart Broad, Tom Browne, Jake Bugg, Samuel Butler, Ben Caunt, Ken Clarke, Eric Coates, Andrew Cole, Kris Commons, Frank Cousins, Thomas Cranmer, Leslie Crowther, Christopher Dean, Bruce Dickinson, Corinne Drewery, Carl Froch, Catherine Gore, George Green, Marshall Hall, Alister Hardy, Robert Harris, Thomas Hawkesley, Sherrie Hewson, Denzil Holles, Mathew Horne, Godfrey Hounsfield, Henry Ireton, Mary King, Harold Larwood, D.H. Lawrence, Andrea Lowe, Robert Lowe, Arthur Mee, Bertie Mee, Stanley Middleton, Samantha Morton, John Ogdon, Sam Oldham, Ian Paice, Donald Pleasence, David Pleat, Su Pollard, John Reynolds, Nathan Robertson, Thomas Robertson, Paul Sandby, Thomas Sandby, Doug Scott, Harold Shipman, Alan Sillitoe; Paul Smith, Graham Taylor, Peter Taylor, Jayne Torvill, Lee Westwood, Dale Winton

Nottinghamshire Maps

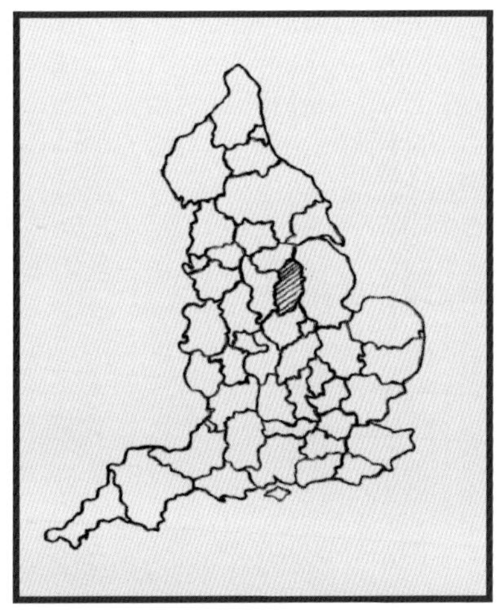

Nottinghamshire 1996-2014

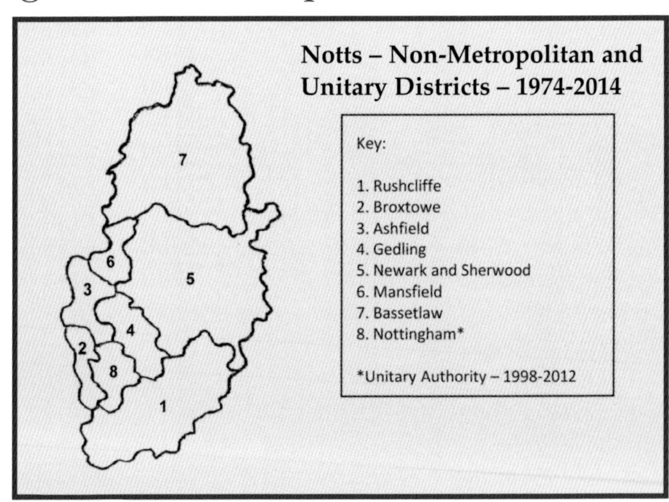

Conventional Nottinghamshire: A County History

Prehistory

The county of Nottinghamshire dates from the 11th century, and was formed towards the end of the protracted conflict between Anglo-Saxon and Viking that took place between the 9th and 11th centuries. Unsurprisingly, the name "Nottinghamshire" means "shire or district of the town of Nottingham", and is clearly derived from the place-name "Nottingham", plus the Old English word *scīr*, meaning "shire or district". The town of Nottingham, however, is much older than the shire it lends its name to – but we'll come to that shortly, for the history of the *area* of Nottinghamshire, goes back much further than that.

We'll start with the history of man in the Nottinghamshire area shortly. But before that, it is appropriate to start over 200 million years ago at the beginning of the Triassic Period – for that is when the Hemlock Stone was formed. Composed of pebbly coarse-grained sandstone, the Hemlock Stone stands completely on its own today at the eastern edge of Stapleford – although the same strata underpins most of Nottingham city centre a few miles to the east and forms the cliffs of Castle Rock on which Nottingham Castle still stands today. It is thought that the land around the stone wore away over the millennia, and the Hemlock Stone remained as it was a much harder piece of rock, with its black baryte-strengthened cap protecting its lower sandstone reaches. Other theories suggest that it was fashioned by ancient man, carving it, perhaps, as a symbol of worship or celebration, while many centuries later, it was also used by Celtic Druids.

> **Quirk Alert:** *George's Grill*
>
> *The Hemlock Stone at Stapleford was used in a somewhat bizarre fashion as part of the Golden Jubilee celebrations for King George III on 25th October 1809; bizarre, because a bullock was roasted on top of the rocky outcrop and cooked slices of meat were given out to the residents of nearby Bramcote and Stapleford!*

The Hemlock Stone, a fascinating pillar of pebbly coarse-grained sandstone near Stapleford that dates back over 200 million years.

As for the history of man in Nottinghamshire, it is thought that permanent occupation of the area occurred during the various Stone Ages when hunter gatherers roamed the hilly tundra. The most startling evidence of these nomadic tribes can be found at Creswell Crags, a limestone gorge on Nottinghamshire's north-western border with Derbyshire. The cliffs of the ravine contain several caves in which flint tools have been found from a number of different cultures and which therefore suggest the caves were seasonally occupied throughout the above-named periods. Finds include Palaeolithic axes and scrapers, possibly fashioned from quartzite by Neanderthals around 40,000 BC before the advancing ice sheets drove them south. When the glaciers retreated, Homo sapiens moved into Creswell Crags and it is from this era that more sophisticated tools were found. After 25,000 BC, the caves were vacated for several millennia before a group known to archaeologists as Creswellian Man took up residence, also leaving behind tools made from flint such as their distinctive so-called Creswell points – thin, elongated and sharp. Other specific items found at Creswell Crags during late 19th century excavations include a bone engraved with a horse's head, plus other worked bone items, while later excavations in the 1920s also revealed the remains of a wide variety of prehistoric animals and other animals now extinct in

Creswell Crags, site of many priceless ancient archaeological finds, plus the location of the only British Stone Age cave art, undiscovered until 2003. The photo shows the Nottinghamshire side of the ravine where the majority of the Stone Age cave art was found in the cave known as Church Hole.

Britain such as the mammoth and the woolly rhinoceros.

As for those engraved artefacts at Creswell, they were widely known throughout the 20th century as being the earliest known art in Britain. But then in 2003, these objects were surpassed when engravings and bas-reliefs were found on the walls and ceilings of some of the caves; surpassed because prior to this discovery, it had been thought that no British Stone Age cave art existed. The engravings were mostly found in the entrance chamber to the cave known as Church Hole, which lies on the Nottinghamshire side of the ravine, and are comprised of around 90 representations of Ice Age animal such as bear, bird, bison, deer and horse. In terms of dating the artwork, scientists used the thin layers of calcium carbonate flowstone that overlay some of the engravings in order to provide approximate dates. With the oldest of these flowstones having been formed 12,800 years ago, scientists and archaeologists concluded it was most likely the engravings were created around 13,000-15,000 years ago.

As well as Creswell Crags, quartzite tools dating from the Middle Palaeolithic period were discovered in the Trent Valley at Attenborough, although it is possible that these were carried down country by the advancing glaciers. The same could be said of even older and cruder tools found in high-level gravels at Beeston and which date from the Lower Palaeolithic period, along with later artefacts found at Cropwell Bishop, while another Upper Palaeolithic site was discovered at Langwith on the banks of the River Poulter.

Moving forward to the Mesolithic period (c.10,000-4,500 BC) and evidence is not as forthcoming, although microlithic tools have been found at Misterton in the north of the county and at Tuxford in the east. As for the Neolithic period (c.4,500-2,000 BC), there is evidence of habitation at the site known as Kingshaugh Camp which lies in between the villages of East Markham and Darlton. Neolithic finds include flints and tools – although the fortifications found here are thought to have been started during the Iron Age, after which the site was developed by the Romans, too. It is a similar story at the Iron Age hillfort of Cockpit Hill, a circular earthen bank near to Calverton, where excavations have unearthed Neolithic flint implements thus suggesting the site may well have been occupied during the Neolithic period, too. And in addition to these sites, many more Neolithic tools have been found including axe-heads at various locations around Nottinghamshire including Aversham, Barton-in-Fabis, Beeston, Car Colston, Collingham, Hoveringham, Netherfield, Thrumpton and Wollaton, while flint arrowheads have been found at Gunthorpe, Newark and Tuxford. Of these, the polished axe-head found at Hoveringham was almost 27 cm long and in mint condition, having been dropped into the prehistoric Trent before it saw sustained use.

The late Neolithic/early Bronze Age period is when the ancient henge's and stone circles appeared around Britain, but the vast majority were established further west and thus none have been recorded in Nottinghamshire. However, Nottinghamshire is home to a handful of Bronze Age burial chambers, dating from between 2100 and 700 BC. These include the one on Catstone Hill which lies just south of Strelley, and at Budby Barrow which lies close to the tiny village of Budby, in Sherwood Forest. Of these, the "catstone" element of Catstone Hill may well be a corruption of cap-stone. It certainly sits in a bowl shaped depression on the hill where there are two sets of boulders which could be passage grave cap-stones. One group of stones is aligned with its mound roughly lying east-to-west, including a vertical blocking stone and a fallen stone two metres in front. The other group lies 20 metres to the south and appears to be set upon packing stones.

Quirk Alert: *Budby Burrow*

Budby Barrow can be found in Sherwood Forest, just north of Edwinstowe, and it is thought to be a possible Bronze Age round barrow, although there is no evidence of a surrounding ditch. However, today, it is more like one big burrow than a barrow thanks to the efforts of the local rabbit population!

This stone on Catstone Hill near to Strelley may be the "capstone" to a Bronze Age grave and which therefore may have lent its name to the hill.

Budby Barrow, just north of Budby, is thought to be another Bronze Age round barrow.

View down the western bank and ditch of Oldox Camp, near Oxton. When viewed from the air, clear entrances are visible from the north, while this stretch here is actually a narrow funnelled entrance to the camp from the west.

As well as the barrows, a number of Bronze Age hoards have also been found. For example, the hoard discovered in Nottingham's Great Freeman Street during building in 1860, included sixteen socketed axe-heads, four socketed spear-heads and a palstave, while another hoard at Newark also consisted of socketed axe-heads and spear-heads along with two perforated bronze discs. In total, around 80 Bronze Age socketed axes have been discovered in Nottinghamshire while further implements have been discovered at Mansfield Woodhouse (a thin butted flat axe), Gotham (a palstave) and at East Stoke (a tri-horned bronze bull's head). The latter was probably the model of a Celtic deity, and it was the religious beliefs of the people of that era that ensured that other important articles have been found at possible cremation sites such as the one at Combs, near Southwell, while another large Bronze Age cemetery was discovered just north-east of Hoveringham.

As Nottinghamshire entered the Iron Age (c.700 BC), extensive settlements and hill-forts began to appear, while by around 300 BC, the move from bronze to iron tools was complete. Nottinghamshire Iron Age sites include those discovered at Arnold, Besthorpe, Burton Lodge near Burton Joyce, Castle Hill near Welham, Cockpit Hill near Calverton, Combs Camp at Farnsfield, and Oldox Camp near Oxton. Geographically, the majority of these Iron Age sites, or camps, or earthworks, lie on a keuper scarp between Burton Joyce and Farnsfield and certainly – Creswell Crags apart – they provide the most visual evidence of ancient sites in Nottinghamshire. Of these sites, the one at Burton Lodge has a ditch which measures 15ft wide and 9ft deep. Ditch sections were cut in the early 1950s and finds included coarse-gritted pottery shards and later medieval pottery. Meanwhile, Combs Camp near Farnsfield is another collection of earthworks that form the remains of an Iron Age hillfort and which enclosed approximately three acres. It was probably in use even further back in time, as excavations have unearthed Bronze Age socketed axes and a flint scraper and knife, while Roman brick and tile finds suggest later use, too. Aerial photographs taken in 2001 also suggest two possibly earlier conjoined enclosures, which may have been overlain by the hillfort, and which are visible to the west of the site. As for Cockpit Hill, excavation of a circular earthen bank in 1974 uncovered a multi-ditched enclosed settlement apparently occupied in the Iron Age and Roman periods while an earlier excavation in 1946 had already revealed the stone footings of a circular Iron Age hut within the earthen ramparts. It is likely, therefore, that a small farmstead existed there within a bank and ditch defence during the years preceding the Roman occupation. Similarly, the site at Besthorpe is thought to have been in use in both the Iron Age and later as a Romano-British settlement, too. Finally, size-wise, Oldox Camp at Oxton measured approximately 942ft by 201ft while the site on Hollinwood Hill at Arnold measured 1,251ft by 720ft – and indeed Iron Age pottery was also found at Ramsdale Park, Arnold, during an excavation there in 1974.

Oldox Camp shown along its south-western profile. The hillfort is roughly triangular and encloses 1.5 acres.

Rearing above Oldox Camp are these two mounds, thought to be Bronze Age burial sites. The left-hand tumulus, known as Robin Hood's Pot, was excavated in the 18th century with finds including a funerary urn, knife, sword and beads.

As well as the hillforts, there are also a number of places in Nottinghamshire that were the site of other Iron Age settlements, such as those at Aslockton, Gamston and Holme Pierrepont. The site at Aslockton was excavated in 1992 revealing a large Iron Age settlement shaped as two linked ovals with an open space at the centre. Also discovered a little earlier in 1967 were three log boats in a quarry at Holme Pierrepont, and which were presumably left here when the River Trent changed course sometime in the Iron Age, with dendrochronology dating the boats to somewhere between 445 BC and 115 BC. Finally, it was also during the Iron Age period that a considerable network of green lanes and ridgeways were created, such as Leeming Lane near Mansfield, while the hillfort at Combs Camp overlooked Stone Street – an ancient trackway that linked the future inland port of Bawtry with Nottingham. These "roads" went on to be used for many centuries afterwards, providing highways for generations of travellers ... including the Romans who, a few decades into the 1st Century, were lying in wait for the Ancient Britons…

Romans, Anglo-Saxons and Vikings

By the time the Romans invaded Britain in AD 43, Nottinghamshire was part of the Celtic *Corieltauvi* tribe that stretched from Lincolnshire down to all but the south-western slice of Warwickshire and thus included all of Nottinghamshire. However, it is likely that just before the Romans invaded Britain in AD 43, the *Corieltauvi* were heavily under the influence of their south-eastern neighbours, the *Catuvellauni*, whose main base was at St Albans in modern-day Hertfordshire, although the *Corieltauvi* certainly issued their own coinage, as coin moulds have been discovered at both Leicester and Old Sleaford in Lincolnshire.

Fosse Road still runs through south-east Nottinghamshire today. This road sign was photographed at Farndon.

By AD 45, the Romans had defeated the *Corieltauvi* and by AD 47, they had built the Fosse Way which stretched from *Isca Dumnoniorum* (Exeter) in the South West to *Lindum Colonia* (Lincoln) in the East Midlands, thus taking it right through territory that would eventually become the south-eastern part of Nottinghamshire. The Fosse Way was also thought to mark the temporary frontier of the embryonic province of *Britannia*, although some temporary military posts were constructed to the west of that line in Nottinghamshire, including at both Broxtowe and Farnsfield – the latter an established Iron Age settlement.

There were also posting stations placed at regular intervals along the Fosse Way, with four of these appearing in future Nottinghamshire territory. The first was 12 miles south-west of Lincoln at a place called *Crococolana* – and which is pin-pointed by the modern hamlet of Brough, a few miles north-east of Newark. This site was excavated by T. C. Smith Woolley in the early 20th century with his greatest discovery being a decorated part of a ceremonial Roman cavalry helmet. Next on the Fosse Way was *Ad Pontem*, which was located a few miles south-west of Newark, and close to modern-day East Stoke. Here, 20th century excavations revealed evidence of a small 1st century garrison of around two acres in size and which later became a larger defended town, while the Roman name for the place appears to refer to a long-since vanished bridge over the nearby Trent.

A further six miles down the Fosse Way a mile south of modern-day East Bridgford, was the largest of these four stations and which was known as *Margidunum*; in fact, it was the largest known Roman settlement in Nottinghamshire. This station was rhomboid in shape and may have covered up to eight acres, perhaps enough to accommodate a thousand men and some cavalry. The site is today located at the point where the A46 meets the A6097 and before work began on the roundabout there (later named the Margidunum Roundabout), excavations of the site were carried out between 1966 and 1968. These excavations repeated the success of earlier ones in this location in 1910 and 1936, and huge quantities of Claudio-Neronian and Flavian pottery were unearthed, thus suggesting that *Margidunum* was founded in around AD 50. Its defences, however, were begun in the late 2nd century and included a 25ft-wide rampart and at least one ditch, while later a second rampart was constructed in front of the first along with two six-foot ditches. Even later still, another wall some nine feet wide was constructed, probably in the late third or fourth century. Excavations also revealed a rectangular building measuring 12ft by 24ft whilst the oldest building uncovered dates to around AD 150. It is likely, therefore, that military occupation of the site ended around AD 75, after which a sprawling town developed. The official staff at *Margidunum* may have included a *benficiarius consularis*, who was probably of centurion rank and responsible for security and the collection of road tolls. The town was occupied until at least the Roman departure from Britain in around 410, and probably remained occupied after then, too, given the evidence of a Saxon cemetery outside the southern defences. Other excavation finds at *Margidunum* include Roman coins from the 1st to the 4th century, and a piece of Roman oak panelling for the lining of a well dating to the reign of Claudius (AD 41-54).

Today's village emblem at Willoughby-on-the-Wolds, revealing its former Roman name.

The final of the four Nottinghamshire-based Roman posting stations on the Fosse Way was located just inside what would eventually become the county's border with Leicestershire at Willoughby-on-the-Wolds, and was called *Vernemetum*. However, excavations in the mid-20th century failed to turn up any pottery earlier than the beginning of the 2nd century, although large quantities from the 3rd and 4th centuries were found. The name and certain other finds suggest that a temple or other place of pagan worship might have once stood there.

The other principal Roman road in the county was a branch off Ermine Street, the famous road that ran from London (*Londinium*) to Lincoln (*Lindum*) and then onto York (*Eboracum*). Before entering Nottinghamshire, this former Roman branch road is known as Tillbridge Lane in Lincolnshire (today's A5100), and commences its westward route from today's Lincolnshire Showground. It enters Nottinghamshire after crossing the Trent at Littleborough – a former Roman posting station known as *Segelocum*. Like other stations on the Fosse Way, *Segelocum* also developed into a small Roman town; in fact, following excavations there by John Wade in the 1960s, he described it as the largest Roman settlement in Nottinghamshire not on the Fosse Way. Roman finds here include altars, coins, pottery and urns. From Littleborough, the old Roman road passed through the modern-day villages of Sturton le Steeple, South Wheatley, North Wheatley and Clayworth, before exiting the county at Bawtry. From there, it went onto Doncaster (*Danum*) and then onto *Eboracum*.

Wrapping up Roman roads in Nottinghamshire, it is believed that another connected the future towns of Mansfield and Worksop and was known as Leeming Lane. However, that's not the end of the Roman Nottinghamshire story as a number of other places were the sites of Roman villas while there have been hundreds of Roman finds elsewhere, too. The villa sites can be addressed in loosely geographical trios, starting with Ratcliffe-on-Soar which was the location of the

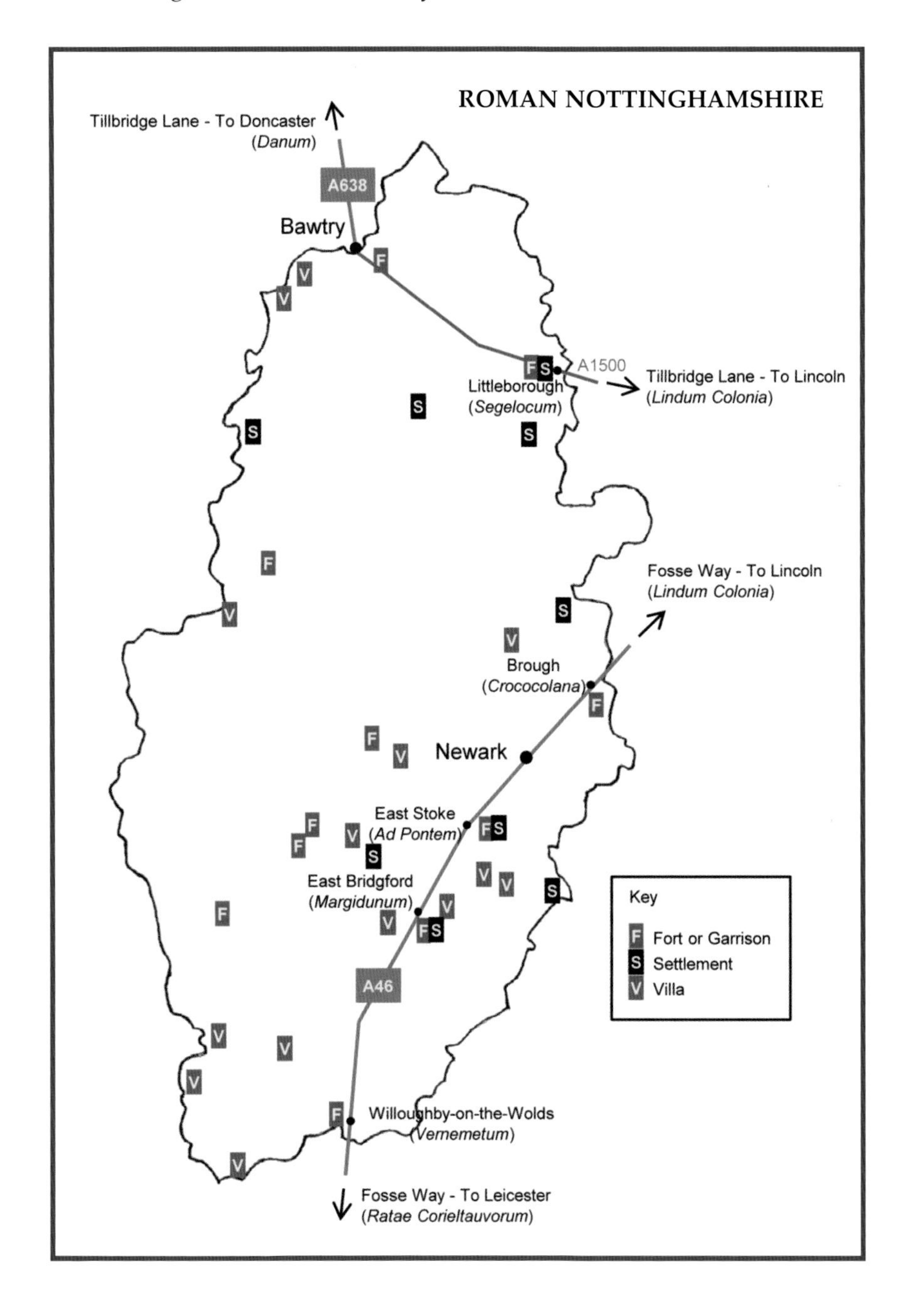

Roman settlement of Redhill, and pretty much occupied the spot now taken up by the coal-fired power station that dominates the area. It also lies close to not only the south-western Nottinghamshire border with both Derbyshire and Leicestershire, but also close to the confluence of the Rivers Trent and Soar – and confluences were a typical place of veneration to the Ancient Britons. This probably explains why the excavations of 1963 revealed that a Romano-British (probably Pagan) temple had been located nearby, along with another Roman villa, suggesting that this may have been near an early ford on the Trent, too. Meanwhile, three miles to the north-east, Barton-in-Fabis was the location of a Roman villa mosaic, discovered in the 19th century at nearby Glebe Farm. And then four miles to the east of Barton-in-Fabis is the site of another Roman villa at Flawford with finds including fragments of floor mosaic.

Quirk Alert: *Lashes to Ashes*

In 1860, the church sexton at Littleborough (Segelocum in Roman times) discovered a stone coffin whilst digging a grave. On opening the coffin, he found the perfect body of a beautiful young woman wearing a garment fastened with a Roman brooch. Or at least that was his story. For in a single breath, she was gone, crumbling to dust and leaving only the brooch behind!

Moving north-east by a dozen or so miles brings us to the second trio of Roman villas. Here, Car Colston was the site of a simple farmhouse-style villa that was identified in the late 19th century, while six miles to the north-west is the site of two villa buildings excavated in the 1950s and 60's between Epperstone and Thurgarton. Completing the second trio is the important Nottinghamshire town of Southwell, famed for its Minster, but also home to what seems to have been the largest courtyard-type villa in the Midlands. The villa was excavated in 1959 and was found to lie under and adjacent to the Minster; in fact, part of the mosaic and wall plaster from the Southwell villa can still be seen inside the south transept of Southwell Minster. The building was clearly of a luxurious status of its time, given the floor mosaics along with a decorated bath-house, exterior industrial structures and retaining walls.

Our final trio of Roman villas are further north in the county, starting at Cromwell, five miles north of Newark, where the outline of a Roman villa can be seen from the air amid complex ancient agricultural markings. Moving right across the county to the north-west, is the tiny village of Styrrup, site of yet another Roman villa. However, we've saved until last Nottinghamshire's best known Roman villa – which was located on the site of modern-day Mansfield Woodhouse, and which was therefore situated close to the aforementioned Leeming Lane. The site was discovered by one of the village's own, Major Hayman Rooke in 1786, and whose name is also immortalised in the Major Oak in nearby Sherwood Forest. The site was also excavated some 150 years later by Adrian Oswald. He found that the main buildings covered an area measuring 142ft by 40ft, and contained rooms with painted wall plaster. A second, but smaller, group of buildings on this site had mosaic floors and wall plaster, painted in purple, red, yellow and green stripes!

One fort that was not on one of the recognised Roman roads was that discovered at Broxtowe in 1937. Many items of jewellery and other artefacts were found there, but alas, the site was obliterated the following year (1938) by a rapidly expanding housing estate; there is no sign of the fort today. Similarly, nothing remains of the two temporary Roman military camps at Calverton that can be made out from the air, although two large Roman coin hoards were found here in 1959 and 1960. Also visible from the air just north-east of Market Warsop is the outline of a temporary Roman army camp. Then there is the outline of a Roman fort at Dorket Head near Arnold while another Roman hillfort was discovered at Osmanthorpe near Edingley and which may have been connected by a Roman road to *Ad Pontem* via another hillfort at Camp Hill.

SOUTHWELL'S ROMAN LEGACY

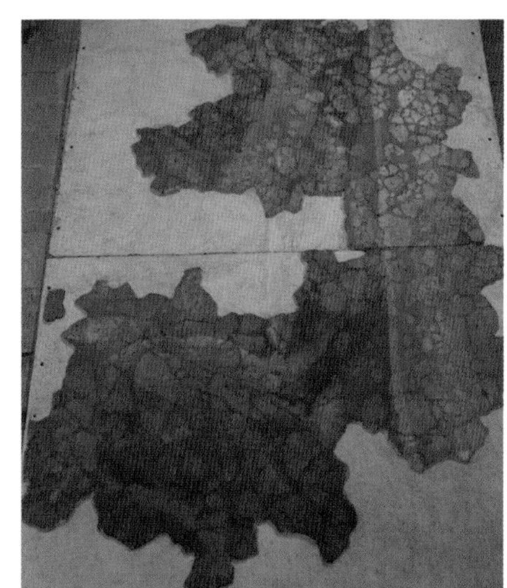

This Roman wall plaster can today be found in Southwell Minster. It was recovered from a cold bathroom of a nearby Roman villa which was excavated in 1959 before the building of the New Grammar School in Church Street.

Part of the mosaic tiles that can be found in the south transept of Southwell Minster, and are thought to have been part of the former Saxon church built on the same site. It is also highly likely that these tiles once graced the floor of a Roman villa that was built close to the site.

Quirk Alert:
He Who Mustn't Be Conveyed!
Amongst the finds at the excavated Roman villa at Ratcliffe-on-Soar were four lead tablets on which were scratched curses. One of these curses includes the only named individual from Nottinghamshire from the Roman era! But to utter his name risks transference of the curse, and therefore he shall remain nameless here!

In addition to this, two Romano-British rural communities have been excavated at Besthorpe in the east of the county, one at Ferry Lane Farm, the other at Mons Pool quarry, while another was found during excavations just north of Retford in 1985 at Lound. Meanwhile, in the south Nottinghamshire village of Gonalston, a rural Romano-British settlement was excavated in the early 1990s ahead of quarrying beside the Trent. Then at Menagerie Wood near Worksop, a Romano-British enclosure settlement was excavated in the 1980s with finds including ancient coppice poles, while at Rampton in north Nottinghamshire, a small Romano-British settlement was excavated that, like *Segelocum*, appeared to have been affected by flooding from the Trent. Finally, large areas of the north-west of the county contain evidence from the air of an ordered Romano-British agricultural landscape known as the brickwork-plan field system.

Further Miscellaneous Roman Artefacts

Bunny	Roman well discovered in 1940
Clifton	Pottery found in 2007
Gringley-on-the-Hill	Roman coins
Hexgrave Park	A heavy Roman inscribed lead ingot found in 1848 and now in the British Museum
Harlow Wood	A large bronze Roman brooch found in the 1970s
Holme Pierrepont	An important Roman cart wheel and three ancient canoes dating from somewhere between the 2nd and 5th centuries, found in 1968
Hucknall	A hoard of 24 silver denarii from the reign of Hadrian
Kirkby-in-Ashfield	Two Roman coin hoards found in the early 1990s
Langar	Site of Roman villa
Laxton	Site of Roman villa
Little Morton	A hoard of over 3,400 Roman coins found in 1998
Meering	Roman pottery and a coin hoard found
Newstead	A hoard of 1,500 Roman coins found in 1990
Nottingham	Coin hoards and pottery
North Leverton	A small cast bronze figurine identified as the mythic consort Attis, found in 1998
Newton	Close to *Margidunum*, with excavations in 2003 suggesting it supported a very large Roman villa described as being 'remarkable' in its dimensions
Oldcotes	Another Roman villa, including a notable labyrinth floor mosaic with the image of Theseus at its centre, found in the 19th century – now lies under St Helen's church
Ollerton	Roman coin hoard
Osberton Hall	Roman altar
Retford	Several important Roman finds, now housed in Bassetlaw Museum
Scaftworth	A small Roman fortlet that guarded the crossing of the River Idle
Shelford	Roman pottery
Shelton	Roman villa
Sibthorpe	Roman villa
Stanford-on-Soar	Possible Roman villa
Staunton	Impoverished Romano-British settlement, excavated in the 1970s
Sutton Bonington	An urn of Roman coins found in the early 19th century
Upton	Roman coin hoard discovered in the early 18th century

As for the local Nottinghamshire population, they continued to be little affected by the Romans during their occupation, and continued to farm and live in thatched round houses in the manner of their Iron Age ancestors, as is evidenced by excavations all the way along the Trent Valley. However, the Roman departure in the early 5th century had a severe effect on both Nottinghamshire and Britain's economy and it didn't really return to similar levels again until the late Anglo-Scandinavian period.

But what of the Nottinghamshire area after the Romans departed? This is a difficult question to answer, for once the literate Romans had departed, the largely illiterate Britons were unable to record their own progress. It is likely that some form of life persisted on the villa sites for an undefined length of time, whilst those who lived in Romano-British settlements and farmsteads must have continued their lives much as before. What we do know, though, is that the country gradually became settled by the Angles and Saxons of northern Europe, with Nottinghamshire playing host to the Angles who came from the Schleswig-Holstein peninsula between modern-day Germany and Denmark. These particular Angles had originally settled in Lincolnshire before pushing their way up the Trent valley into Nottinghamshire and Derbyshire, as evidenced by mid-6th century heathen burial sites found from Newark to Burton. It was only therefore the fertile districts to the south and the east of Nottinghamshire that were significantly populated, probably because the whole region from Nottingham to within a short distance of Southwell was at that time covered by Sherwood Forest. That said, by the end of the 6th century, those same Angles had colonised areas in and around the forest, with evidence of settlements found at both Oxton and Tuxford.

Meanwhile, throughout Britain, the Anglo-Saxon ruling class gradually replaced the weak and divided British. Also gradually replaced, were place-names, with only river-names (like the Trent and the Maun) and places deriving from river-names (like Clumber) and other topographical features retaining their Celtic origins.

By the end of the 6th century, the majority of the Nottinghamshire area had become part of the Anglo-Saxon Kingdom of Mercia. The Kingdom was centred on the valley of the River Trent and its territories covered much of modern South Derbyshire, Leicestershire, Nottinghamshire, Staffordshire and northern Warwickshire. The most authentic source of information at this time was from the Northumbrian monk and scholar who became known as the Venerable Bede, and who describes Mercia as being divided in two by the River Trent. As for the northern-most part of Nottinghamshire, this may have been part of Northumbria; certainly King Edwin of Northumbria is known to have defeated his predecessor, King Athelferth, on the banks of the River Idle in the early 7th century. Furthermore, having married the Christian daughter of the King of Kent, Edwin and his court are said to have been baptised in 627 in the waters of the Trent at a place chronicled as *Tiorulfingacestir*. Given that the *cæster* element of the name means that the place was almost certainly the site of a former Roman fort or small town, the logical assumption is that the place was the Northumbrian successor to *Segelocum* (present-day Littleborough), and built at the crossing point over the Trent on the Roman Road known as Tillbridge Lane.

It was also at around this time that King Edwin was acknowledged as *Bretwalda* – the leader of the Anglo-Saxon Heptarchy. However, King Penda of Mercia forged an alliance with the Welsh, and on 14th October 633, Mercia and Northumbria met at the Battle of Heathfield, where King Edwin was killed. The exact location of this battle is not known, and a number of places stake a claim, including Edwinstowe in central Nottinghamshire, allegedly named after King Edwin himself; indeed, a chantry chapel dedicated to St Edwin is also known to have existed between Edwinstowe and Warsop.

Meanwhile, another vanquished Northumbrian King, Oswald, was also killed by Penda in battle, this time on 5th August 641. And although his body was hacked to pieces and bits sent off to various churches around the country, it is likely that the route of the body-part transporters followed the Trent, since a string of churches in that neck of the woods are dedicated to St Oswald, including those at Dunham-on-Trent, East Stoke and Ragnall.

By c.600AD, Nottingham was part of the Kingdom of Mercia, but was still known by its Celtic name of Tigguo Cobauc – meaning "place of cave dwellings". And this is where some of those cave dwellers lived, in the caves hewn out of the sandstone outcrop that would later support Nottingham Castle.

The other two pointers to life during these times are burial sites and place-names. The former enable estimation of the location of early Anglo-Saxon settlements in Nottinghamshire, and cremation cemeteries have been discovered at Holme Pierrepont, Kingston-on-Soar, Netherfield, Newark and Sutton Bonington, whilst interments have been recorded at Aslockton, Bingham, Oxton and Cotgrave. Of these, 76 burials were found at Cotgrave whilst the excavation at Oxton revealed the burial of a man of some importance.

As for Anglo-Saxon villages, we don't know exactly how many there were since many of these places had their names subsequently changed by Danish settlers. But certainly those places ending in *–ing*, *-ingham* and *–ington* are believed to be amongst the first settlements, while later Anglo-Saxon endings of *–ton* and *–worth* also abound in the area. Remarkably, over forty per cent of all Nottinghamshire place-names come into these two categories, while another twenty five per cent are related to topographical features such as *–beck*, *-field*, *-ford*, *-ley* and *–well*. The latter bracket of place-names also provide us with an insight into the *landscape* of Mercian Nottinghamshire – such as those based upon islands such as Bunny, Cuckney, Holme, Holme Pierrepont and Mattersey, where these places derive their island-meaning names from either the Old English word *ēēg* (meaning "island or land partly surrounded by water") or from the Old Scandinavian word *holmr* (meaning "island or river-meadow"). And you can add to these Beeston and Tuxford (relating to rushes), Headon (relating to heather), Bramcote (broom) and Farndon and Farnsfield (fern). Then there are those places relating to trees, such as Bircotes (birch), Eakring (oaks), Linby (limes), Ollerton (alders) and Willoughby (willows). And then finally, there are a whole raft of place-names based upon Anglo-Saxon animals such as Bulwell (bulls), Calverton (calves), Everton (boars), Gotham (goats), Rampton (rams) and Lambley (lambs).

Quirk Alert: *An Evens Chance*

Close to the Anglo-Saxon church tower at Carlton-in-Lindrick is what is known as the Devil Stone (shown below), and which wasn't actually discovered until 1937. However, legend has it that that if you run around it seven times, you will either have good luck or an encounter with the devil!

Of course, churches also abounded during Anglo-Saxon times, but very little remains of these today – other than "successor to successor" churches standing in virtually the same place. However, it is clear that, even back then, Southwell was an important Nottinghamshire minster, or mother church – i.e. one which covered a large area in the days before parishes were introduced. The earliest church on the site is believed to have been founded in 627 by Paulinus, the first Archbishop of York, when he visited the area while baptising believers in the River Trent. Then in 956 King Eadwig gave land in Southwell to Oskytel, also an Archbishop of York, on which a minster church was established. This was followed by an early 12th century Norman version, while the magnificent Early English minster church that survives today (*see page 25*) dates from the mid-13th century.

In terms of Anglo-Saxon remains, the church of St John the Evangelist at Carlton-in-Lindrick has stonework at the base of its tower that probably dates back to the 9th century – although Arthur Mee suggests the western side of the arch into the nave dates to c.650 and the eastern side to 1060. A rather interesting observation then follows, suggesting that the 1060 builders left the western side of the tower unaltered because "the tower, being a place of refuge and defence against enemies, was full of materials for dealing with unwelcome marauders and was not regarded, therefore, as being part of the church." Meanwhile, a number of ancient Anglo-Scandinavian preaching crosses, or bits of crosses, survive in churchyards throughout the county. The cross in St Helen's churchyard at Stapleford is the oldest in Nottinghamshire, and is thought to date to between 680 and 780 when the settlement was first established as a Christian place of worship. Probably the most important pre-Conquest monument in Nottinghamshire, it is carved with Anglo-Saxon imagery, including what is thought to be the symbols of St Luke (an ox) and St John (an eagle). Between 1200 and 1760, the cross was dismantled and thus lost its transverse arms. However, in 1760 it was erected on a stepped base outside the churchyard and opposite the Old Cross Inn (which also survives to this day). The cross was then moved inside the churchyard in 1928 to safeguard it against an increase in traffic. The square cap and ball was added in 1820, but was destroyed in 1916 when struck by lightning; the latest stone ball was added as recently as 2000 as a result of a local public campaign.

As for other Anglo-Saxon finds, two fragments of an Anglo-Saxon cross were found under St Peter's church at East Bridgford during restoration carried out in the early 20th century, while another shaft decorated with a cross and plait-work was found at Hawksworth St Mary and All Saints, and moved into the church in 1908. Then at Shelford All Saints during restoration work carried out in 1877-78, the top section of a Saxon or early Norman Cross was discovered built into a brick buttress that used to support the south aisle. The sculpture on one side of this cross is the Virgin and Child, and another side is a four-winged angel, while a third side demonstrates typical interlaced Anglo-Saxon ribbon-work. Finally, three fragments of an Anglo-Saxon cross were found at Holy Trinity church in Rolleston in 1895, while a smaller fragment built into a wall actually has the name of the maker, Radulf,

The church of St John the Evangelist at Carlton-in-Lindrick. It is thought that the stonework at the base of the tower dates back to the 9th century.

This Anglo-Saxon cross in St Helen's churchyard at Stapleford is thought to date to between 680 and 780.

inscribed in Saxon capitals. Other crosses include those at Bilsthorpe, Coates, Kneesall and Screveton.

By the end of the 9th century, the Vikings were in charge of Nottinghamshire and they heavily influenced the county for around a century and a half. It all started in the late 860s when after harrying much of England, the Danish army under Halfdan established a base at Nottingham where he was joined by a second army led by Guthrum. By 877, they had partitioned Mercia and it is at this point in time that the area of Nottinghamshire began to take shape, along with Derbyshire, Lincolnshire and Leicestershire, with each new "shire" named after their respective military stronghold. This area became known as the Five Boroughs, the name deriving from the Old English word *burh* meaning "fortified place or stronghold", and the strongholds in question being at Derby, Nottingham, Lincoln, Leicester and Stamford. Then in the following year (878), King Alfred of Wessex and the Danish King Guthrum agreed to carve up England between them following the Treaty of Wedmore and a temporary peace was established. The Five Boroughs became occupied by separate divisions of the Danish army, and the Danes who settled the area introduced their native law and customs known as the Danelaw. Each of the Five Boroughs was ruled as a Danish Jarldom, controlling lands around the fortified *burh*, which served as the centre of political power.

Meanwhile, the Anglo-Saxon half of Mercia ended up forging strong links with its old enemy Wessex. Æthelflæd, 'Lady of the Mercian's' then set about fortifying Mercia's eastern borders, before taking the Danish fortress at Derby in July 917 and annexing the whole region back into English Mercia again. When Æthelflæd died in 918, the Mercian's accepted Edward the Elder of Wessex as their king. He proceeded to take back Nottingham where he then built a second *burh* in 920, this time on the south side of the Trent to further fortify the area from Danish attack, whilst leaving the area under the rule of the Earls of Mercia. Then in 934, Athelstan assembled an army at Nottingham to drive off another threat, this time from the Scots. However, this was not the end of the Anglo-Scandinavian power struggle, for in 941, King Olaf of York reoccupied the five former Danish *burhs*. Danish rule was not restored for long, though, for King Edmund I recovered the Five Boroughs for Wessex in 942, and drove the Danes back to the Humber. Edmund's sons, Edwy and Edgar, then granted extensive estates, mainly in the Southwell area, to two successive Archbishops of York, Oskytel and Oswald. It was also at this point that the next Southwell Minster was built along with a residence for the archbishops while the county of Nottinghamshire found itself transferred to the diocese of York.

The Five Boroughs continued to oscillate between Anglo-Saxon and Viking during the early 11th century; Sweyn Forkbeard seized them in 1013, but only survived for another five weeks after which the formerly ousted Æthelred the Unready returned to reclaim his crown – only for the Danish King Cnut to invade in 1016 and claim it back. By 1035, what was

Quirk Alert: *Score Draw*

The Vikings exerted a huge influence over Nottinghamshire during their occupation and, as a result, a number of Scandinavian place-names appear, with many found in the Trent Valley – site of their first incursion into the county. The two most common Viking place-name endings are -thorpe (outlying farmstead or hamlet), and -by (farmstead, village or settlement). And as chance has it they occur 22 times apiece in Nottinghamshire!

Quirk Alert:
Pancakes and Chauvinism

A local legend claims that the pancake was invented by the women of Linby, to celebrate the defeat of the Vikings. The legend also suggests that the menfolk of Linby had long-since fled, leaving their stout wives to tackle the Viking hordes alone!

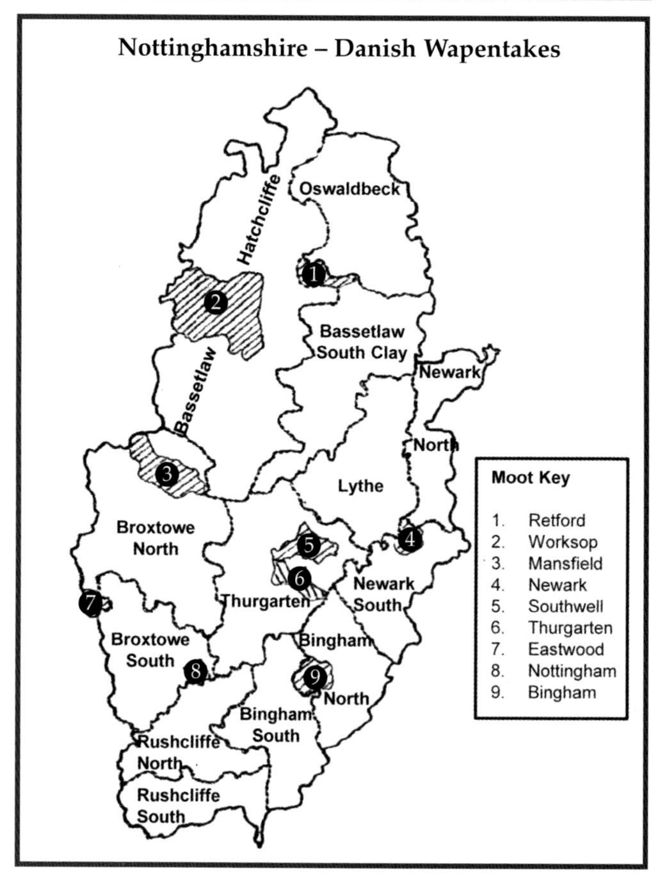

Once Nottinghamshire fell under Danish rule at the end of the 9th century, it was subdivided into Danish wapentakes – the equivalent of the Anglo-Saxon hundreds. Each of these local government divisions chose its "moot place" where regular assemblies were held to administer its own area. Broxtowe met on the site of the future Broxtowe Hall in the parish of Bilborough while Thurgarton moot was held at a place called Iverishaghe within the Oxton parish. Meanwhile, Bingham's moot assembled at Moot House Pit, a shallow depression beside the Fosse Way in the parish of Cropwell Butler while Rushcliffe's is thought to have met near Court Hill, Gotham. Of the above wapentakes, Lythe was eventually merged with Thurgarten while the three most northerly wapentakes merged into one called Bassetlaw … and thus much of today's regional Nottinghamshire map was already in place.

now the *Earldom* of Mercia was back in Anglo-Saxon hands, under Leofric, Earl of Mercia. He also happened to be the husband of the legendary Lady Godiva, who also owned a certain area in eastern Nottinghamshire known as the "new work" – as distinct from the "old works" – plus the former Roman stations of *Crococlana*, *Ad Pontem* and *Margidunum*. This "new work", of course, became Newark and guarded the crossings of the Rivers Devon and Trent as well as the Fosse Way itself. By the time that Lady Godiva presented Newark to the important Lincolnshire monastery of St Mary Stow, the town was already Nottinghamshire's second most important behind Nottingham itself.

As already stated, it was in the middle of this 200-year Anglo-Saxon/Viking struggle that Nottinghamshire was first created, and with very similar borders to those that it has today. Internally, the shires of the Danelaw were divided into wapentakes, the equivalent of the Anglo-Saxon hundreds. Over time, the names and areas changed; for example, after the Norman Conquest, the wapentakes largely took on the boundaries of the ecclesiastical deaneries. However, during the 10th century, we see evidence in various charters where distinct areas within Nottinghamshire are allocated to Mercian thegns (Anglo-Saxon noblemen), and which closely resemble our modern-day parishes. The Domesday Book of 1086 then became the first concise recording of towns, villages and estates in Nottinghamshire, recording most of the county's current settlements, bar those that emerged during the Industrial Revolution. Nottinghamshire itself is first referenced as a shire in 1016, when it was harried by Cnut. However, it had clearly been recognised as a distinct *area* long before that, particularly throughout its Five Boroughs lifetime. As for Nottingham, the town is considerably older than the shire that it lends its name to, as the following Quirk Alert demonstrates…

Quirk Alert: *Snot Funny!*

Nottingham was built on top of hundreds of man-made sandstone caves that date back to the pre-Anglo-Saxon period. The Brythonic Celts who inhabited the area, named the place Tigguo Cobauc, meaning "place of caves", and it was still known as that in c.600, when the area had become part of Anglo-Saxon Mercia. Indeed, the name appears again in The Life of King Alfred, *written by the Welsh monk, Asser, Bishop of Sherborne, and who visited the place in 893. However, 26 years earlier in 867, the Anglo-Saxon Chronicle of that year also records the place as Snotengaham, while it is still similarly recorded as Snotingeham in* Domesday Book *of 1086. The name means "homestead of the family or followers of a man called Snot", and is derived from the somewhat unfortunate Old English personal name, Snot, plus the Old English words inga and hām, meaning "of" and "homestead", respectively. It is thought that the leading "S" was dropped from the name in the 12th century, due to Norman influence – so the good folk of Nottingham are probably blissfully unaware that they are somewhat indebted to their Gallic cousins! As for the original Mr Snot, he was not, to the best of my knowledge, one of Roger Hargreaves' characters, but he would almost certainly have been an Anglo-Saxon chieftain, and therefore the place was presumably known as Snotengaham before the Danes arrived in 867.*

From the Normans to the Wars of the Roses

Following the Norman Conquest of 1066, Nottinghamshire was soon subjected to the same ruthless overhaul of ruling class that was to be repeated in most other English counties. In other words, out went the previous Anglo-Scandinavian incumbents, to be replaced by Norman gentry. The outgoing Anglo-Saxons had names such as Alfric, Wulfric and Wulfsi, and the outgoing Danes had names such as Odincar, Swein and Ulfkell – although, intriguingly, there were already some Norman landowner names prior to 1066, such as Reginald (at Clarborough, Hawton and Kirton), Richard (at Keyworth and Kingston-on-Soar) and William (at Widmerpool). Despite the overhaul, though, there is little evidence of fighting or destruction, and the structure of these Nottinghamshire estates remained largely intact. Also surviving in Nottinghamshire were the former Danelaw parishes which had been expressed in Danish units of carucates divided into eight bovates (as opposed to the Anglo-Saxon equivalents of hides and virgates).

In terms of new ownership, William the Conqueror himself became one of the major landowners in Nottinghamshire, while he also bestowed extensive estates upon his illegitimate son, William Peverel, who acquired land in some 49 different manors stretching from Barton-in-Fabis in the south of the county to Sibthorpe in the north-east. Following the murder of Earl Edwin of Mercia in 1071, William I placed the house of Ferrers (by then, the Earls of Derby) in overall charge of Nottinghamshire, thus making them effectively Earls of Nottinghamshire, too. Peverel was also granted the important feudal fife known as the Honour of Nottingham and was ordered by William I to erect a castle there on a rather convenient natural promontory! Other Norman beneficiaries included Roger de Busli who held land in 107 manors with the largest concentration in the Bassetlaw wapentakes. He also owned

NOTTINGHAMSHIRE'S "NORMAN CASTLES"

Part of the remaining earthworks at Laxton, the site of an 11th century castle consisting of a motte with inner and outer baileys.

Another mound on which a former motte stood is this one at Aslockton. The feature is also known as Cranmer's Mound, named after Thomas Cranmer who was born at Aslockton in 1489.

St Mary's church at Cuckney was erected in the late 12th century on the site of the bailey of the medieval castle built here in the late 11th or early 12th century. The church and its graveyard have destroyed any surface evidence of the former castle although there are a few low remains of the motte, which is partly enclosed by a wide ditch.

Newark Castle was yet another Nottinghamshire castle founded in the mid 12th century, this time by Alexander Bishop following a charter thought to have been granted by Henry I in 1135. Originally a timber castle, it was later rebuilt in stone towards the end of the 12th century. It was then dismantled after the English Civil War, but was restored in the 19th century.

eleven houses in three different plots in Nottingham, while another Norman, Geoffrey Alselin, owned 21 houses.

As for non-Norman-held tracts of land, these were owned by the Archbishop of York (who held onto extensive estates throughout the county) and the newly-appointed Bishop Remigius of Lincoln, who was granted the majority of lands in the Newark wapentake – these having been taken from the bishops of Dorchester-on-Thames. St Peter's Abbey at Peterborough also owned estates in Collingham and North Muskham.

At around this time, the North Midlands also underwent the other standard Norman process: that of fortification. We've already mentioned William Peverel's remit to build a castle at Nottingham, but the majority of other key castles weren't built until the 12th century. The exception appears to be that built in the late 11th century, just north of Laxton. According to an early 20th-century report by the British Archaeological Association, the site is notable not only as "the most striking specimen of a mount and court stronghold" in the area, but also for "the nearly perfect condition of its two courts". The motte-and-bailey castle first built on the site was constructed by either Geoffrey Alselin who was granted the property in 1066, or by his son-in-law, Robert de Caux, who inherited the seat after Alselin's death, and was almost certainly a wooden structure. The second wave of castle construction may have followed de Caux's appointment to Hereditary Keeper of the Royal Forests of Nottingham and Derbyshire. Much later, in 1204, the castle was seized by King John, while by 1230, the property and title had passed to the Everingham family until they were stripped of the title in 1286 after which the castle fell into disrepair. The site of the ruined castle also became the location of a 16th-century manor house known as Laxton Hall.

As for the 12th century castles, these include a motte-and-bailey castle built at Aslockton, although only the earthworks survive today. The motte is also called Cranmer's Mound, named after Thomas Cranmer who was born at Aslockton in 1489. As for the motte, it is a scheduled ancient monument today and stands about 16 feet high, while to the south-east, two rectangular platforms or courts are enclosed by ditches and are the sites of later houses of the Cranmer family. Meanwhile, another 12th century motte-and-bailey castle was built at Cuckney between Worksop and Market Warsop. Built by Thomas de Cuckney, the castle was slighted after The Anarchy of the mid-12th century, having been classed as one of the so-called "adulterine" (or illegal) structures built during the reign of King Stephen (1135-1154). Today, all that remain are the lower parts of a motte partly enclosed by a wide ditch, and the faint remnants of a bailey. And sticking with Norman castles, another wooden structure was built at Bothamsall overlooking the Meden valley, and was situated in the part of Sherwood Forest that belonged to Roger de Busli. Only its earthworks remain today.

Probably the *second*-most famous castle in Nottinghamshire is Newark Castle, founded a little later in the mid-12th century by Alexander, Bishop of Lincoln, following a charter generally thought to have been granted by Henry I in 1135. Originally a timber castle, it was rebuilt in stone towards the end of the 12th century – and it was in this stone castle that King John famously died on the night of 18th October 1216, having been allegedly poisoned. Meanwhile, the castle became a favourite stopping place of Edward I on his journeys between England and Scotland. Alas, none of Bishop Alexander's castle remains today as most of it was dismantled in the 17th century after the English Civil War. It was then restored in the 19th century, first by Anthony Salvin in the 1840s and then by the corporation of Newark who bought the site in 1889. Nevertheless, the castle is still a Scheduled Ancient Monument and a Grade I listed building.

However, it is, of course, Nottingham Castle that commands the greatest interest, courtesy of its affiliation with the legend of Robin Hood – and where it features as the scene of the final showdown between Robin and the Sheriff of Nottingham. But we'll come to that shortly. First, we need to jump back to the castle's inception during the 11th century. William Peverel's initial Norman Nottingham Castle of 1067 was a wooden structure and of a motte-and-bailey design, and it wasn't until 1170 that a far more imposing stone castle was built there, with this comprising an upper bailey at the highest point of Castle Rock, a middle bailey to the north which contained the main royal apartments, and a large outer bailey to the east. However, in between these times, the castle became a key battleground during the struggle between King Stephen (1135-1141 and 1141-1154) and his cousin, Matilda (1141), the daughter of Henry I. Matilda's forces initially raided Nottingham in 1140 but failed to storm the castle. Nevertheless, Peverel was captured the following year at the Battle of Lincoln and he was forced to hand over the castle to William Pegenal of Bingham, as custodian on Matilda's behalf ... only for Peverel, on his release, to seize the castle back for the King. Matters swung back the other way in 1153, though, when Matilda's son, Henry of Anjou, laid siege to Nottingham. Peverel set fire to the town to drive Henry out – an act that earned him little favour when the latter was crowned Henry II, the following year! Peverel was driven out and replaced by the Earl of

Quirk Alert:

The Bell of a Thousand Years

The church of St Michael the Archangel at Halam has two bells. One dates from the 18th century, but remarkably, the other dates back to Norman times. Even more extraordinary is the fact that the Norman bell still rings true, while its 18th century companion is cracked and never struck!

THE MEDIEVAL NOTTINGHAM CASTLE

The Castle Gate House at Nottingham Castle, demonstrates the old and the "new". The bridge and the lower stonework shown here is medieval, while the upper part of the tower and gatehouse is Victorian.

At the foot of Castle Rock is what is known as Mortimer's Hole, the opening to a 150m tunnel that led to the upper bailey of the medieval Nottingham Castle. It was from here that a pivotal moment in British history took place in 1330, when Edward III's soldiers gained entry to the castle and captured the Regent, Roger Mortimer.

Chester – who was subsequently poisoned, almost certainly by Peverel, who promptly reinstated himself at the castle – before having to flee to Lenton Priory disguised as a monk when Henry II returned to the town in 1155!

Moving forwards a few years, we finally arrive at the nucleus of a legend. For whilst Richard I (1189-99) was away on the Third Crusade along with many other English noblemen, his younger brother, John, was given responsibility for six counties, including Nottinghamshire. By 1192, John had wrested control of the castle from Richard's Justiciar, Bishop William Longchamp and he was thought to have installed the infamous Sheriff of Nottingham in his place. However, on March 25th 1194, the returning King Richard was then said to have besieged the castle with the siege machines he had used at Jerusalem, aided by Ranulph de Blondeville, 4th Earl of Chester, and David of Scotland, 8th Earl of Huntingdon. This is believed to have been the only occasion when the defenders of the castle suffered a defeat and, of course, the event became woven into fiction in the centuries to come – but more on that shortly.

As for Nottingham Castle, it continued to serve as one of the most important in England. It was a particular favourite with both royals and nobility thanks to its proximity to the Royal Forest of the Peak to the north-west and Sherwood Forest to the north-east; in fact, the castle also had its very own deer park and which is still known today as The Park. In terms of incident, though, the castle was held for Simon de Montfort during the Second Barons' Wars of 1264-67, but surrendered to the forces of Henry III, who appointed John de Grey as its royal constable. He didn't last long, though, for following the capture of the King at the Battle of Lewes, de Montfort re-established control of the castle and appointed Hugh Le Despenser in his place. It was also during this struggle that Nottingham's town walls were started, some standing as high as 30 feet in places and up to seven feet thick.

As for Nottingham Castle's most famous (and non-fictional) incident, this occurred in 1330 when Edward III staged a coup d'état at Nottingham Castle against his mother Isabella of France, and her lover, Roger Mortimer, 1st Earl of March. Both were acting as Regents during Edward's minority following their murder of his father, Edward II, at Berkeley Castle. Edward III was assisted in the 1330 coup by William Montagu and his companions, who were also accompanied by William Eland, castellan and overseer of Mortimer's castle, and who knew the location of a cave leading to a secret tunnel which would take them up to a normally locked door high up in the castle. However, on the night of 19th October 1330, the door was deliberately left unlocked and Montagu and his companions gained entry, overpowered Mortimer and killed his personal guards. Mortimer was sent to the Tower of London, and hanged a month later while Isabella was forced into retirement at Castle Rising in Norfolk. The cave and tunnel survive to this day and are still known as Mortimer's Hole.

The next significant event at Nottingham Castle occurred at the end of the War of the Roses – but we're getting a bit ahead of ourselves there and so we will return to Norman Nottinghamshire. For records show that shortly after the Conquest, Nottingham began to see growth *outside* of its earthworks as suburbs began to spring up beyond the town's limits. These areas became collectively known as the "New" or "French" town, distinguishing them from the "Old" or "English" town, with these terms used until at least the mid-15th century. The French town also had its own code of laws and quarter sessions until the close of the 17th century, although the "English" and "French" towns did share a common market place – albeit divided by a wall until 1713! Medieval Nottingham also grew as a trading town, particularly along both the Trent valley and its Nottingham-related tributary, the River Leen, with the latter acquiring a wooden quay built by the Franciscan Friars in the 13th century. As for the county's industries, the late 11th century saw a number of fisheries in Nottinghamshire, particularly on the Trent and its tributaries, such as those at Clifton, Dunham-on-Trent, Holme Pierrepont, Laneham, Netherfield, Newark, Norwell, Saundby and South Muskham. Another c.12th century fishery at Colwick was investigated in 1973, revealing six rows of oak and holly posts forming a "V", the neck of which pointed downstream. The likelihood is that eels were ensnared during their autumnal migration.

From the 12th to the 14th century, Nottingham continued to prosper courtesy of its trade from the Trent, partly due to a charter granted by Henry II which gave the town the right to exact tolls on shipping from Thrumpton to Newark. This charter also granted Friday and Saturday markets to Nottingham along with a local monopoly in the manufacture of dyed cloth. A subsequent charter issued by King John granted permission for merchants to establish their own guild in the town, and to be exempt from paying tolls throughout the whole of the King's territories. Several decades later in 1284, Edward I then gave Nottingham the additional right to elect a mayor while at the same time there was a grant for the holding of an annual fair for 15 days during November. As an aside, six years later, Edward I and his wife, Eleanor of Castille, were staying at Harby, the eastern-most settlement in Nottinghamshire. However, Eleanor was taken ill and died here on 27th November 1290. Grief-stricken, Edward ordered that crosses were to be erected at their stopping points on the sombre journey back to London, and they are still known today as Eleanor crosses.

Alongside these medieval developments in Nottingham, Newark also grew as a commercial town, similarly hosting a thriving wool industry, although the town wasn't allocated its own burgesses (Nottingham had two) to represent the town in Parliament until the reign of Charles II, this thanks to Newark's loyalty to Charles' father. The medieval market at Newark was also impressive, an area that is marked today by the beautifully-restored White Hart Inn and which dates back to the 14th century – and which makes it contemporary with a truly remarkable man born in Newark in 1307. His name was John Arderne and he is considered by many to be England's first surgeon and one of the first men to devise genuinely workable cures, while many of his treatments are still in use today, most notably the usage of anaesthetic. Other remarkably modern concepts adopted by Arderne were the recording of procedures, a code of conduct for the medical practitioner, and a belief that the rich should be charged as much as possible, but that the poor should receive his services free of charge. As for medieval Mansfield, the town possessed a mill, a fishery and two churches while East Retford became a market town of repute, particularly attracting the folk who dwelled in Sherwood Forest as did the eight-day fair that was granted to East Retford in 1259.

Quirk Alert:

Ye Olde Legends of Inebriatalem!

The 12th century pub in Nottingham known as Ye Olde Trip to Jerusalem is set against caves carved out of sandstone rock. Some of the larger ground-level caverns are used as modern-day drinking rooms, while the network of caves beneath was used as a brewery for many centuries and dates from 1068. The pub is also home to a small wooden model of a ship known as the "cursed galleon". Legend has it that anyone who cleans it will meet with a mysterious death. Needless to say, it is now caked in inches of thick grime! It is also now kept in a glass container, as previously, clumps of dust were known to float off and drop into the pints of appalled drinkers! Finally, the pub is also home to an antique chair for which it is claimed that any woman will increase her chances of pregnancy by sitting in it!

NOTTINGHAMSHIRE'S MEDIEVAL PUBS

Ye Olde Trip to Jerusalem in Nottingham is thought to date from c.1189, and takes its name from the 12th century Crusades to the Holy Land. It is one of 20 English pubs that claim to be the oldest in the country. That said, the front of the building is only around 300 years old, although its foundations are considerably older.

The White Hart, Newark, dates from the 14th century and is considered to be a building of national importance.

As the Middle Ages progressed, not only did the wool trade expand in Nottinghamshire, but the cloth industry did, too – with Nottinghamshire cloth described as "northern cloth" thanks to it being manufactured "yon side of the Trent", while Lenton Fair, which was established in 1300, was described as the finest cloth market in the county. Another 13th century industry that thrived in Nottingham was ceramics, and the town was famous for its manufacture of what was known as Green Glaze Ware. The late 14th century also saw the establishment of the bell-founding industry in Nottingham.

Of course, coal was due to become a major Nottinghamshire industry in later centuries, but coal mining is actually mentioned as far back as 1282 at Cossall with further references to mining at Selston also recorded in the late 13th century. However, it was the monks of Newstead Abbey who controlled the mining at Cossall while those at Beauvale controlled Selston, as well as later mines at Kimberley and Newthorpe. By the end of the 15th century, Beauvale had also been granted the rights to sink further shafts in western Nottinghamshire, although they allocated a certain proportion of their coal to Lenton Priory.

Also mined and quarried in Nottinghamshire during these times was alabaster or gypsum, and which was originally centred on Gotham in the south-west of the county and Orston in the east – with the latter described as "the finest in the Kingdom". But whereas foliated gypsum was used mainly for tough, fire-resistant floors, alabaster was used extensively for carving into effigies. The 14th century saw a certain "Peter the Mason" become nationally famous for his alabaster work, which included the reredos for the high altar in St George's Chapel at Windsor … and which had to be transported in sections by 10 wagons each pulled by an octet of horses! Other customers of Nottinghamshire alabaster came from as far afield as Italy, Iceland, and the Abbot of Fécamp in Normandy, while local churches are also graced with effigies from this era such as those of Sir Hugh de Willoughby at Willoughby-on-the-Wolds, Sir Henry Pierrepont at Holme Pierrepont, and Sir Robert Goushill at Hoveringham.

Quirk Alert: *To Dye For*

Many of the medieval trades also lent their names to the streets of Nottingham, since certain trades tended to cluster in the same area. As well as the rather obvious Fishergate and the less obvious Fletchergate (named after fleshers or butchers rather than the makers of arrows), there was also a Smithy Row, a Bridlesmithgate and a Wheelergate, while also less obvious was Pilchergate (named after fur merchants), Barkergate (named after tanners) and finally, Listergate – named after dyers – since the Old English word "litster" means "to dye".

The aftermath of the Norman Conquest saw much of Nottinghamshire become subject to the forest laws, based upon areas of the English countryside where Norman kings and barons had exclusive rights to hunt. The term "forest", though, represented more than just dense woodland; it included moor, heath and fen, too. And unfortunately for the resident peasants, a special set of harsh laws were imposed by forest courts, including the prevention of the clearing of new land for farming or from fencing existing crops to keep the game out. As for the "forests" of Nottinghamshire, they were dominated by Sherwood Forest, one of the largest Royal Hunting Forests in the country and which covered all of central Nottinghamshire, accounting for roughly one quarter of the county's area. Sherwood Forest is first referred to in the Pipe Roll of 1130 with its name implying a common forested area belonging to the whole shire. It was not until the reign of Edward I (1272-1307) that Sherwood Forest is referred to as a royal forest, although it is highly likely to have belonged to the royals since Norman times. The area is certainly referred to in the Domesday Book of 1086 as containing both "woodland pasture" and "waste", where the former would have been oak and beech woods that were home to deer, and wild boar, and the latter being the area to which the animals were driven by hunters prior to the kill.

Quirk Alert: *A Blinding Sentence*

During medieval times, all of Sherwood Forest came under the jurisdiction of the Forest Laws. These were administered by the Royal Justiciar for the Forests Yon Side Trent, and covered not only the protection of game, but also the carrying of weapons in the area by anybody other than valid travellers, who were themselves restricted to using just the highways that traversed the woodland and waste. Foresters, woodwards and rangers had the right to arrest any poachers, trespassers or rustlers, with offenders forced to attend the six-weekly verderers court that were held in various locations within Sherwood; Linby on a Monday, Calverton on a Wednesday, Mansfield on a Thursday and Edwinstowe on a Friday. Sentences for those found guilty of breaching the Forest Laws included blinding and/or the amputation of fingers or a complete hand, although following Magna Carta these were replaced in 1217 by more humane punishments such as fines and imprisonment.

Of course, it would be impossible to complete a review of Sherwood Forest without considering the legend of Robin Hood and which is usually dated at around the late 12th century, perhaps during the reign of Richard I (1189-1199). Alas, there are certain anachronistic flaws in that theory, one being that his band of merry men included Friar Tuck – since friars didn't appear in England until the 13th century. Also, it appears as though Robin Hood was not actually associated with

The statue of Robin Hood that sits in the ditch beneath Nottingham Castle's walls.

Richard I in legend until the 16th century, since early ballads such as *A Gest of Robin Hood* name his king as Edward. But even if you chose the earliest King Edward (Edward I, 1272-1307), that is still significantly later than Richard I's time. That said, there are records of a certain Robin Hood in the Pipe Rolls of 1225, 1226, 1228, 1230 and 1231, although he is actually called Robert Hod and appears to be a fugitive from the justice administered by the Sheriff of ... well ... Yorkshire, actually! And appearing to back this controversial shift in county location, the early tale originally called *Lytell Geste of Robyn Hode*, and which is thought to date from the 14th century, sees the action take place in the Wakefield area! However, there is another twist ... for the tale also sees Robin kill the Sheriff of Nottingham!

This latter tale also includes the characters of Little John, Will Scarlett and Much (the miller's son), but Friar Tuck and Maid Marian only appear to have been added at a much later date. For example, Friar Tuck's character starts to appear regularly in the play *Robin Hood and the Sheriff* from around 1475 onwards. Whether Tuck was based on a living character is also open to debate, for there were certainly two royal writs in 1417 which refer to Robert Stafford, a Sussex chaplain who had assumed the alias of Frère Tuk. As for the legend, the most recognised background for the character is that he was a former monk of Fountains Abbey who was expelled by his order because of his lack of respect for authority – and not forgetting his taste for good food and wine, too! Of course, following his expulsion, he becomes the chaplain of Robin Hood's band of outlaws, after encountering Robin in Sherwood Forest. The famous first encounter involving staffs on a log spanning a river, was first performed in the play *Robin Hood and the Curtal Friar*, during the May games in 1560. Interestingly, the aforementioned chaplain, Robert Stafford, came from Lindfield in Sussex, and

SOUTHWELL MINSTER

View of Southwell Minster from the north-west (left) *and from the south* (right). *Built on the site of at least two former churches, work began on the Norman version in 1108 and was completed by c.1150. The Norman church was then replaced by another in 1234 and which was built in the Early English style.*

Left: *The ruin of the Archbishop of York's palace which lies alongside the minster.* Right: *Inside the nave looking towards the pulpitum, built in 1350.*

close to there is the village of Fletching where the compounded surname of Robynhood is recorded several times after 1296! As for Maid Marian, she appears to have been a romantic addition to the tale during the Tudor era.

As mentioned earlier, Southwell Minster was founded in 627 by Paulinus, the first Archbishop of York, and then succeeded by the 956 version built by another Archbishop of York, Oskytel. However, the Norman reconstruction of the church began in 1108 and was probably a rebuild of the Anglo-Saxon church, and which would have started at the east end so that the altar could be used as soon as possible. The Saxon building would then have been progressively dismantled as work on the new building proceeded but with many of the stones from the Saxon church reused in the construction. Today, the tessellated floor and late 11th century tympanum in the north transept are the only parts of the Saxon building remaining intact. Work on the nave began after 1120 and the church was completed around 1150. The church was originally attached to the Archbishop of York's Palace which stood next door and is now ruined. It served the archbishop as a place of worship and was a collegiate body of theological learning, hence its designation as a minster. The Norman church was then largely replaced by another in the Early English style during the 13th century because its predecessor was too small, while the celebrated octagonal chapter house was built between 1290 and 1300. Arthur Mee describes the entrance to it as "probably the most beautiful doorway in any cathedral in England", whilst its eight walls contain 36 seats with triangular canopies over them for which he states: "the carving of these canopies is one of the stone wonders of the world".

Entrance to the celebrated octagonal Chapter House at Southwell.

One of the many carvings in the above Chapter House.

The only church in Nottingham in early Norman times was St Mary's, which lay within the King's lordship. The church is certainly mentioned in Domesday Book and a predecessor church is believed to date back much further to Saxon times. However, the main body of the present building – and which is the second largest church in the county – probably dates from the 14th and 15th centuries. Within a decade of Domesday, the parish churches of St Peter and of St Nicholas had also appeared.

Of course, there are many more churches in Nottinghamshire that still retain either Norman features or work dating from the late 12th century merge of Norman and English styles, and most of these are captured in the table opposite … which is rather northern and eastern-heavy…

EX-NORMAN CHURCHES IN NOTTINGHAM

Above: *St Mary's church, High Pavement. This was the only church in early Norman Nottingham and is still the second largest church in the county today. The current incarnation, however, dates from the late 14th/early 15th century with the nave notable for its uniformity of the Gothic Perpendicular style.*

Right: *St Peter's church, St Peter's Gate. The church evidences many stages of construction from about 1180 onwards, this following the destruction of its predecessor by fire in around 1100. The parish of St James' church, Standard Hill, founded in 1807 was united with St Peter's in 1933, but the latter was demolished a few years later.*

LOCATION	CHURCH NAME	DISTRICT	NORMAN FEATURES
Averham	St Michael & All Angels	N&S	Norman and some Anglo-Saxon masonry.
Balderton	St Giles	N&S	Norman porch and Norman (north) doorway.
Bilsthorpe	St Margaret	N&S	Norman font.
Blyth	St Mary and St Martin	Bassetlaw	Built in 1088 by Roger de Busli as part of a Benedictine Priory. The nave is Norman, as are the two arcades, the clerestory, the triforium on the south side and the north aisle.
Carburton	St Giles	Bassetlaw	Norman chancel, nave, doorway, windows and font.
Church Laneham	St Peter	Bassetlaw	Norman (south) doorway, pillars and arch, plus an original and extremely rare Norman door. Also possesses a Norman chancel arch and font.
Church Warsop	St Peter and St Paul	Mansfield	Largely Norman tower, small Norman window with a Maltese cross cut on one side, plus Norman arch and priest's doorway.
Clayworth	St Peter	Bassetlaw	Base of tower dates from the early 11th century, maybe even Anglo-Saxon times, as is part of the wall between the nave and chancel. There are also two Norman doorways.
Collingham	St John the Baptist	N&S	Norman north aisle with zigzag arcades.
East Leake	St Mary	Rushcliffe	Early Norman or Saxon herringbone masonry on the north wall of the nave.
Edwinstowe	St Mary	N&S	Priest's doorway in chancel.
Egmanton	St Mary	N&S	Norman doorway, Norman pillars in the nave and a Norman chancel arch, plus a Norman font.
Elston	Elston Chapel	N&S	Norman masonry and a Norman (south) doorway.
Farndon	St Peter	N&S	Herringbone masonry in north wall is early Norman or Saxon.
Fledborough	St Gregory	Bassetlaw	Lower half of tower is late 12th century.
Halam	St Michael the Archangel	N&S	Norman bell known as "the bell of a thousand years". Norman chancel arch and late 12th century font.
Hayton	St Peter	Bassetlaw	Norman doorway and Norman masonry in the nave.
Keyworth	St Mary Magdalene	Rushcliffe	Norman font.
Lambley	Holy Trinity	Gedling	Norman arch into the nave.
Linby	St Michael	Ashfield	Norman masonry, doorway and window.
Littleborough	St Nicholas	Bassetlaw	Norman doorway, Norman arch from nave to chancel on Saxon pillars, and a Norman font, while the exterior includes Saxon herringbone masonry with Roman tiles also built in.
Mansfield	St Peter	Mansfield	Lower stages of the tower are Norman, and there is a Norman arch into the nave.
Newark on Trent	St Mary Magdalene	N&S	Norman vaulted crypt and the piers of the central crossing.
North Leverton	St Martin	Bassetlaw	North wall of chancel.
North Muskham	St Wilfrid	N&S	Fragments of a Norman arcade.
Norton Cuckney	St Mary	Bassetlaw	The nave and aisles, while there is Norman stringwork in the porch, and a Norman doorway.
Norwell	St Lawrence	N&S	Norman doorway in 14th century porch.
Rampton	All Saints	Bassetlaw	A Norman font, while parts of the north aisle are even older, almost certainly Saxon.
Rolleston	Holy Trinity	N&S	Norman piscina and Norman masonry along the lower walls.
Sookholme	St Augustine	Mansfield	Norman chancel arch and Norman font plus Norman masonry in the north and south walls.
South Muskham	St Wilfrid	N&S	Norman masonry inside and outside of north wall of chancel, a Norman font and a Norman (north) doorway.
South Scarle	St Helena	N&S	Norman nave and Norman bays in the north arcade.
South Wheatley	St Helen	Bassetlaw	Chancel arch.
Sutton-cum-Lound	St Bartholomew	Bassetlaw	Norman arch over doorway.
Teversal	St Katherine	Ashfield	South arcade and font.
West Markham	All Saints	Bassetlaw	Priest's door and piscina, while much of the masonry is Saxon.
Worksop	St Mary & St Cuthbert (aka Worksop Priory)	Bassetlaw	Virtually all of it – nave, aisles and the two west towers plus west doorways, the triforium, clerestory, arcade arches, and south doorway. The church was part of an Augustinian Priory founded in 1120, but the eastern part was demolished during the Dissolution in 1539.

From left to right:
Balderton, St Giles' – north door.
Carlton-in-Lindrick, St John's – west door.
Church Laneham, St Peter's – south door.
Norton Cuckney, St Mary's – south door.

NORMAN CHURCH TOWERS IN NOTTINGHAMSHIRE

The church of St Peter and St Paul, Church Warsop.

St Gregory's church, Fledborough.

St Mary and St Cuthbert, Worksop, also known as Worksop Priory.

Although Elston Chapel sports a genuine Norman doorway, the majority of the building dates from the 14th to the 16th century.

The box pews should date to the Georgian period … but sadly fell victim to 20th century vandals and therefore much of the panelling had to be restored.

Nottinghamshire's importance as a county during these times was emphasised by the fact that a single shire court held at Nottingham served both Nottinghamshire and Derbyshire until 1256, while the sheriff of Nottingham actually had jurisdiction over Derbyshire until the 16th century. Nottinghamshire was also home to many important abbeys and priories, including its sole Benedictine priory at Blyth which was founded in 1088 by Roger de Busli of nearby Tickhill Castle. His home town was Rouen in Northern France and the priory at Blyth was a daughter house of the Abbey of Holy Trinity at Rouen. Its Norman church still survives to this day.

The county's only Cistercian house, Rufford Abbey, was founded in 1147 just south-west of Ollerton and was populated by Cistercian monks from Riveaulx Abbey in Yorkshire. It was founded by the descendants of one of the original Norman conquerors, Gilbert de Gant, Earl of Lincoln, and its church was dedicated to the Blessed Virgin Mary. Meanwhile, the most celebrated Cluniac priory was founded at Lenton by William Peverel in the early 12th century and was dedicated to the Holy Trinity (see *Quirky Nottinghamshire [Lenton]* for more).

Also of significance was Welbeck Abbey, the site of a monastery belonging to the Premonstratensian order, and which was founded by Thomas de Cuckney in 1140, and dedicated to St James the Great. After the Dissolution of the Monasteries, a country house was eventually built here in the early 17th century by Sir William Cavendish and designed by John Smythson, and survives to this day as a Grade I listed building. Then there was also Newstead Abbey – although it was never actually an abbey! It was initially known as the priory of St Mary of Newstead, and was a house of Augustinian Canons founded by Henry II in around 1163. Converted to a domestic home following the Dissolution of the Monasteries, Newstead "Abbey" is now best known as the ancestral home of Lord Byron.

Other religious houses included the Priory of Beauvale (Carthusian) at Greasley, near Eastwood and which was dedicated to the Holy Trinity (see *Quirky Nottinghamshire [Kimberley]* for more), the Priory of Felley (Augustinian) founded in 1156 by Ralph Britto of Annesley (see *Quirky Nottinghamshire [Friezeland]*), and a number of other Augustinian houses including one founded at Worksop in 1103 by William de Lovetot and another founded at Thurgarten in the 12th century by Ralph d'Eyncourt. Meanwhile, a Gilbertian house was founded in 1185 at Mattersey and a Benedictine house for nuns was founded at Wallingwells by Ralph of Chevrolcourt.

ABBEY AND PRIORY REMAINS IN NOTTINGHAMSHIRE

St Mary and St Martin's church at Blyth is a former Norman priory church, parts of which date back to the time when a Benedictine priory was founded here in 1088.

All that remains of Beauvale Priory. This Carthusian priory was founded in 1343 by Nicholas de Cantelupe.

The gatehouse to Worksop Priory. The priory was founded in c.1120 (see p28) while this gatehouse was added later in c.1330 to house guests and visitors, perhaps even Edward III who visited the priory.

The remains of Mattersey Priory, founded in 1185 as a Gilbertian establishment by Roger FitzRanulph, and dedicated to St Helen.

Newstead Abbey – although it was only ever a priory known as St Mary of Newstead, and which belonged to the Augustinian order. The façade above includes the original west front of the priory.

Rufford Abbey, originally a Cistercian Abbey founded by Gilbert de Gant in 1146, but which was first converted into a country house in the 16th century following the Dissolution of the Monasteries.

This is the ruinous Great Hall from the first Rufford Country House, and which was built above the Frater and Cellarium of the original abbey in the late 16th century by the 6th Earl of Shrewsbury, George Talbot, and his second wife, Bess of Hardwick. The house then passed to the Savile family in 1626 and George Savile, first Marquess of Halifax, demolished much of the old house and the abbey and rebuilt another between 1678 and 1680.

And here is the Frater (or dining room) in question a survivor from the original 12th century abbey at Rufford.

Finally, Nottinghamshire was also home to two Friaries, both situated in Nottingham. The Grey Friars (Franciscans) established a 13th century site in Broadmarsh and eventually erected a preaching cross in what became known as Greyfriars Gate. The White Friars (Carmelites) then established a church between Moothall Gate and St James's Lane in around 1270 from which the names Friar Lane and Friar Row derive. There were also a number of hospitals run by medieval religious institutions, too, including those at Blyth, Newark, Nottingham, Southwell and Stoke, while homes for the aged poor existed with two in Nottingham – including a third outside the city walls called the Hospital of St John the Baptist.

It was mentioned earlier that medieval Nottingham was divided into the "Old" or "English" town and the "New" or "French" town, with the former inside the town's earthworks and the latter without, and with each having their own bailiff. However, in 1448, both bailiffs were elevated to the status of Sheriff when Henry VI raised Nottingham to county status, and they were thus both able to hold monthly county courts.

> **Quirk Alert:** *Key Monk Business*
>
> *Did you know that the Black Death of 1348-1349 took out 48.5% of all priests in the Newark deanery? Meanwhile, in 1402, Robert Leycestre, a Nottingham Franciscan monk, was hanged at Tyburn for preaching that King Richard II was still alive! Then in 1532, the Nottingham Carmelites' Prior, Richard Sherwood, had to obtain a royal pardon after killing one of his friars, William Bacon, during a drunken brawl! Six years later in 1538, three of the canons at Shelford were accused of "unnatural sin" and another three of incontinence! Although it is widely thought that the charges were trumped up! Finally, and also in 1538, Prior Nicholas Heath of Lenton was convicted on the circumstantial evidence of an alleged treasonous conversation.*

Towards the end of the Middle Ages, Britain was dominated by the Wars of the Roses, and Nottinghamshire played a significant role in affairs. The Lancastrian King Henry VI found that although many

MEDIEVAL CHURCHES

St Helen's church, Stapleford, dates from between 1240-50 and was built in the Early English style.

St Nicholas's church at Tuxford has a few feet of Saxon herringbone masonry but the rest is largely medieval. The tower and spire both date from the 14th century and demonstrate the passing of the broach and arrival of the parapet.

significant local lords aligned themselves to his cause (such as the Earl of Shrewsbury, Lord Roos of Belvoir and Sir Robert Strelley), so too did many others to the Yorkist cause (Lord Cromwell, Sir Richard Illingworth of Bunny and Sir Henry Pierrepont, to name but three). Henry VI was then deposed by Yorkist Edward IV in 1461 and the latter visited Nottingham on several occasions between 1469 and 1471 when he built a great octagonal tower at the castle, work completed by his successor, King Richard III. And indeed, Richard III himself was in Nottinghamshire, at his hunting lodge in Bestwood, on the fateful day of August 11th 1485 – for this was the day Richard learned that his bitter rival for the throne, Henry Tudor, had landed an army at Milford Haven. Richard returned to Nottingham immediately, and left shortly afterwards to meet his fate on Bosworth Field on 22nd August 1485.

However, it was events two years later that saw Nottinghamshire at the fore of the struggle, and which revolved around Lambert Simnel's claim to be the Earl of Warwick. Fashioned as the son of the late George, Duke of Clarence – and therefore alleged nephew to Edward IV and Richard III – the 10-year old Simnel became the figurehead of a Yorkist rebellion organised by John de la Pole, Earl of Lincoln. Having drummed up Yorkist support in Ireland, and crowning him as King Edward VI in Dublin, a force of Irish troops and 2,000 Flemish mercenaries then landed at Piel Island off the coast of Lancashire on 5th June 1487. Joined by some English supporters, they marched south, advancing towards Newark.

A memorial in St Oswald's churchyard at East Stoke, to those who died at the Battle of Stoke Field.

At this point, Henry VII was at Kenilworth, but rapidly moved his forces through Leicestershire and into Nottinghamshire, passing through Bunny on June 12th and arriving in Nottingham shortly afterwards. Here the king attended the Corpus Christi Day service, probably at St Mary's church, and then joined his army with that of Lord Strange, which had camped at Lenton. The combined force of around 12,000 soldiers moved off to Radcliffe-on-Trent on Friday 15th June and commenced their advance up the Fosse Way the following day – the same day that the 8,000 Yorkist troops crossed the Trent near to Fiskerton. They then took up positions along a ridge that crossed the Fosse Way between the villages of East Stoke and Elston – and it was here that the Earl of Lincoln attacked the vanguard of Henry's army, knowing that the latter's force would outnumber his own once they all arrived. And indeed, the Lancastrians did suffer heavy losses, but the battle turned back in their favour with the arrival of the main part of their army. It was at this point that many of the Irish mercenaries tried to do a runner back across the Trent, but most of them were cut down in their flight, earning the site of their massacre the name of "Bloody Gutter". In fact, in all, two thousand Lancastrians died along with four thousand Yorkist's. The rebellion now crushed, Simnel was actually pardoned by Henry VII, and was thereafter employed in the Royal kitchens as a servant.

From the Dissolution to the English Civil War

The most intriguing village crosses in Nottinghamshire can be found at Linby, just north of Hucknall, as Linby actually has *two* crosses. The larger medieval one at the western entrance to the village is known as Linby Top Cross, and is unique in that its steps are seven-sided. The other cross a few yards to the north-east on the B6011 is known as Linby Bottom Cross and, although it only has mere four-sided steps, it is also remarkable in that it is built over an ancient spring head seen by some as a holy well. Both crosses are actually thought to be boundary crosses used to mark the extent of Sherwood Forest. However, the medieval Top Cross was destroyed in the 1560s but restored in the 1860s. Meanwhile, the Bottom Cross dates from 1663 and was actually set up to replace its older counterpart long before its restoration; in fact talking of Restoration's, the Bottom Cross was also set up to celebrate the crowning of Charles II, too!

> **Quirk Alert:** *Evil Exit*
>
> *The tower of the church of Holy Rood at Edwalton was built in the 16th century, and included a door known as the Devil's Door. This was always left open during christenings to allow evil spirits to escape.*

Events in Nottinghamshire during the mid-16th century were dominated by the Dissolution of the Monasteries in the late 1530s, and the resulting fate of the county's abbeys, priories and monasteries. First to go in 1536 were Blyth, Broadholme, Felley, Rufford and Strelley, with Thurgarten, Welbeck, Mattersey and Worksop following in 1538, and the remainder in 1539, including Beauvale, Newstead and Wallingwells. Unfortunately, the subsequent plundering of these sites means that little remains today. At Blyth, the priory church was stripped of its chancel and the eastern end of the church, and this fell into ruin alongside the former monastery buildings to the north, and which had been separated from the church by the cloisters and garth. However, the remains of the priory – largely the late 14th century tower and the Norman nave and aisles – were used as part of its reconstruction as a parish church for the local inhabitants. The priories at Thurgarton and Worksop suffered a similar fate, while

Newstead was purchased by Sir John Byron of Colwick. He actually retained the west front of the priory church and then worked a number of the monastic buildings into his new home. A similar story applies to Rufford Abbey, which was purchased after the Dissolution by Sir George Talbot, 4th Earl of Shrewsbury. It was then developed into a country house by the 6th Earl between 1560 and 1590. Other monasteries were less fortunate and were completely demolished, although the ruins of Mattersey Priory still survive up in the north-east of the county. As for the dispossessed former occupants, a number went onto become parish priests, while the people of Nottinghamshire did not rise up against the Reformation like they did in neighbouring Lincolnshire and Yorkshire. That said, there were dissenting voices, with Dutchman Van Baller preaching Lutheran doctrines at Worksop, John Lascells executed at Tyburn in 1546, and alleged heretic Anne Askew supplying the most poignant tale of these times as a result of her steadfastness and subsequent horrific execution in 1546 (see *Quirky Nottinghamshire [Nuthall]* for more).

Quirk Alert: *Three Wives and Twenty Five Little Whalleys*

The church of St Wilfrid in Screveton contains an alabaster tomb of Richard Whalley, who died in 1583. However, he was a very busy chap in life, having three wives and fathering 25 children!

NOTTINGHAMSHIRE'S ANCIENT MEDIEVAL CROSSES

This cross at Collingham probably dates from the 14th century and its crocketing suggests a former much grander edifice than most villages possessed. However, its purpose and the reason for its grandness are unknown, as Collingham is not listed as having a medieval market.

This cross at Gringley-on-the-Hill is Grade II listed and described by English Heritage as of medieval origin. Whether it dates back as far as 1252 which was when the village was granted its market charter is not known.

Kirkby Cross in Kirkby-in-Ashfield dates from the 13th century and is another scheduled ancient monument.

Top Cross, Linby, dates back to medieval times and is Grade II listed.

Bottom Cross, Linby, dates from 1663, and was built over an ancient well.

In addition to the Dissolution, a number of significant political events also occurred in Nottinghamshire in the 16th century. Perhaps the most notable occurred in 1567, when the Shrievalties of Nottinghamshire and Derbyshire were divided, having been combined under one Lord Lieutenant since at least 1066. Having said that, the post wasn't occupied on a permanent basis until the 17th century, and in Tudor times, the post was only occupied during times of crisis. Meanwhile, many of Nottinghamshire's M.P.s from the 16th century came from the county's gentry, such as the Byron, Markham, Pierrepont and Stanhope families, while they were joined in the latter half of the century by the Cavendishs, fruit of the union of William Cavendish and Bess of Hardwick in neighbouring Derbyshire. By the early 17th century, others joined their ranks by purchasing titles, with Sir John Holles paying £10,000 for the Baronetcy of Haughton in 1616, and adding the vacant earldom of Clare to his collection in 1624 for a further £5,000. Similarly, Sir William Cavendish acquired the Viscountcy of Mansfield in 1620 followed by the earldom of Newcastle in 1628, while Philip Stanhope secured the Baronetcy of Stanhope in 1616 and the earldom of Chesterfield in 1628.

It was also in the 16th century that coal mining began to take off, with Lenton Priory granting Wollaton's Sir Henry Willoughby (1451-1528) the permission to extract coal on their patch, mainly on the Wollaton estate. It has been estimated that the Wollaton pits were producing around 20,000 tons of coal per year, and the huge profits accrued from the coal allowed Sir Henry's second son, Sir Francis Willoughby (1546-1596), to build the magnificent Wollaton Hall between 1580 and 1588. Designed by the famous Elizabethan architect Robert Smythson, the building consists of a high central hall, surrounded by four towers while the floor plan is thought to be based on Giuliano da Majano's late 15th century Villa Poggio Reale near Naples.

As well as coal, Sir Francis Willoughby also owned one of the first ironworks in Nottinghamshire while he also became a pioneer in the manufacture of glass. Meanwhile, the first railroad was built in Nottinghamshire as early as 1604, and that was on the Willoughby patch, too – constructed by Huntingdon Beaumont who was partnered by Sir Percival Willoughby, the second occupier of Wollaton Hall. The railroad was known as the Wollaton Wagonway and ran from Wollaton Lane to Strelley Pits. Despite having wooden rails and the coal trucks being pulled by horses, it was still perhaps the first such industrial line in England.

In the mid-16th century, William Lee of Calverton invented the first ever stocking frame knitting machine, and which ultimately led to him presenting Queen Elizabeth I with a pair of silk stockings in 1598. Despite this, the queen failed to encourage him, fearing trouble from redundant knitters, and twice turned him down for patents. Lee therefore took his machinery to Rouen in France, taking with him his brother, James, as well as nine workmen and nine frames. He found better support from Henry IV of France, who granted him a patent. The Lee's began to prosper but alas, that all changed after Henry's assassination in 1610. William died in 1614, but James returned to Thoroton where William's apprentice had continued to work on the frame and produced a number of improvements. This led to the establishment of two knitting centres, one in London and one in Nottingham, and the machinery that the Lee's developed provided the foundation for the blossoming lace industry in Nottingham nearly a century later.

Wollaton Hall built between 1580 and 1588 and paid for by the coal mined by the Willoughby family.

The Willoughby Almshouses at Cossall, donated by George Willoughby in 1685.

Quirk Alert: *Out of the Frame*

William Lee's historically important stocking-frame invention of 1589 may never have happened but for infatuation. For it is alleged that it was the indifference to his wooing of a certain lady obsessed with knitting that drove him to develop the machine, so that it could take the place of her needles and she might finally notice him!

It was also during the 16th century that many new religious denominations came to the fore, and although neither the Nottinghamshire Catholics nor Jesuits made any impact, a number of Puritans certainly did. One of them was William Brewster of Scrooby, who became one of the main figureheads of the Pilgrim Fathers who, following persecution in England, moved to Holland before sailing for North America on the *Mayflower* in 1620 to become founders of the Plymouth colony in New England (see *Quirky Nottinghamshire [Scrooby]* for more). A handful of other Nottinghamshire clergy were ejected from their posts for their views throughout the early 17th century, while 1659 saw Quaker meetings in Newark broken up with violence, and the 1665 Five Mile Act drive dissenters out of the towns and into the countryside. Nevertheless, the Conventicles Act of 1669 saw over 2,000 non-conformists registered in Nottingham alone, and by 1689, the Toleration Act enabled dissenters to build their own chapels with the earliest in Nottinghamshire dating to the Quaker meeting house in Blyth (1700) and another in Mansfield (1702).

Quirk Alert: *Out of Order*

In 1574, Elias Okedeane of Greasley was charged in the ecclesiastical court with failing to wear a surplice, while in 1593, Richard Clifton of Babworth was charged with not making the sign of the cross as well as not observing fast and holy days!

Thurland Hall, where Charles I set up his temporary headquarters after raising his standard in Nottingham on 22nd August 1642.

The Governor's House, Newark-on-Trent, and the main headquarters of the Royalists in the East Midlands during the English Civil War.

Before launching into Nottinghamshire's role in the English Civil War, it is worth summarising the cause, the main events, and the effects of this hugely important historical event, which took place in three distinct phases between 1642 and 1651. Of course, England had been ruled by monarchs for centuries until the reign of King Charles I. However, having ascended the throne in 1625 Charles, like so many of his predecessors, believed in the Divine Right of Kings, but this was a time when Parliament was beginning to assert greater control and were seeking to limit the royal prerogative. Nevertheless, Charles ploughed on with his unpopular religious policies, leading to costly intervention in Europe in 1627, a move which was opposed by Parliament. The intervention also proved a disaster, Parliament thus opened impeachment proceedings against him, at which point Charles promptly dissolved Parliament!

Despite his desperate need for money, and which could largely only be raised with the support of Parliament, Charles refused to recall Parliament for another decade, a period which became known as "the personal rule of Charles I". Unable to raise funds through Parliament, Charles resorted to a series of deeply unpopular taxes that gradually turned large parts of the country against him. Moreover, his religious desire to impose High Anglicanism had already antagonised many in England, but when he attempted to enforce this on the Scots in 1637, rebellion broke out north of the border, leading to what became known as the Bishops Wars of 1639-1640. Again without sufficient funds, Charles' forays into Scotland were another disaster and ultimately led to the Scots taking Newcastle and Charles having to pay Scotland war expenses.

Desperate for cash, Charles finally recalled Parliament in England in 1640 – an opportunity for Parliament to discuss grievances against the Crown and to oppose an English invasion of Scotland. True to form, Charles took offence to this slight on his Divine Rule, and promptly dissolved Parliament again – thus introducing the term "Short Parliament" to British history. He also still forged ahead with his attack on Scotland, but had learned nothing from his previous attacks. Not only did he lose again, but the Scots promptly occupied Northumberland and Durham and Charles had to pay them £850 a day to stop them from advancing further!

So, in November 1640, Charles had no choice but to recall Parliament again. Naturally, by now, Parliament was openly hostile to Charles. There is much more history to impart here, but suffice to say that there was much bartering between Charles and what now became known as the "Long Parliament", a number of high profile executions, and even more Acts of Parliament. Throughout it all, Charles clung to his belief of Divine Right, while trouble in Ireland and accusations of improper use of the army there culminated in the King attempting to arrest five members of the House of Commons. Once again he failed, at which point, presumably sensing that control was slipping away, he withdrew to the Royalist stronghold of the north of England, albeit adding another failure to his long list – that of attempting to requisition the arsenal at Hull. The military governor refused, and when Charles attempted to use force, he was driven away.

By this stage, most areas had already declared for King or Parliament, and war was inevitable. It only remained for it to be sparked ... in Nottingham. The resulting English Civil War is generally regarded to have been fought in three distinct phases. The first phase ran from 1642 to 1646, and like the other two phases, was fought between the Parliamentarians (the Roundheads) and the Royalists (the Cavaliers). The first phase ended in February 1646 when the King surrendered to Scottish forces in Southwell (more on that shortly). Alas, Charles refused to accept Parliament's demand for a constitutional monarchy, and temporarily escaped captivity in November 1647. He managed to form an alliance with Scotland in 1648, and hence the second phase of the war (1648-1649), but which again resulted in his capture, this time by Oliver Cromwell's now established New Model Army. This time, he was tried, convicted and executed for high treason on 30th January 1649. The monarchy was subsequently abolished and the Commonwealth of England established in its place. However, the third phase of the war took place between 1649 and 1651, when supporters of Charles II battled with Parliamentarians, and which ultimately resulted in Royalist defeat at the Battle of Worcester on 3rd September 1651. So, that's the background, now onto Nottinghamshire's role...

St Nicholas's church, Maid Marian Way, Nottingham. Nothing remains of the Norman church, thanks to the Royalists who used the tower as a battery from which to bombard the Parliamentarians in Nottingham Castle. Determined to prevent the church falling into Royalist hands again, Colonel Hutchinson had it pulled down. Re-building began in 1672.

Despite having traditionally been a Royalist stronghold, on the eve of the English Civil War, Nottinghamshire had divided loyalties thanks to deeply unpopular measures imposed by Charles I. The most controversial of these was Ship Money, a tax imposed on coast dwellers to help pay for defences against piracy or enemy forces, but which was also outrageously imposed on inland counties like Nottinghamshire. Nevertheless, on the 22nd August 1642, Charles I raised his standard in Nottingham and made Thurland Hall his temporary headquarters. He was joined here by his nephews, the young German princes Maurice and Rupert, as well as his two eldest sons, Charles and James. Unfortunately, only around 300 people enlisted and sure enough, as soon as the King departed for the Battle of Edgehill, Nottingham was secured by the Parliamentarians, led by George and John Hutchinson, with the latter appointed as Governor of the Castle in June 1643. Around 700 men held Nottingham for Parliament, but there were still Royalist strongholds around the county with the Earl of Shelford and Lord Chaworth holding Shelford House and Wiverton Hall respectively for the King, whilst the Marquess of Newcastle commanded one of the King's armies. However, it was Newark that became the most important place for the Royalists, not only in Nottinghamshire but in the East Midlands, too. The town was occupied for Charles I by Sir John Digby as early as December 1642, although Sir John Henderson commanded the town's garrison, setting up his headquarters at the Governor's House in the Market Place. Newark itself was fortified, with a narrow ditch and rampart constructed around the town, and just in time for the first of three sieges by Parliamentarian forces. Fierce fighting first ensued during February 1643 when the attackers managed to breach the defences before being repelled. However, by June 1643, Queen Henrietta Maria had arrived along with 4,500 troops to reinforce the garrison and it was from this improved position of strength that a force from Newark attacked Nottingham three months later, holding Trent Bridge for around two weeks. Unfortunately, all attempts to capture Nottingham Castle by force were repelled, while the alternative tack of bribery also failed, with George Hutchinson refusing a title and £10,000 to surrender the garrison. In fact, the Royalists were left in no doubt where Hutchinson's allegiance lay: "If my Lord would have that poor castle he must wade to it in blood". January 1644 then saw another Royalist attempt to storm the castle with 1,500 troops, but again they failed, while conversely, a month later, Newark was attacked by Parliamentarians again. Led by Major-General Sir John Meldrum, the Roundheads bombarded the town for a month with cannons before Prince Rupert arrived on 20th March with 6,000 troops and defeated the Roundheads on Beacon Hill.

Quirk Alert: *Seventh Heaven*

One Nottinghamshire Royalist was Sir Gervase Clifton of ... well ... Clifton! But despite his great political achievements – at varying times a Justice of the Peace, an MP for Nottinghamshire, MP for Nottingham and High Sheriff of Nottinghamshire – he is most remembered for having had seven wives! He also outlived the first six of them, the sixth being called Jane Eyre! There must be a story in there somewhere...

Meanwhile, Nottingham remained in Parliamentarian hands, but consistently under attack from Royalists, with the latter also plundering West Bridgford and Wilford in April 1645. However, two months later, the decisive Battle of Naseby took place in Northamptonshire, resulting in the defeat of King Charles's main army, and it was all downhill for the Royalists from there. September 1645 saw the final siege of Newark, which started with Major-General Poyntz gathering a Parliamentarian army in Nottingham. They then advanced to Shelford House, and on 3rd

November they slaughtered its defenders – including its commander, Colonel Philip Stanhope – and then razed the house to the ground, before turning for the other Royalist stronghold at Wiverton Hall.

However, here, Sir Robert Therill's garrison surrendered, although that didn't prevent a similar destruction, with only the gatehouse of this 15th century moated manor house surviving. Poyntz then besieged Belvoir Castle, starving its garrison into submission, before finally turning his attention on Newark. At the same time, an army of 9,000 English and 7,000 Scots headed down from the north under the command of the Earl of Leven before arriving at Muskham Bridge on 26th November. They camped on an island to the north-west of Newark formed by the rivers Devon and Trent, naming their base as Edinburgh! As for Newark itself, the town had been heavily fortified during Royalist occupation, with a series of small square camps linked by a network of ramparts and trenches. This included two large earthworks that became known as the King's Sconce and the Queen's Sconce, and back in May 1646 it harboured around 2,000 Royalist troops. However, knowing that he was beaten, on 5th May 1646, King Charles I disguised himself as a beardless priest (he was well-known for his pointed beard), and gave himself up to the Scots at the King's Head in nearby Southwell. In an attempt to avoid further bloodshed, he also sent orders onto Newark to surrender, which they duly did on the 8th May. The Earl of Leven allowed the garrison and their commander, Lord John Bellasis, to march out honourably. The temporary fortifications were then levelled and filled, while Newark Castle was dismantled and remained a ruin until its restoration in the 1840s and then again in the 1890s. Nottingham Castle suffered a similar fate, although the order for its destruction didn't arrive until May 1651.

The Saracen's Head at Southwell. Formerly known as the King's Head, this is where King Charles I gave himself up on 5th May 1646.

However, that's not quite the end of Nottinghamshire's involvement in the English Civil War, for the Royalists attempted to take Newark again in the second phase of the war in July 1648. The Parliamentary forces based at Bingham were sent to intercept them and a minor skirmish occurred at Widmerpool, followed by the Battle of Willoughby-on-the-Wolds where the Royalists were defeated and Colonel Gilbert Byron was captured. It was this second phase of the war that ended in the execution of Charles I. During his trial, Colonel John Hutchinson (MP for Nottinghamshire) and Gilbert Millington (MP for Nottingham) both sat in the special court, and added their signatures to the royal death warrant – thus effectively making them both guilty of regicide! Other local signatories were Edward Whalley and Henry Ireton – and apart from Hutchinson, who was supported by the Royalist Lord Byron, the other three paid dearly for those signatures. Millington was sentenced to life imprisonment on Jersey where he died in 1666, while Whalley escaped to America where he lived in exile until his death in 1674. Ireton's fate, however, is worthy of its own *Quirk Alert* (see *The Final Hurdle* below).

Quirk Alert: *The Final Hurdle*

One of the signatories on the royal death warrant of Charles I was Henry Ireton, the eldest son of German Ireton of Attenborough. He was also the son-in-law of Oliver Cromwell, having married his daughter, Bridget … and for this he suffered a bizarre posthumous fate. For after the Restoration of the Monarchy in 1660, Charles II had Ireton's body exhumed. Then, on 30th January 1661 (the 12th anniversary of the execution of his father), he had him drawn on the hurdle through the streets of London, and then hung, drawn and quartered at Tyburn. His head (or what was left of it) was then placed in a prominent position at Westminster Hall, where it remained until at least 1685! Fortunately for Ireton, he had died of a fever in Ireland in 1651, aged only 40!

Following the demise of the monarchy, most prominent Royalists were allowed to reclaim their land after paying a fine. However, the exceptions were the Marquess of Newcastle and Sir John Byron who were both barred from repossession at any price. But we're not quite done with Nottinghamshire and the English Civil War, for two more Royalist plots took place during the Commonwealth period. The first on 8th March 1655 saw 300 conspirators meet at the New Inn near to Rufford Abbey along with a cartload of weapons. However, this particular group lost its nerve and dumped the arms in a pond … although the ringleaders were later rounded up and imprisoned. The second plot saw Richard, Lord Byron, assemble a force of 120 men in Sherwood Forest on 12th August 1659. They then marched towards Nottingham, but diverted to Derby before surrendering there on the 14th. The final act of this remarkable period in British history saw the army of General George Monck march through Nottinghamshire on 2nd January 1660, en-route from Scotland to London, where he began the process that resulted in the Restoration of the Monarchy at the end of May 1660.

Finally with respect to the English Civil War, we'll

return briefly to Sherwood Forest. For many centuries, the felling of oaks for use in building was strictly controlled and royal permission was required, with permission only likely to be granted for churches, chapels ... and siege engines. It wasn't until the Commonwealth period of 1649-1660 that a sizeable number of oaks began to be felled, with the Navy demanding timber for ship construction to help in their struggle against the Dutch – a demand supported by the fact that the monarchy had been abolished, and the forest was therefore no longer "Royal"! However, at the Restoration, a royal warrant was issued in 1661 for the import from Germany of red and fallow deer to replace the large numbers slaughtered during the Commonwealth period. Nevertheless, demand for timber continued, notably for the rebuilding of St Paul's Cathedral following the Great Fire of London in 1666 with trees taken from the estates of the Duke of Newcastle at Welbeck Abbey. Eventually, the size of the forest began to dwindle, with 3,000 acres syphoned off for Clumber Park, while numerous other enclosures also took land throughout the following 18th century.

Quirk Alert:
Eakring Rude and Eakring Crude

In 1669, the Reverend William Mompesson arrived at Eakring, having left behind harrowing memories of Eyam in Derbyshire where he had presided over the burial of over 260 of the village's 350 inhabitants between September 1665 and October 1666, including those of his wife and children. His reward at superstitious Eakring was banishment to a hut in Rufford Park and delivery of sermons from an ash tree which became known as Pulpit Ash. Mompesson remained at Eakring for another 40 years, before dying of old age in 1709. Meanwhile, a short distance from Pulpit Ash is a number of oil wells, with the first strike having been made on June 8th 1939 to a depth of 1,914 feet.

Quirk Alert: *Vamping Diaries*

East Leake's church of St Mary the Virgin is one of only six English churches to retain a tin trumpet known as a vamping horn – a kind of megaphone that came into fashion during the reign of Charles II. East Leake's vamping horn also happens to be the largest of the six, measuring 7 feet 9 inches long when fully extended, and 21 inches across the mouth. It was used as part of the gallery orchestra until 1855.

From the Restoration to the Industrial Revolution

As covered in the previous chapter, Nottingham Castle was slighted towards the end of the English Civil War, but following the Restoration, the site was acquired by the Duke of Buckingham who, in turn, sold it to the Duke of Newcastle in 1674. However, although he commenced the preparation for a grand new mansion, he died in 1676, leaving his son, the 2nd Duke, to complete the work.

It was also during the late 17th century that old timber-framed Nottingham began to be replaced with brick and stone, with much of the brick having been sourced from the nearby Mapperley Plains. The fact that its foremost citizens were wealthy enough to fund the rebuild largely stemmed from the growing prosperity in the area from its many industries, particularly coal. The town's first banker duly arrived in 1696 – Thomas Smith of Tithby – while the turn of the century saw mansions with formal gardens laid out around what was shortly to become the Lace Market.

In the years following the Restoration, we've already mentioned that nonconformists were persecuted, but the beginning of the 18th century saw greater toleration and those that benefitted the most were the Methodists. John Wesley himself visited Nottingham 28 times during his career, the first time being 11th June 1741, while toward the end of his career in 1777, he remarked

THE "NEW" AND THE OLD NOTTINGHAM CASTLE

This is the Ducal mansion that took the place of Nottingham Castle after it was slighted at the end of the English Civil War. It was built by the second Duke of Newcastle between 1674 and 1679.

One of few remains of the medieval castle, this is part of the fortified approach to the middle bailey, built by Henry II in the late 12th century.

that: "There is something in the people of this town which I cannot but much approve of". Conversely, he held great affection for the society formed in Misterton in north-east Nottinghamshire which he visited regularly. By the late 18th century, the meetings in members' houses had been superseded by permanent chapels, including those in Nottingham (1764), Newark (1776), Worksop (1780), Retford (1786) and Mansfield (1799). As for Nottinghamshire Catholics, they remained restricted to a few squires and members of the aristocracy, so Bonnie Prince Charlie's march south in 1745 found little support in the county. Indeed the Duke of Kingston actually provided a troop of horse which was involved in a skirmish with the Scots near Congleton, and which later pursued them back to Scotland, while a year later, they also fought at Culloden.

One area that the church did benefit was schools. A Grammar School attached to Southwell Minster had been established as far back as 1543 by an Act of Parliament, and it joined the Magnus Grammar School at Newark which had been founded in 1532 by Thomas Magnus and was affiliated to the church of St Mary Magdalene – with both schools effectively being re-founded and based on their medieval predecessors. Similarly, Nottingham Grammar School had been re-founded in 1512 with its predecessor possibly dating back to 1137, while East Retford Grammar School was re-founded in 1518, having received a benefaction from Thomas Gunthorpe, the vicar of Babworth. The first free Grammar School followed in Mansfield in 1561 and All Saints Grammar School at Elston in 1615, before the 17th century began to see village schools established, including those at Ruddington (1641), Sutton-in-Ashfield (1669), West Drayton (1688), South Leverton (1691), Misson (1693), Morton (1695) and Bunny (1700). By 1800, 66 Nottinghamshire parishes had their own school, while by 1802, it is estimated that 1,700 children were attending Sunday school in Nottingham alone.

The late 17th century also saw the brewing industry establish itself in Nottinghamshire, with Daniel Defoe remarking that the liquor brewed in Nottingham was the best in the East Midlands, while his co-commentator of the day, Celia Fiennes, stated in 1695 that at Newark she had "met with the strongest and best Nottingham ale that looked very pale but exceedingly clear". As for Nottingham, some of the sandstone caves underneath the castle were used by brewers as cellars, including one excavated in 1966 where a well, a malt roasting oven with a firing pit and a large room for steeping the grain were discovered. By 1800, Nottingham was home to three established breweries, Henry Green & Co, Thomas Simpson, and Messrs. Teverill & Co. Meanwhile in Newark and nearby Fiskerton, the local brewers had to pay a measure of beer known as a "tolsester" to their lords of the manor for the right to brew. This led to the founding of the Tolsester Court of Brewers, Tippers and Huccsters, a body which met annually. Finally, there's much more on brewing in the Arnold, Kimberley, Mansfield and Old Basford chapters of the *Quirky Nottinghamshire* section.

Sticking with industry from the 17th and 18th centuries, bell-founding continued as a Nottingham tradition with Nottinghamshire and its neighbouring counties regularly purchasing Nottingham bells. One such manufacturer was Henry Oldfield of Lister Gate and his family continued the tradition for generations until they sold out to Daniel Hedderly of Bellfounders' Yard in 1747 who, in turn, kept the tradition going until 1850, while another 18th century bell-founder was Tatham who worked in Castle Gate and latterly Bridlesmith Gate.

Looking down the final stretch of the former turnpike road that ran from Retford to the ferry over the Trent at Littleborough, and which was built by the Retford and Littleborough Turnpike Trust in 1825. The turnpike was managed by trustees called Sir W.B. Cooke and Company, a private Bank located in Retford and known locally as "The Retford Bank". The building undergoing renovation (you can't win 'em all!) is the original toll house.

Quirk Alert: *The A-peel of Elopement!*
In the 18th century, the remote village of Fledborough was something of a Nottinghamshire Gretna Green. It would appear that a generous rector, the Reverend Sweetapple, developed a reputation for granting marriage licenses to anyone, thus bringing a flood of hopeful elopers to the village. They were joined in 1820 by a certain Dr Arnold, a well-known headmaster of Rugby, who came to Fledborough to marry the rector's daughter – who presumably before her marriage, possessed the rather appealing name of Miss Sweetapple! One would assume that this wasn't an elopement given that the service would have been delivered by her father!

Two significant developments that occurred during the 18th century were the enclosure of land and the emergence of turnpike trusts. Before 1700 only 12 per cent of Nottinghamshire's land had been enclosed, but the 18th century saw 158 Enclosure Acts passed. These Acts brought about the enclosure of open fields and common land in the country, creating legal property rights to land that was previously considered common. The 18th century Acts in Nottinghamshire covered over half the county, with the greatest concentration in the Dukeries while a further 79 Acts were passed in the 19th century to enclose a further 35 per cent of the land. As for turnpike trusts, these were bodies set up by Acts of Parliament with powers to collect tolls in order to maintain principal highways. The first turnpike road in Nottinghamshire was opened between 1725 and 1726 on the part of the Great North Road between Grantham and Little Drayton, and thus passed through Newark, while a later stretch to East Retford was turnpiked in 1765. Nottingham to Loughborough was the second road to be turnpiked between 1737 and 1738 (the present A60), but it wasn't until half a century later in 1787 that the more northerly stretch from Nottingham to Mansfield was also turnpiked. The 19th century then saw the emergence of stagecoaches while the Royal Mail coaches brought even more routes and Nottinghamshire towns into play, like Ollerton and Worksop. By 1836, there were 27 cross-country stages in Nottinghamshire, varying from local routes from Nottingham to Ilkeston and Nottingham to Heanor, to long-distance routes passing through the county in all directions.

Quirk Alert: *The Swan with Two Necks, The Bull and Mouth, and a Beautiful Savage!*

During the 18th century, road conditions became much improved following the emergence of Turnpike Trusts. For example, W. Chaplin & Company was able to run a stagecoach service from London to Nottingham. Operated from the Swan With Two Necks in Lad Lane, London, the 124 mile route was worked by four stagecoaches each seating four passengers inside and eight outside, with the daylight trip taking 14 hours 45 minutes, and the overnight trip taking 18 hours 30 minutes. Other coaches passing through Nottingham included "The Express" operated by E. Sherman & Company which ran from the Bull and Mouth in St Martin-Le-Grand in London, and "The Courier" operated by J. Francis & Company and which ran from the Belle Sauvage on Ludgate Hill, London. As for travellers from Newark and Retford on the Great North Road, they had a choice of "The Union", "The Rockingham" (both Leeds), "The Lord Wellington" (Newcastle-upon-Tyne), "The Royal Express" or "The Highflyer" (both York).

Moving back to late 17th century industry, and framework knitting had become Nottingham's principal industry, with many company's having transferred their business up to the Midlands from London due to lower costs. The industry soon spread to places like Mansfield, Sutton-in-Ashfield and Southwell, although by 1750, the employment of paupers in the trade led to the phrase "as poor as a stockinger". Successive Bills presented by Nottingham M.P.s Abel Smith and Robert Smith to regulate wages failed in 1776 and 1779, leading to the first instances of rioting and frame-smashing. Alongside these events, Robert Frost invented a square net in 1777 to be used by the lace industry in the manufacture of gloves, mitts, purses, shawls and wig foundations, while 1784 saw a Mr Ingham introduce warp lace to the town and William Dawson establish a factory in Turncalf Alley to manufacture it. Then in 1786, the fast-point net was invented by John Rogers of Mansfield. Nevertheless, these developments were superseded by the arrival of much finer yarn in 1804, and by 1808, Joseph Page of Nottingham was able to produce the first piece of double-press print net using doubled fine yarn. Thus began the lace industry in Nottingham, and by 1810, 15,000 people were employed in the town using around 1,800 frames.

Nottingham's lace industry then took a dip in the mid-19th century thanks to the illegal smuggling of frames out to France where the industry paid wages of up to 60 per cent higher, thus tempting a number of emigrations from the Nottingham area. However, the industry recovered towards the end of the 19th century, with the number of frames climbing from 1,050 to 2,250 between 1873 and 1883 and, by 1890, there were more than 130 lace factories in Nottingham alone, and over 500 in the town and its outlying areas of Arnold, Basford, Beeston, Lenton and Radford, which employed a combined workforce of 17,000 people. Unsurprisingly, therefore, Nottingham became the lace capital of the world throughout the 18th

NOTTINGHAM'S FAMOUS LACE MARKET

The Grade II-listed Adams Building on Stoney Street, probably the largest and finest example of a Victorian lace warehouse to survive in the country.

A former Lace Market warehouse on the corner of Stoney Street and Barker Gate.

and 19th centuries, and was centred on the area of central Nottingham known as the Lace Market – although it was never a market in the sense of having stalls, but comprised a series of salesrooms and warehouses for storing, displaying and selling the lace. The most impressive buildings can be found on Stoney Street and St Mary's Gate where lace manufacturer Thomas Adams (1817-1873) built his factory and warehouse buildings, including the Adams Building, opened in 1855. Born in Worksop, and a strong Quaker and philanthropist, Adams provided humane conditions for his workers as well as supplying a chapel, indoor toilets and a tearoom. He also ran a book club for his workers as well as a savings bank and a sick fund, while he also founded six churches in Nottingham, too. Today, the Lace Market is a protected heritage area, and these impressive lace and textile factories have been converted into shops, restaurants, cafes, bars, offices, apartments and even a college campus.

This building on High Pavement has, in the past, been a Victorian courtroom, a gaol and a police station, but has today been converted into a tourist attraction known as the Galleries of Justice. It was also the Shire Hall in the mid-20th century, making it the smallest civil parish in England, for it was a tiny bit of the county nestling in the centre of the Borough of Nottingham.

The previous paragraph on the lace industry runs from the late 17th century to the late 19th century, meaning that it spans the entire period of the Industrial Revolution. This period is largely agreed to have begun in earnest with Richard Arkwright's water-powered cotton-spinning machines that he developed at Cromford in Derbyshire in 1771. However, before he arrived at Cromford, he had moved to Nottingham from his native Preston in 1768, and it was here that he developed his spinning frame at Hockley. These machines, though, were powered by horse gins, which is why he moved to Cromford where he could harness fast-flowing water to power his machines. Nevertheless, by 1794, there were eight cotton mills in Nottingham, with dozens more springing up around the county at places like Arnold, Basford, Cuckney, Fiskerton, Gamston, Langwith, Lowdham, Mansfield, Newark, Papplewick, Pleasley, Retford, Southwell and Worksop. By 1809, Mansfield alone had five mills, one of which employed 160 hands operating 2,400 spindles.

However, times were about to change somewhat, thanks to the Napoleonic Wars which brought about a blockade of British goods meaning that exports suffered adversely. This, along with new machinery being introduced into the hosiery industry, led to both unemployment and to considerable unrest ... and ultimately to the birth of the Luddites – so-named because some of their public pronouncements were signed by King Lud or Ned Lud. The first Luddite trouble kicked off in Nottingham market place on 11th March 1811 when a protest meeting led to the destruction of around sixty frames. The fashion soon spread to outlying Nottingham areas such as Bulwell, Lambley and Woodborough with around 100 more frames destroyed; by the end of the month, they were smashing machines in Sutton-in-Ashfield and Mansfield, too. The practice abated for a little while, but the first fatality (a man from Arnold) occurred with a resurgence of violence in November 1811, when up to 200 machines were destroyed, while 1812 saw the destruction extended to lace and silk frames. By March 1812, though, the authorities were hitting back, and the first Luddite transportations occurred. Thereafter, the practice diminished somewhat, although a further outbreak in 1814 resulted in the murder of one man and the attempted murder of another from New Basford. Sentences were extended from transportation to execution and the practice finally fizzled out, with the last ever act of Luddism occurring at Bulwell on 2nd November 1816. Despite all of this negativity, the textile industry continued to flourish on the western side of the county, and by 1839, the area was employing 2,272 workers in 21 different mills.

Earlier, we talked of the 18th century transport improvements brought about by turnpike trusts. Of course, the other 18th century transportation break-

Quirk Alert: *All Men Must Die!*

The 18th century saw ceramics still popular in Nottingham, with a certain Mr Morley running an establishment at Mug-house Yard, Mug-house Lane, Beck Street. He specialised in brown mugs for use in public houses, while he had also been making a range of brown products known as Nottingham Ware since at least 1726. Typical of the product at the time was a brown stoneware mug of Queen Anne, set between two beefeaters, with dogs and a hare round the base and on the rim. An example of one such mug made for William Marsh in 1729 was also accompanied by a verse which read:

"On Banse downs a hair were found
Thatt led uss all a Smoaking Round".

But here is an example of another mug – and only a certain group of people will realise how extraordinary this fact is. For this particular mug was made for one Edward Stark in 1727, and was decorated with wolves and a stag. Valar morghulis!

through involved canals, with James Brindley constructing Britain's first major canal, the Bridgewater Canal, between 1759 and 1761. However, it was 1769 before Brindley turned his attention eastwards, for that was when he designed the Chesterfield Canal which ran from Chesterfield, entering north-west Nottinghamshire at Shireoaks and then running largely eastwards across the county, termniating at Stockwith on the River Trent. The canal consisted of 65 locks across its 46-mile length. The project ran from 1771 to 1777 and linked up to other canals such as the Erewash Canal on the Derbyshire/Nottinghamshire border, in order to service Derbyshire and Nottinghamshire's burgeoning coal and ironworks. By 1789, the Chesterfield Canal was aiding the transport per annum of 3,862 tons of lead, 42,379 tons of coal, 7,569 tons of stone, 4,366 tons of corn, 3,955 tons of lime and 1,544 tons of iron. Meanwhile in 1772, two large locks were built on the River Trent near to Newark. Then in 1793, the Trent was surveyed from Cavendish Bridge on the Derbyshire/Leicestershire border all the way downstream to Gainsborough, with most of the intervening 71 miles running through Nottinghamshire; 65 miles of this stretch was revealed to have an appropriate minimum depth of three feet, with the remaining six miles consisting of a number of shallows. This led to locks being constructed at Thrumpton, Beeston and Holme Pierrepont, and ultimately to the river being navigable by barge throughout its entire Nottinghamshire course. Within five years, there were over 140 crafts using the thoroughfare and by 1817, a steam packet service was running between Nottingham and Gainsborough. As for the river's exports, these included beer kegs, Cheshire cheese, coal, copper, ironstone, lead, pottery and salt, while imports included Swedish flax, hemp and iron ore, and Norwegian timber.

Nottinghamshire was also home to two other late 18th century canals. The Nottingham Canal was built between 1792 and 1796 and ran for 14.7 miles from the terminus of the Cromford Canal at Langley Mill to the River Trent at Nottingham. Although most of it was closed in 1937, the southern part has now been absorbed into the River Trent Navigation and the northern part from Wollaton to Langley Mill is used as a walking trail and a nature reserve. Meanwhile, the Grantham Canal was built between 1793 and 1797 and ran for 33 miles from Grantham to West Bridgford where it joined the River Trent. After the railways put the usefulness of canals into the shade, it was actually the Ambergate Railway Company who bought both the Grantham Canal (1854) and the Nottingham Canal (1855). Both canals eventually fell into disrepair though and the Grantham Canal was closed in 1936 a year before the Nottingham Canal. Since the 1970s, the Grantham Canal has been partly restored with two stretches now navigable to small vessels. The Erewash Canal and most of the Chesterfield Canal was also abandoned in 1962, although the Worksop to Trent section of the latter remains in use today.

NOTTINGHAMSHIRE'S 18TH CENTURY CANALS

A peaceful stretch of the Nottingham Canal at Awsworth. Built between 1792 and 1796 to provide an alternative coal route to Nottingham, this northern stretch of the canal is now home to walking trails and nature reserves.

Part of the Chesterfield Canal at Worksop and which is still navigable. The canal was the first to be built in Nottinghamshire between 1771 and 1777 and traversed the width of northern Nottinghamshire.

A disused part of the Grantham Canal just north-west of Cotgrave. It was built between 1793 and 1797 and, although closed in 1936, part of it has been restored by the Grantham Canal Society and is navigable again.

Of course, the heyday of the canals only lasted for around sixty years, as most were superseded by the railways in the mid-19th century. However, initially, they worked in tandem. A small railway line was built in 1805 in the Greasley parish, and was called the Giltbrook Bend, Greasley to Watnall Hall & Wool Pit line! It consisted of a mile and a quarter of track and, like many that followed it, linked coal mine with canal. Others included one linking North Brinsley Colliery with Brinsley Wharf (3.25 miles), Brinsley Colliery with Langley Bridge (2 miles), and Old Engine with the Robinettes Arm of the Nottingham Canal (0.5 miles). Of course, this was only a precursor to the railway explosion that began in 1836 when a Bill was presented to Parliament for two lines for the newly-formed Midland Railway Company whose headquarters were in Derby. The first of these lines was to connect Nottingham with Derby and the 15.5 mile line was officially opened on the 30th May 1839, with the locomotive achieving a top speed of 40 mph. The public service commenced on 4th June, ran four return services a day, and called at Beeston, Long Eaton, Breaston and Borrowash in between Nottingham and Derby.

By 1844, the Midland Counties Railway Company had merged with two others to form the Midland Railway Company, and this new company was soon laying track between Nottingham and Newark and then onto Lincoln with the line opening in August 1846. The line from Nottingham to Mansfield followed in October 1849 and from Nottingham to Grantham in July 1850. Meanwhile in the north of the county, the Manchester, Sheffield & Lincolnshire Railway Company opened the Woodhouse Junction (Sheffield) to Gainsborough section in July 1849, with the line passing through Worksop and Retford. By the end of the 19th century, hundreds of miles of track had been laid in Nottinghamshire alone, initially to satisfy local industrialists but also to link all towns via the primary transport system of its age. For example, the Nottingham Suburban Railway began serving most of the city's expanding commuter villages in 1889, although it was soon superseded by Nottingham's electric tram system and was forced to close in 1916. Finally, in 1893, the Manchester, Sheffield & Lincolnshire Railway obtained Parliamentary aproval to build a line south of Nottingham connecting to the Metropolitan Railway line from Marylebone, and thus the Grand Central Railway Company was born. The line opened to passengers in March 1899, while Nottingham's Victoria Station was opened on the Queen's 81st birthday on 24th May 1900, boasting 12 platforms and having cost £1,000,000. The station was shared by both the Great Central Railway and the Great Northern Railway, but was sadly demolished in 1967 to make way for the Victoria Centre – although the old station clock tower was incorporated into the main entrance of the shopping centre.

Moving briefly back to the beginning of the 19th century again, by 1815, overcrowding had become a real issue especially within the old walled medieval Nottingham where 8,000 back-to-back houses were

Quirk Alert:
The Font of No Knowledge

A most curious event happened in the early 19th century at Holy Cross church, Epperstone, for a rector buried the Norman font and substituted a smaller one. The reason behind the burial remains unknown, but the font was retrieved decades later in 1853 and still survives in the church today.

Quirk Alert: *In Loving Memory*

The church of St Luke at Kinoulton was built in 1793. However, the graveyard of its predecessor was put to questionable use by a 19th century Kinoulton farmer, who used some of its gravestones to mend his oven! He actually got away with it, too, until a farm labourer, about to tuck into his bread, was alarmed to see the words "In Loving Memory" stencilled down the side of his meal!

Quirk Alert: *Ann Burton, Aged 248*

So, clearly she isn't. However, she would be if it were construed that the date of her death was invalid and therefore she wasn't "officially dead". In which case, this premise could apply to Ann Burton, born 1766, and who – according to her gravestone in Sutton-in-Ashfield churchyard – died on 30th February 1836!

Nottingham railway station on Station Street. Originally known as Nottingham Midland, this is the third incarnation of the station which was built between 1903 and 1904.

Part of the 1875-built, 15-arched viaduct in Mansfield, all of which survives, despite the town being without a railway station between 1964 and 1995. Originally built to serve the Nottingham to Worksop line, this Grade II-listed structure stretches for 240 metres and is 25 metres high.

Quirk Alert: *Rail Wars*

The Nottingham to Grantham railway line that opened in 1850 was built by the Ambergate, Nottingham, Boston & Eastern Junction Railway Company. At the same time, the Great Northern Railway was in the process of expanding its Towns Line northwards and already had its eye on Grantham and expansion into Nottinghamshire. It therefore offered to join forces with the ANB&EJRC, an act which prompted the Midland Railway to take drastic action to protect its Nottingham to London service. And so as a GNR locomotive passed Colwick, a MR train trailed it. The GNR driver then made a charge at its MR counterpart, an act which ended in failure, eviction from his engine cab and the capture of his locomotive ... which was then spirited away to a MR engine shed and the approaching rails completely removed! With no way out of its shed, the GNR locomotive actually stayed there for seven months. However, the GNR had the last laugh, as in April 1855, the Ambergate Railway was leased to the GNR for a total of 999 years!

crammed into 132 streets, that were connected to 308 courts and alleyways. Disease was rife, the infant death rate high, and life expectancy of the poorest fell shockingly below 20 years of age. Alas, the Duke of Newcastle's castle mansion and Lord Middleton's Wollaton Hall prevented overspill into the suburbs until after the Nottingham Enclosure Act of 1845. Nevertheless, the town still had facilities, with two Assembly Rooms on Low Pavement and a theatre in St Mary's Gate joined by Nottingham General Hospital in 1781 and a local asylum in 1812, while gas lamps first arrived in 1819. Despite this, reform was desperately needed, so when the Reform Bill was first rejected in 1831 mobs took to the streets of Nottingham in protest and one attempt to break open the prison resulted in three deaths. Unsurprisingly, the Hussars were called out to help control the situation. Then on Monday 20th October, 20,000 people attended Reform Rally in the Market Place, and although most protestors conducted themselves peacefully, one mob attempted to storm the prison again while others sacked Colwick Hall, and set fire to the empty shell of Nottingham Castle and Lenton Hall, with Wollaton Hall only surviving a similar fate thanks to the presence of the Yeomanry. In January 1832, three of the rioters were sentenced to death while the Duke of Newcastle was awarded £21,000 as compensation for the "loss" of his semi-derelict Nottingham Castle!

Southwell Workhouse was built in 1824 and was cited by the Royal Commission on the poor law as the country's best-run workhouse, before the resulting New Poor Law of 1834 led to the construction of improved workhouses across the country. Today, it is run by the National Trust as one of England's best-preserved 19th century workhouses.

Quirk Alert: *The Forest Hackers*

In 1865 a group of youngsters attached to St. Andrew's church on Mansfield Road, Nottingham formed a football club and since they played on the Forest Recreation Ground, they called themselves Nottingham Forest. It was one of their players, Samuel Widdowson, who invented the shin pad in 1874, and which became a particularly valuable asset in those days as the hacking of shins was an acceptable part of the game – along with tripping, elbowing and charging down the goalkeeper!

BUILDINGS OF NINETEENTH CENTURY NOTTINGHAMSHIRE

Mansfield market place, including the memorial built in memory of Lord George Bentinck, younger son of the 4th Duke of Newcastle.

This Grade II-listed market cross in Bingham was erected in 1861 in memory of the Earl of Chesterfield's agent John Hassall of Shelford Manor.

Retford Town Hall, built in 1867 by Bellamy and Pearson.

Thoresby Hall, built between 1868 and 1874 for the 3rd Earl Manvers.

The New Trent Bridge was built in 1871. In the background is Nottingham Forest's City Ground; Forest were founded six years earlier in 1865.

Ossington Coffee House, Newark, built in 1882 by Viscountess Ossington to promote the cause of temperance.

From the Late Victorians to Present Day

Towards the end of the 19th century, some other familiar landmarks began to arrive, none more iconic than the New Trent Bridge that replaced its 17th century predecessor in 1871 and also allowed larger vessels to pass upstream. Also appearing during this era, were three firms which went onto become internationally famous, and remain so to this day. The first was a cigarette manufacturing company founded by John Player. Initially a drapery assistant, Player set up his own business in the 1860s but was soon supplementing his income with tobacco. By 1877, he had purchased a small tobacco factory in Broadmarsh and began manufacturing cigarettes. Then following the purchase of a 30-acre site at Radford he built and opened a much larger factory there in 1884. By 1893, his two sons had taken over the business and in 1898 two more factories were built on the Radford site. By this stage, the company workforce had expanded to around 1,000, and this total included around 200 girls who went by the name of Player's Angels – and who also made up to 200 cigarettes a day, by hand – a stark contrast to the five machines deployed at the site, which made 200 cigarettes per minute! The next significant event occurred in 1901 when, in response to hostile competitive threats from America, John Player & Sons merged with 12 other British manufacturers to form the Imperial Tobacco Group. Having survived the American threat, the company flourished and by 1914, the Radford site was employing 2,500 workers, while the onset of World War I also saw the issuing of patriotic cards with their cigarette packs. With the ever-increasing popularity of cigarettes, the business continued to expand and the work-

Quirk Alert: *The Loot of Boot*

When in 1928 University College Nottingham moved from Shakespeare Street in the city centre to its current location on the western edge of Nottingham, D.H. Lawrence commented as follows:

In Nottingham, that dismal town where I went to school and college,
they've built a new university for a new dispensation of knowledge.
Built it most grand and cakeily out of the noble loot
derived from shrewd cash-chemistry by good Sir Jesse Boot.

THE BIRTH OF NOTTINGHAM'S UNIVERSITIES

Nottingham University was originally founded as University College Nottingham in 1881, as a constituent college of the University of London, and this is part of the building where it all began. Today it is known as Arkwright Building and is part of Nottingham Trent University, but its foundation stone was laid in 1877 for its older sister university by none other than former British Prime Minister, William Ewart Gladstone. Formerly Trent Polytechnic, Nottingham Trent University achieved university status in 1992.

Following considerable expansion, University College Nottingham moved to the western outskirts of Nottingham, financed by an endowment fund, public contributions, and the generosity of Sir Jesse Boot who donated 35 acres that were to become known as University Park. The above Trent Building dominates the site and was formally opened by King George V on 10th July 1928. The university was granted a Royal Charter in 1948 and formally became known as the University of Nottingham.

force had increased to around 7,500 by the early 1930s following the building of two more factories on the Radford site. Of course, as the 20th century progressed, the harmful side-effects of smoking came to light, but the company still flourished, building a huge new facility known as the Horizon Factory on a new 45-acre site at Lenton in 1972. However, on the 15th April 2014, Imperial Tobacco announced that the Horizon Factory would close in early 2016, and which will bring an end to around 130 years of cigarette and tobacco manufacture in Nottingham.

The second of Nottingham's three internationally famous firms was founded by Jesse Boot in the late 19th century. Young Jesse had originally left school at the age of 13 to help his widowed mother run her small herbal shop in Nottingham's Goose Gate, eventually taking over the business in 1877, aged 27. Starting as he meant to go on, he used clever advertising to promote his products including the employment of a bellringer to walk Nottingham's streets announcing his bargain prices for soap. By 1885, he had moved to larger premises that were equipped with a workshop in which he developed his own products. By the 1890s, his business was doing so well that he was opening additional stores in Nottingham and in the surrounding towns. Boot's first factory accompanied these stores in 1892 and was followed by many more, including a soap works opened in 1928. However, it was just before his death in 1931 that he acquired the 300-acre site between Beeston and Lenton that would eventually grow into

NOTTINGHAM'S EARLY 21ST CENTURY CORPORATE GIANTS, FOUNDED LATE 19TH CENTURY

The former John Player & Sons main works, built in the early 1970s on a 45-acre site at Lenton. The company is now known as Imperial Tobacco. And alongside it is...

... the Head Office of Boots the Chemist, largely hidden by the trees. It is deeply ironic that this was as close as I could get, having worked exactly there for 18 years, but having left last year! The two buildings in question are D90 West and D90 East, just two of many (some of them listed) that occupy a vast site the size of a small town that stretches from Lenton to Beeston.

the "small town" that it resembles today, and which is populated by a large array of offices and factories built using many different styles of architecture, and with some of the buildings now holding listed status. There are also some beautifully landscaped gardens and woodland walks on the site, some of which are accompanied by impressive sculptures. All in all, a wonderful place to work – I should know, as I worked there from 1995 until the early 21st century, and would still be there now if they hadn't outsourced their IT department to a huge American IT company! Talking of which, that may not have been necessary had events unfolded differently after Jesse's death ... for in the 1920s, he had sold his controlling interest in the company to the United Drug Company. However, in 1933, the new controlling American company got into difficulty, and Jesse's son, John Campbell Boot, led a consortium of British financiers to re-purchase the company. Hats off to JCB! As for Jesse Boot, he was knighted in 1903, created a baronet in 1917 and raised to the peerage as 1st Baron Trent in 1929.

The final member of the trio of internationally renowned Nottingham firms founded in the late 19th century was the Raleigh Cycle Company Ltd. The company was effectively formed in 1889, but both Tom Humber from Beeston and another partnership headed by mechanic R.M. Woodhead had been building bicycles in Nottingham throughout the previous decade, with the latter company adopting the name Raleigh for their products which were named after a nearby street. Impressed by the products, businessman Frank Bowden bought out Woodhead's partnership, launched Raleigh as a company, and by 1889 was applying what were then new Dunlop tyres to his products. Within three years, Raleigh had entered the racing field and was soon winning prestigious races. The company then went onto become one of the leading manufacturers of racing cycles in the world in the 20th century, while it also produced iconic bicycles for children such as the Chopper (1969), the Grifter (1976) and the Burner (1982).

The turn of the 20th century also revealed some startling population figures, courtesy of the great censuses that commenced in 1801, and proved what a huge change the Industrial Revolution brought to Nottinghamshire. Using census-recorded Registration County figures, Nottinghamshire grew from a population of 152,573 in 1801, to 596,705 in 1901 – a population increase of 391%. However, if we analyse the population increase in the *towns* using Registration District and Council Parish figures, it is clear that the Industrial Revolution led people away from rural and into urban areas, with the urban population of Nottinghamshire jumping from 40% to 70% between 1801 and 1901. Leading the way was Nottingham itself, having grown from 28,861 in 1801 to 239,743 in 1901 – an increase of 830%! Hucknall Torkard saw an even greater rate of increase (1,018%), climbing from 1,497 to 15,250 while Kirkby-in-Ashfield saw a similarly huge increase from 1,002 to 10,318 (1,029%). However, Mansfield only increased from a population of 5,988 in 1801 to 21,445 in 1901 (a rise of a mere 358%), while Newark only jumped from 6,730 to 14,992 (223%) – although Mansfield still managed to leap-frog Newark to become the county's 2nd largest town in 1901, while Newark dropped to 5th place; the county's former 2nd largest place now found itself behind Worksop, which had climbed from a population of 3,263 in 1801 to 16,112 in 1901 (a 494% increase) and Hucknall Torkard (15,250), while 6th place Sutton-in-Ashfield had grown from a population of 3,311 to 14,862 (449%).

Wilford Suspension Bridge over the River Trent was opened in 1906 by the Nottingham Corporation Water Department. It was used as both a pedestrian footbridge linking West Bridgford to Meadows, and also to carry water to Wilford Hill reservoir.

These vastly inflated populations also needed transporting in the early 20th century: step forward Tom Barton. He began transporting people from his native Long Eaton in 1908 using a char-à-banc, and his transport network gradually expanded, including the transport of workers from Nottingham to the Chilwell Shell Works during World War I. In time, Barton rolled out his diesel engine buses with the now famous Robin Hood badge on red, maroon and cream livery. Meanwhile, 1919 saw the launch of Skills Motor Coaches in Nottingham, another firm still going strong today, and specialising in long-distance coach journeys, while the South Notts. Bus Company Ltd was formed in Gotham in 1928. The expanding public transport network also brought about the growth of West Bridgford as a dormitory town, and its population exploded from 293 in 1881 to 11,632 in 1911 – an absolutely enormous population increase of 3,970% in just 30 years!

Before moving forwards into the 20th century, the impact of the coal mining industry on Nottinghamshire throughout the Industrial Revolution period must be emphasised. Without doubt, it was this industry in the west of the county that largely accounted for those dramatic 19th century population increases in the surrounding towns. Dozens of pits were in use by 1801, with the output being shipped along the Erewash and Nottingham Canals, while the pits were mining to ever-greater depths. Nuthall's was sunk to 480 feet in the early 19th century, but when the centre of the mining industry switched to the Duke of Newcastle's Cinder Hill pit at Basford in 1841, depths of 666 feet were reached, followed by ever-deeper pits thereafter. By 1860, there were 21 collieries in Nottinghamshire, a figure that rose to 31 by 1907. Unsurprisingly, output increased dramatically, too, rising from 732,666 tons in 1862 to 11,728,886 tons by 1907, by which time the industry was employing 35,415 Nottinghamshire miners. Meanwhile, brewing remained a strong industry in Nottinghamshire throughout the 19th century, and Newark remained the most important brewing centre.

Statue of Harold Larwood in the centre of his home town of Kirkby-in-Ashfield.

Statue of Brian Clough at the top of the Old Market Square, Nottingham.

Sport also began to take off in Nottingham in the latter part of the 19th century. Nottinghamshire County Cricket Club's first recorded away game was at Sussex way back in August 1835, although some state 1841 as the club's founding date. What is for sure is that Nottinghamshire won the County Championship seven times between 1875 and 1886 and also shared the title three times between 1873 and 1889. During the 20th century, Trent Bridge established itself as one of the key test match grounds in the country, while Nottinghamshire produced legendary players such as Harold Larwood (1924-38) and hosted world-class players such as Sir Garfield Sobers (1968-74) and Sir Richard Hadlee (1978-1987). It was Sobers who also hit those legendary six sixes off poor Malcolm Nash during a Sunday League game against Glamorgan in August 1968. Meanwhile the oldest football club in the world is Notts County, founded in 1862. Alas, their only honours include a very early FA Cup success (in 1894) and an Anglo-Italian Cup success in 1995, but which is a slightly better return than Mansfield Town's Football League Trophy won in 1986. The trophies won by Nottingham's other club, Nottingham Forest, are considerably more impressive. These include two FA Cup triumphs in 1898 and 1959, but which were all superseded during the 18 year reign of the legendary Brian Clough between 1975 and 1993, during which time they won the League Championship in 1977/78, two European Cups (1979 and 1980), four League Cups and two Full Members Cups. Finally, no mention of Nottingham-based sport is complete without a mention of the superlative Clifton-born Jayne Torvill and Calverton-born Christopher Dean, who won World, European and Olympic gold medals for ice dancing, including their memorable *Bolero* routine at the 1984 Sarajevo Olympics when they posted a full house of sixes! More recently, they have both starred in the ITV show *Dancing on Ice* which ran annually between 2006 and 2014.

As for transport in the 20th century, the first electrified trams ran in Nottingham on New Year's Day, 1901, with Mansfield opening their electric tram service on 11th July 1905. The electric trams in Nottingham were then gradually replaced by trolleybuses with the first one introduced in 1927 and which ran between King Street and Basford, while motorbuses also began to appear throughout the 1920s; indeed, motorbuses had replaced the electric tram service in Mansfield by 1932, too, while the last of the *original* trams in Nottingham ran on 5th September 1936. The trolleybuses then lasted until 1966 by which stage they had been replaced by diesel buses. Also of note during the early 20th century was the Nottinghamshire & Derbyshire Tramways Company that was created in 1903 and later immortalised in the works of D.H. Lawrence's short story *Tickets Please* – and which featured the Ripley Rattler, which connected Ripley with Nottingham. Although this tram service was also superseded in the 1930s by the trolleybuses, trams have made an emphatic return to Nottingham in the 21st century. The first line opened on 9th March 2004 and cost £200 million to construct. It starts from Nottingham railway station just south of the city centre, and runs generally northwards for around nine miles (2.5 of them on roads), taking in numerous city centre stops before heading out for Basford, Bulwell and Hucknall, with a branch line running to a large Park and Ride facility at Phoenix Park to the north-west of the city. The trams have been so successful that two new multi-million pound lines are currently under construction. The first

Quirk Alert: *Blyth and Blidworth's Blessed Blend*

The 20th century saw the revival of the medieval custom of hanging an ale-garland each Christmas outside the Angel Inn at Blyth – to indicate that ale and food are provided within. Also revived was an old tradition at Blidworth St Mary's church whereby on the first Sunday in February, the last baby boy to have been baptised is dedicated at the altar and then rocked in a cradle. The child is then listed on what is known as the Register of Rockings that hangs on a wall above the font. Meanwhile, the spring which carries the pendulum of the clock in the church tower at Blidworth is made from a sword which saw action at Waterloo!

will link Nottingham Station to Toton via the Queen's Medical Centre, Nottingham University and Beeston, and the second line will link Nottingham Station to Clifton via Meadows and Wilford.

The previous paragraph mentions D.H. Lawrence, one of Nottinghamshire's most famous sons. Born in a typical mining home in Eastwood in 1885, Lawrence went onto write many classic novels and short stories in his short life (he died in France, in self-imposed exile, aged only 44). His most famous novels have all been adapted for television, sometimes numerously, and include *Sons and Lovers*, *The Rainbow*, *Women in Love* and *Lady Chatterley's Lover*. Alas, many of his novels tackled controversial subjects and were subject to heavy censorship in the early decades of the 20th century, while Lawrence himself suffered persecution as a result; indeed, at the time of his death, he was widely viewed as a pornographer who had wasted his considerable talents!

Up until the middle of the 20th century, coal mining in Nottinghamshire had been largely restricted to its western borders. However, 1945 saw the first of many modern collieries established further east at Cotgrave. Many more followed in the Dukeries, including the deep pits sunk at Bevercotes and Harworth (see *Quirky Nottinghamshire [Bevercotes]* for more) which, at a depth of more than 1,000 metres, were some of the deepest in the UK. Others further east included those at Calverton, Clipstone, Ollerton and Thoresby. The 1960s and 1970s saw a mass migration of miners from closed coalfields, particularly from the North East, to work in the expanding Nottinghamshire coalfield. To accommodate the immigrants, vast modern housing estates were built by the National Coal Board at Cotgrave, Calverton, Clipstone, Forest Town and Ollerton. At around the same time, a series of coal-fired electricity-generating stations appeared along Nottinghamshire's stretch of the River Trent, including those at Staythorpe (1950 and 1962), High Marnham (1962), Cottam (1969) and West Burton (1969), making Nottinghamshire a major player in the "Powerhouse of Britain".

The 1970s then saw the National Union of Miners begin to exert their influence via a number of strikes. However, that influence was short-lived, as anyone who watched the scenes unfold on their TV's in 1984 will confirm. Alas, picket lines were crossed daily at the Nottinghamshire pits, with the Notts NUM membership having voted in a secret ballot by 20,188 to 7,285

Quirk Alert: *Seismic 93*

The region around Thoresby Colliery at Edwinstowe was recently described by the British Geological Survey as the most seismically active area in the country. Between mid-December 2013 and mid-April 2014 alone, there were 93 small tremors, while 28th October 2014 saw an earthquake measure 2.6 on the Richter Scale. Of course, all of these tremors are largely attributed to mining!

D.H. LAWRENCE AND TRAMS

The D. H. Lawrence Birthplace Museum on Victoria Street, Eastwood. The great man was born here on 11th September 1885.

Also belonging to D. H. Lawrence Heritage is Durban House Heritage Centre on Mansfield Road. It contains an exhibition on the social history of Eastwood during Lawrence's lifetime, including the mining industry and trams.

Trams were the main method of transport at the turn of the 20th century, and they feature in D. H. Lawrence's short story, "Tickets Please". Many years later in the 21st century they have made a major comeback. The tram above outside Nottingham City Hall (built 1927-29) is one of many running on a multi-million pound network that, once again, links Nottingham City Centre to its outlying areas. As for the City Hall, its impressive dome contains five bells one of which, Little John, is one of the largest in England and is so heavy that the hammer that strikes it weighs a quarter of a ton!

Cottam Power Station, one of four huge power stations aligned along the River Trent in north-eastern Nottinghamshire, thus earning the area the nickname "The Powerhouse of Britain".

Entrance to Thoresby Colliery at Edwinstowe, currently the only surviving colliery in Nottinghamshire ... but alas, not for long.

not to join the national strike against pit closures, claiming it was unconstitutional. This led to many ugly scenes with one Yorkshire miner killed during a pithead demonstration at Ollerton. It was all in vain, too, as the near year-long strike ended in defeat for the miners, while the Nottinghamshire pits secured no favours from the Thatcher government. Pit closures followed and by 1997, only six collieries survived, all by this stage operating in private hands. Today, only one colliery survives – Thoresby Colliery at Edwinstowe – and UK Coal announced in April 2014) that the pit would close in 2015. One final word for the coal industry, though – for a special place in cricket folklore is owed to Annesley Colliery near Kirkby-in-Ashfield. This is because at one time there were five men working underground who were destined to go on to play for England, including the legendary "bodyline"' pace-bowling partners, Harold Larwood and Bill Voce.

Part of Robin Hood Way, as it passes through Sherwood Forest between Bothamsall and Ollerton.

Clumber Bridge, designed in 1770 by Stephen Wright and now part of Clumber Park which is run by the National Trust.

The Horse and Groom sits in the middle of the pretty village of Linby which, until 1988, also had a working colliery in its midst.

Part of the Queens Medical Centre, Nottingham. Until February 2012, it was the largest hospital in the UK and the largest teaching hospital in Europe.

Throughout the 20th century, Nottingham – along with most of the other major towns in the county – had its centre cleared of old housing and slums to be replaced by offices and shops. Former working class residents moved out to the fast-growing suburbs, while wealthier middle class residents moved out to villages within easy commuting distance of their place of work. The last few decades of the 20th century also saw the tourism industry grow in Nottinghamshire, with the two main focal points being Nottingham and Sherwood Forest. Numerous visitor centres also sprung up around the county, while other tourist hotspots include Clumber Park, Newstead Abbey and Rufford Abbey. Then there is the Robin Hood Way, a 104-mile footpath that stretches from Edwinstowe church to Nottingham Castle via a roundabout route that takes in amongst many other places, Sherwood Forest, Creswell Crags, Beauvale Priory and King John's Palace.

As we come towards the end of Nottinghamshire's history, it is worth clarifying the local government and county border changes implemented towards the end of the 20th century, and which still remain in place today (2015). The first and second of the maps below show the vague change in county shape following the Local Government Act 1972, and which came into force on the 1st April 1974. A number of counties disappeared completely as a result of this Act while others had their borders severely diminished. Nottinghamshire got off lightly, losing only the Finningley area from the northern-most tip of the historic county, which went to the new county of South Yorkshire. However, Nottinghamshire's "new" border with Humberside only lasted for 22 years after the latter was abolished in 1996, meaning that things are still pretty much the way they've been for around 1,000 years, save for the re-division of Yorkshire on the county's north-western frontier.

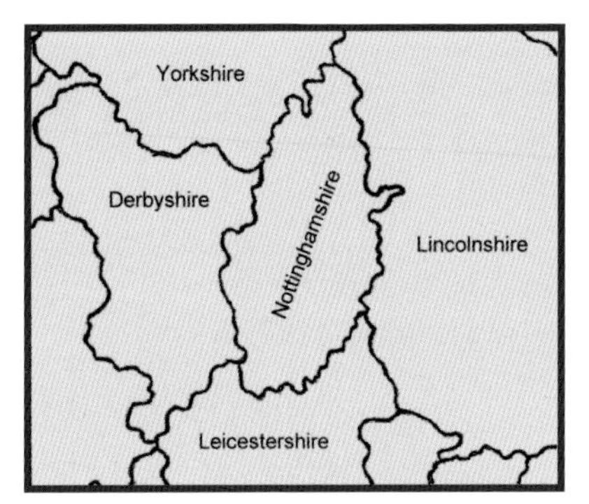

Historic Counties

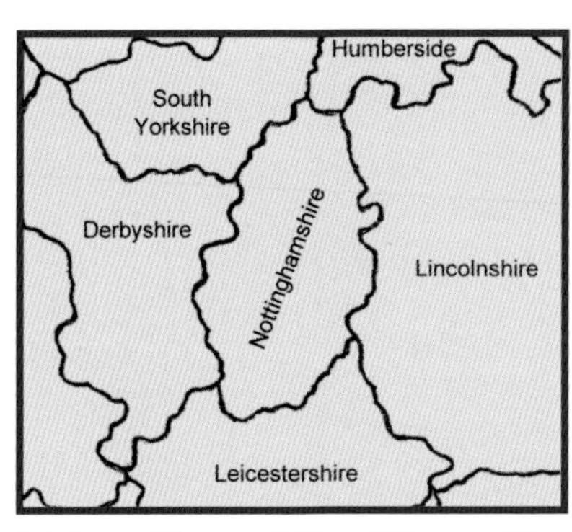

Metropolitan and Non-Metropolitan Counties – 1974-1996

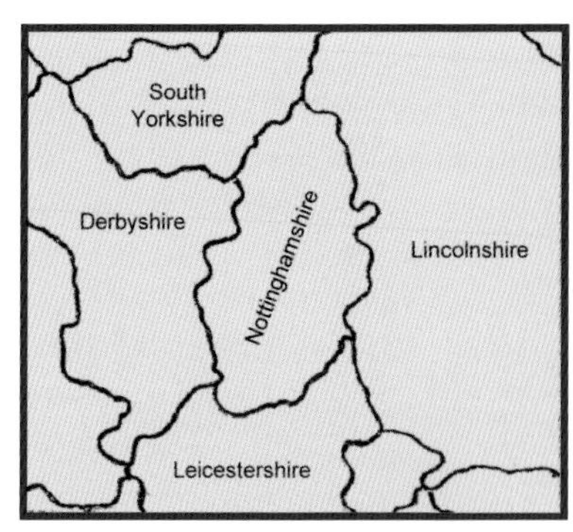

Ceremonial Counties – 1996-2104

Above: *The Double Diamond Jubilee commemoration at Laxton ...*
... and (left) *the Double Diamond at Tuxford. See Quirk Alert, opposite for the background.*

Some Quirky Nottinghamshire Stats

To complete the Conventional Nottinghamshire section, here are some unique and quirky statistics. For starters, Nottinghamshire is the county with the most individually named oaks, the obvious one being the Major Oak, but which is joined in Sherwood Forest, among others, by Parliament Oak, Old Churn Oak, the Greendale Oak, the Byron Oak and the Porter Oaks, each with their own story to

Quirk Alert: *Double Diamond*

Within three miles of each other at Laxton and Tuxford are two very different artefacts celebrating a double commemoration of the Diamond Jubilee of Queen Victoria and Queen Elizabeth II. At Tuxford, the artefact in question is known as The Victorian Lamp and can be found at the crossroads in the centre of the town. Originally erected in 1897 to celebrate the Diamond Jubilee of Queen Victoria, the lamp was restored in 1968 to commemorate the 750th anniversary of Tuxford receiving its market charter from Henry III in 1218. It was further restored in 1997 to mark the centenary of the Victorian Diamond Jubilee and then further enhanced in 2012 to commemorate the Diamond Jubilee of Queen Elizabeth II. The top of the lamp is marked with a golden crown and between the lamps are the crests of VR and ER while underneath, the crossroads are represented, pointing to Laxton, London, Lincoln and York.

As for Laxton's commemorative artefacts, these take the form of a time capsule buried underneath a commemorative plaque in 2012 to mark the Diamond Jubilee of Elizabeth II, while Queen Victoria's Diamond Jubilee is represented by a plaque on the trunk of a tree which was planted back in 1897 to celebrate the event. However, in the first photograph (opposite page, bottom left), the eagle-eyed amongst you will have already noticed the two ceramic interlopers standing on top of the tree plaque, while a poor third interloper lies in two halves at the foot of the tree!

tell. An even better tree-related story to tell is that of the Bramley apple, which was first seeded by pips planted by Southwell's Mary Ann Brailsford, but which took its name from the butcher, Matthew Bramley, who in 1846 bought the house (and by now, the tree) that Mary had seeded in 1809.

Church-wise, the font at Babworth All Saints' church is definitely the only one in Britain made from the Devon cider vat that was also used to make the pins which fastened the timbers of *Mayflower II* (1955), while Headon's St Peter's church is the only one to have a genuine crown of thorns collected from the site in Jerusalem where Jesus was tried before Pilate. Kingston-on-Soar's church has a sculpture containing the most babes in barrels (200), while the predecessor to Kilvington's 19th century St Mary's church must be the only one to have been used as a sheep fold – a similar scenario to the crumbling predecessor to Kimberley's 19th century Holy Trinity church, which was used for cock fights! Then we have the churches at Carburton and Perlethorpe which are two of only three in the country (the other is in Cambridgeshire) to have church registers pre-dating 1538, while the grandest of them all, Southwell Minster, must surely be the only church in the land to include work spanning 17 centuries.

We then have Bilsthorpe's old hall which presumably has the only remaining cupboard in which a 16th century monarch (Charles I) once hid! Thomas Cranmer of Aslockton is certainly the Archbishop who annulled the most royal marriages (Henry VIIIs marriages to Catherine of Aragon, Anne Boleyn and Anne of Cleves), while Maplebeck's pub was once the smallest pub in England with the largest landlord! Newark and Sutton-in-Ashfield are home to the biggest antique fair and the largest sun-dial in Europe, respectively, while Laxton is the last village in Europe still practising the medieval open field system of farming.

The Horseshoe Pile at Scarrington – the largest such structure in the world!

As for Nottingham, it is one of eight core cities recognised by the Government and was also the place where ibuprofen was discovered in 1961. Also hailing from Nottingham is a whole host of other discoveries including traffic lights (1868), football shin pads (1874), HP sauce (1895), tarmac (1901), three-speed gears for bicycles (1936), the video cassette recorder (1956) and the MRI machine (1977). Nottingham's Council House is also home to the deepest-toned bell, and loudest clock bell in Britain, while the first aerial press photo was taken in Nottingham in 1910. Nottingham was also the location of the first police forensic laboratory in 1934, while it also sent the first radio message by police car in 1932. Finally, Notts County is the oldest professional football club in the world, formed in 1862, while the screen room on Broad Street, Nottingham, is the smallest public cinema in the world, having just 22 seats.

However, we're going to leave the last word to a Nottinghamshire world best – for the village of Scarrington is home to the largest known pile of horseshoes in the world – around 50,000 of them and standing at 17 feet high and 19 feet 6 inches in circumference at the base. It was originally the work of the local blacksmith at Scarrington Forge between June 1945 and April 1965. George Flinders was blacksmith here for 51 years and his record-breaking structure weighed around 17 tons. The structure was then bought by Nottinghamshire County Council in 1973 when they heard that an American wanted to buy it and ship it to the USA. However, over the years, the stack began to weaken and to lean, thanks to treasure-hunters taking souvenirs, so in 2006, the entire stack was dismantled and re-built with new shoes and a steel girder added through the centre.

Quirky Nottinghamshire

Introducing the Shire-Ode

A Shire-Ode tells the story – in rhyming verse – of fictitious, eccentric inhabitants of the county in question. However, in so doing, it also incorporates into the flow of the verse, many place-names that can be found within that county – places which then go on to form a county almanac, of sorts. Each place appears in roughly alphabetical order, although some of the smaller places are batched up into trios known as a "Three's Up". The location of all of the places is also pinpointed in the map on the page following the Shire-Ode.

As for the *Nottinghamshire* Shire-Ode, this tells the tale of *Arnold's Daughter*, the former referring to a town just north-east of Nottingham and the latter a reference to Kimberley, an adjacent town to the north-west of Nottingham. And what trouble she proves to be…

Nottingham Shire-Ode: Arnold's Daughter

She was born the youngest of **Arnold**'s three
There was **Elton**, then **Trent**, and then sweet **Kimberley**
But while Kim was a rower; did her **Awsworth**, for sure
The boys' greater success soon stuck in her craw.

For Elton played footie for **Mansfield** at first
But when **Everton** called, Arnold's pride almost burst
Whilst Trent's sport was cricket – he'd bat and he'd **Bole;**
On **Edingley** debut, gave his heart and his soul.

Alas this success made Kim **Kersall** her kin;
Made her **Idle** and **Thorney**, not proper and prim
Not the same little girl Arnold thought that he knew
Who'd eat sweets watching **Thrumpton**, and then **Scrooby** Doo.

She left home for a job where she'd tease and she'd flirt
As a **Bunny** girl serving in **Little Green** skirt
Then next she went **Commonside**; the "girl" was long gone
As she cavorted on stage with next to **Norton**.

Her shows became famous, earned plenty of dough
She'd **Trowell** on the makeup and the money would flow
Then out went the **Oldcotes** and in came the new
Mink, fox and ermine – and **Bevercotes**, too.

As the **Kirton** fell, in her **Coates** she'd take solace
With her dosh, bought a **Holme** – her own **Beckingham** Palace
At the back was a **Grove**, of pear and **Plumtree**
And there 'cross the **Meadows**, **Sherwood Forest** she could see.

But she was **Misson** her Dad, and his love, plus his sweets
How she'd **Lenton** him so, for reassurance and treats
Plus her new fella, **Stanley**, as well as being posh
Was a crafty **Old Basford** who was after her dosh.

Descended from **Cromwell**, he sure could **Bulwell**
But with her daft **Headon**, Kim just couldn't tell
"**Askham**, **Gotham**, then **Dunham**," was his call
And she fell for the cad; line, sinker, **Huck'n'all.**

They soon had a child, but this just **Boughton** fights
Got no sleep 'cos the poor kid had **Colwick** all night
With the bust-ups and moods, they just couldn't **Chilwell**
Though **Friezeland** did sum up the atmosphere well.

One step from the **Nuthall**, Kim struggled, Kim cried
And took solace in sweets which she **Scofton** the side
But though she disliked Stan, he felt pure **Hayton** top -
So he just **Upton** left – for a lass at **Spion Kop**.

So she'd suffered her **Rainworth**, but Kim didn't **Maun** -
Ryton cue, sought out Dad, to begin a new dawn
Her bro's took some work, a bit harder to soothe
Humble pie was **Eaton**; the **Ruffs** with the smooth.

Reunited with Dad, and all she held dear,
Kim then met Mr Wright, with the sweetest career
He was gentle and kind, but his tastiest asset:
He was Bertie's son – Mr **Colston Bassett**!

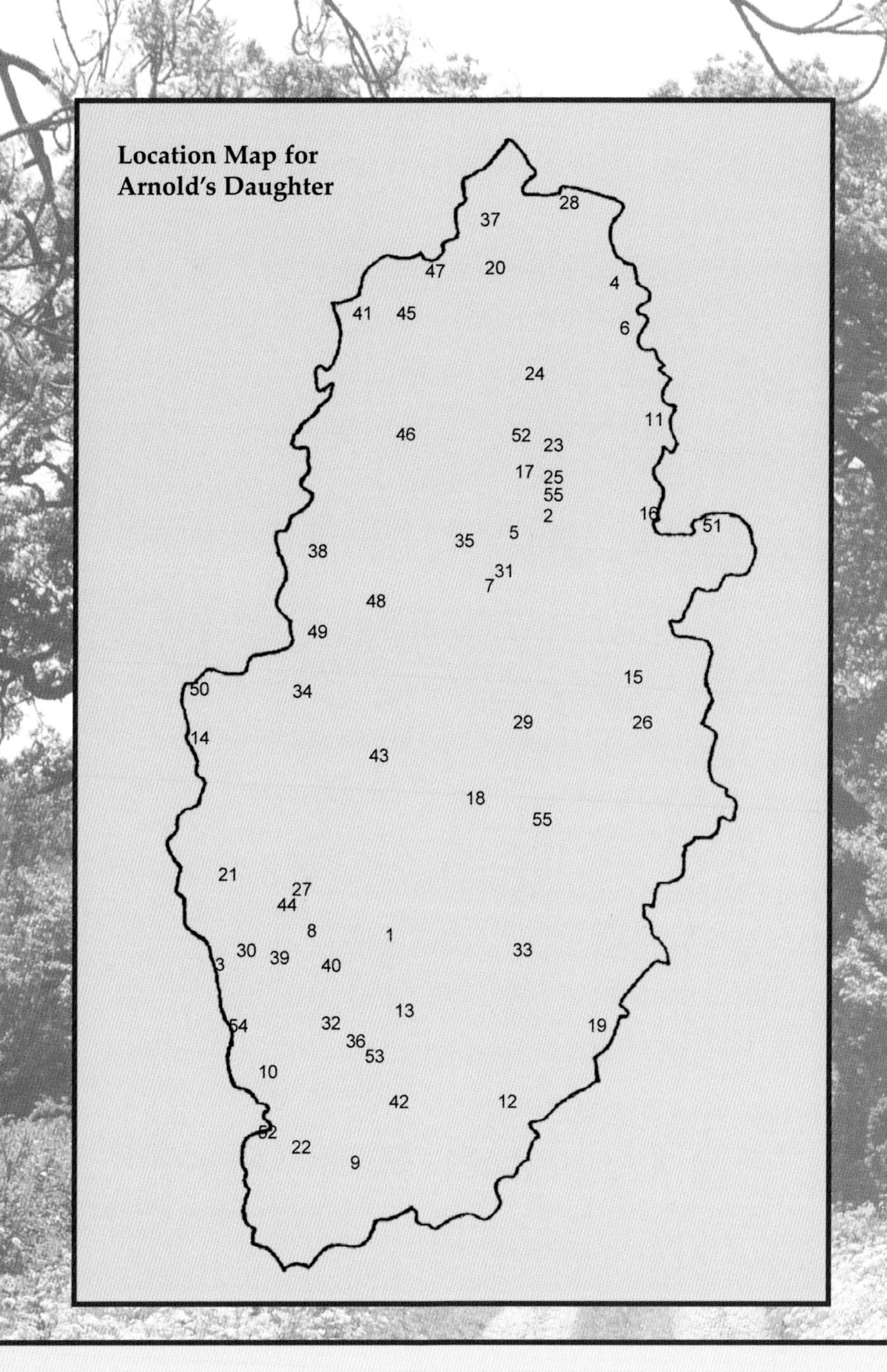

PLACE-NAME TABLE FOR ARNOLD'S DAUGHTER

1	Arnold	2	Askham	3	Awsworth	4	Beckingham	5	Bevercotes
6	Bole	7	Boughton	8	Bulwell	9	Bunny	10	Chilwell
11	Coates	12	Colston Bassett	13	Colwick	14	Commonside	15	Cromwell
16	Dunham	17	Eaton	18	Edingley	19	Elton	20	Everton
21	Friezeland	22	Gotham	23	Grove	24	Hayton	25	Headon
26	Holme	27	Hucknall[1]	28	Idle	29	Kersall	30	Kimberley
31	Kirton	32	Lenton	33	Little Green	34	Mansfield	35	Maun
36	Meadows	37	Misson	38	Norton	39	Nuthall	40	Old Basford
41	Oldcotes	42	Plumtree	43	Rainworth	44	Ruffs	45	Ryton
46	Scofton	47	Scrooby	48	Sherwood Forest	49	Spion Kop	50	Stanley
51	Thorney	52	Thrumpton	53	Trent	54	Trowell	55	Upton[2]

[1] Featured in the poem as Huck'n'all.
[2] Place appears twice in Nottinghamshire.

NAME (STATUS):	**ARNOLD** (Town, Suburb)
POPULATION:	37,768
DISTRICT:	Gedling
EARLIEST RECORD:	*Ernehale*, 1086 (Domesday Book)
MEANING:	Nook of land frequented by eagles or herons
DERIVATION:	From the Old English words *earn* (eagle) or *heron* (heron) and *halh*, (nook or corner of land)
FAMOUS RESIDENTS:	**Richard Parkes Bonington** (1802-1828), landscape painter; **Thomas Hawksley** (1807-1893), civil engineer; **Arthur Henry Knighton-Hammond** (1875-1970), landscape, portrait and industrial painter; **Sir John Robinson** (1824-1913), founder of the Home Brewery; **Andrea Lowe** (b.1975), actress

Arnold Pub: The Ernehale

The Ernehale Inn on High Street, Arnold, is named after Arnold's ancient Anglo-Saxon name, meaning "nook of land frequented by eagles or herons". Meanwhile, the Friar Tuck is one of a quartet of Arnold-based pubs that refer to the legend of Robin Hood – with another on Mansfield Road named after the outlaw himself and the Sherwood Manor, located a little further up the road, while the Major Oak is located to the east of the town.

The Ernehale Inn, Arnold.

Arnold Church: St Mary's

St Mary's church dates from the late 12th century, although the nave and chancel are 14th century while the pinnacled tower was built in the 15th century. The church was then restored during 1868-69 and again in 1877 under the direction of Nottingham architect Richard Charles Sutton. The year 1958 then saw the church floated on an enormous concrete raft to prevent subsidence damage, as the National Coal Board had begun to mine beneath the church. Today, St Mary's contains one of only three Easter Sepulchres in Nottinghamshire. Meanwhile, another impressive church in the Arnold area is St Paul's church on Mansfield Road, although this church is much newer than St Mary's, having been built in the 1890s. It was built by the well-known Nottingham architect, J.L. Pearson, was started in 1893 and completed with one of Pearson's attractive spires in 1897. The church was re-dedicated to St Paul and St Timothy in 1993.

St Mary's church, Arnold.

St Paul's with St Timothy's church, Daybrook, Arnold.

Arnold Historic Trivia: Luddites, Landscapes and Liquor

The earliest traces of occupation in the Arnold area date from the late Bronze Age, and take the form of defensive earthworks, while excavations at Ramsdale Park, in 1974, revealed Iron Age, hand-made pottery dating to pre-50 BC. As for the place-name, that is Anglo-Saxon, deriving from either the Old English words *earn* (eagle) or *heron* (heron). However, due to the local topology, Arnold was unlikely to have been the haunt of eagles, as they tend to inhabit areas of rocky outcrops and the nearest of those is at Creswell Crags, some 20 miles to the north-west. That said, the European white-tailed eagle *might* have once resided here, as they feed on fish and the Trent lies around four miles away to the south-east – so they may have flown home to roost in the heavily wooded Arnold area thus giving the place its name. Nevertheless, it is likely that the derivation comes from somewhere else and hence the other theory that it was originally called *Heron-halh,* meaning "nook of land where herons live" – and that lazy pronunciation over the centuries mutated the first part of the name from *Heron* to *Eron* to *Erne* and then to *Arn*. Given that there are brooks, streams and wetlands around the town, this seems to be the most likely explanation. The *halh* part of the name is certainly less open to question, as Arnold is surrounded by a circular ridge running from the north-west around to the south-east, and with raised ground to the west. This bowl-like topography is therefore certainly in keeping with a "nook of land".

The Daybrook Almshouses, founded by Sir John Robinson in memory of his son, John Sandford Robinson, who died on April 21st, 1898.

Much later during the 18th century, the framework knitting of stockings became hugely popular in Arnold. Initially introduced as an extra form of income during the winter months, the industry soon became the main form of employment in the town and, at its height, around 1300 frames were in use in Arnold, with only Nottingham and Sutton in Ashfield employing more. The late 18th century then saw the Industrial Revolution in full swing. A Worsted Mill was built in Arnold in 1788 and became the largest of its type ever built, employing over 1200 people at its height, while the

The house on High Street, Arnold, where Richard Parkes Bonington was born.

town continued into the early 19th century as a centre of the framework knitting industry. The result was a rapid influx of people into the town from all over the county. However, by 1811, changing fashion had resulted in a decreasing demand for their style of hosiery. This, in turn, resulted in a decrease in pay coupled with poorer standard of living and conditions of employment, and therefore in March 1811, the Arnold workers rebelled and smashed 63 frames … and in so doing became the site of the first Luddite riots in Britain.

It was also into these times that Arnold's most famous son was born. His name was Richard Parkes Bonington, and in his short life, he went onto become one of England's greatest Romantic landscape painters and most influential artists. Bonington learned water-colour painting from his father at a very young age, and was exhibiting paintings at the Liverpool Academy at the age of eleven. However, in 1817, the family moved to Calais, where his father had set up a lace factory – a move which merely accelerated young Bonington's flair. He soon began taking lessons from the painter Louis Francia who, ironically, taught him the English water colour technique, having recently returned from England himself. In 1818, the Bonington family moved to Paris to open a lace shop and whilst here, young Richard met and became friends with Eugène Delacroix. He worked for a time producing copies of Dutch and Flemish landscapes in the Louvre, but after

The former home of Home Ales between 1875 and 1996.

Left: *The old gates to Home Brewery are still intact today.*

attending the École des Beaux-Arts in Paris in 1820, he began to sketch the suburbs of Paris and the surrounding countryside. His first paintings were exhibited at the Paris Salon in 1822, and it was here in 1824 that he won a gold medal along with John Constable. It was also at this time that he began painting coastal views in Dunkirk and developed the style for which he is most well-known – coastal scenes with a low horizon and large sky, and demonstrating a masterful grasp of light and atmosphere. By 1825, he was turning his hand to historical painting, too, while he also developed a technique mixing watercolour with body colour and gum, achieving an effect close to oil painting. Further visits to Venice and London over the next two years saw him add to his repertoire, but it all tragically came to an end in 1828 when he contracted tuberculosis. He died in London on 23 September, aged only 25. A statue was erected in his honour outside the Nottingham School of Art, while a primary school, a theatre and a number of roads in Arnold are named after him. The Wallace Collection also includes a large number of both his landscapes and history paintings.

Towards the end of the 19th century, Arnold became the location of Home Ales brewery which brewed in the town between 1875 and 1996, and which was famous for its Robin Hood logo on beer-mats. At the peak of its success, the brewery owned 450 public houses and many people of a certain age will remember Home Ales pubs! The brewery managed to remain independent until 1986 when it was eventually purchased by Scottish & Newcastle for £123m. However, the new owners gradually moved production to its Mansfield brewery site, resulting in the eventual closure of the Arnold brewery in 1996. Home Bitter is still brewed under contract at Everards in Leicester, although many of the public houses that used to serve it now sell Theakston's beers instead.

Arnold Quirk Alert: The Ram

Somewhat controversially, Arnold is home to a pub called The Ram. Now anyone not from the area, or unfamiliar with East Midlands football, might wonder at the quirkiness of, what on the surface, appears to be a fairly tame name for a pub. But given that Arnold marks the heart of Nottingham Forest territory, it is almost inconceivable that a pub in this area would have the nickname of their bitter local rivals, Derby County. But there it stands on Mansfield Road – and with all of its windows intact, too! Maybe there's some secret Nottingham-based irony that only Arnold folk are party to! More likely, though, is some sort of affiliation to Ramsdale Park, a mile up the A60!

The Ram Inn, Arnold.

NAME (STATUS):	**AWSWORTH** (Village)
POPULATION:	2,517
DISTRICT:	Broxtowe
EARLIEST RECORD:	*Ealdeswyrthe*, 1002; *Eldesvorde*, 1086 (Domesday Book)
MEANING:	Enclosure of a man called Eald
DERIVATION:	From the Old English personal name, *Eald*, plus the Old English word *worth* (enclosure, enclosed farmstead or settlement)

The Gate Inn, Awsworth.

Awsworth Pub: The Gate Inn

The Gate Inn is located at the point where Main Street becomes Awsworth Lane. It is a popular pub that runs numerous themed nights, comedy evenings, and also regularly hosts Morris dancing (see *Awsworth Quirk Alert* for more).

Awsworth Church: St Peter

The parish church of St Peter dates from 1746, having benefited to the tune of £300 in 1749 from the Queen Anne Bounty Fund, with an additional £200 supplied in 1793 for church augmentation. The original chancel still survives today, but the nave was re-built in 1902-03 by Naylor and Sale of Derby in a Gothic style.

Awsworth Historic Trivia: Glassworks and Viaducts

During the early 17th century, a glass-works was established in Awsworth and survived until at least the end of the 17th century. Indeed, an official document of 1621 states that glass-making furnaces existed in Awsworth along with London, Milford and Newcastle; collectively they employed around 4,000 people.

By the 1870s, Awsworth station had been opened on the Great Northern line from Nottingham to Derby and which crossed the Erewash Valley to Ilkeston over the Bennerley Viaduct which adjoins Awsworth to the east. At Awsworth Junction, a short distance further east, a branch line curved away towards Pinxton where another viaduct almost half a mile in length took the railway across the Giltbrook Valley, and which was known variously as Awsworth Viaduct, Giltbrook Viaduct and Kimberley Viaduct, but more commonly in the local area as the Forty Bridges – although the actual combined number of arches and girder spans was 43. This viaduct was demolished in 1973 to make way for the A610, but the Bennerley Viaduct is still in place. Still an impressive structure, the Bennerley Viaduct is 1452ft long and rises over 60ft above the River Erewash. It was built between 1876 and 1877 and, although most railway viaducts of that time were built of brick, this one was built of lighter wrought iron lattice work due to the potential for subsidence in this major coal mining area; indeed, this part of the Great Northern Railway Derbyshire Extension was built with the exploitation of the Derbyshire and Nottinghamshire coalfields in mind, sweeping up from West Hallam and Ilkeston and across the border into Nottinghamshire via Awsworth, Kimberley, Basford and Bulwell, Daybrook, Gedling and Carlton and then doubling back to Nottingham Victoria station. Today, the Bennerley Viaduct still consists of its sixteen 76ft 7in lattice-work spans, each supported on wrought iron columns with stone capped blue brick foundations. There were also three additional iron spans at the Ilkeston end of the viaduct which carried the railway line over the Erewash Canal and the Midland Railway's Erewash Valley Line, while at the Awsworth end there was a section of embankment including bridges of more conventional brick construction through which the Nottingham Canal passed. Bennerley Ironworks was originally due north of the viaduct served by sidings connected to both the Great Northern line and the Midland Railway Erewash Valley line. After the demolition of the ironworks a

St Peter's church, Awsworth.

The Bennerley Viaduct, just west of Awsworth, built between 1876 and 1877 and with its sixteen enormous wrought iron lattice-work spans still intact.

British Coal distribution depot served by sidings from the former Midland Railway occupied the same site. This has now also been demolished, and a vast concrete wasteland has been left behind. As for the railway line and its branch line to Pinxton from Awsworth Junction, both eventually succumbed to the Beeching Axe in the early 1960s.

As an addendum to the Bennerley Viaduct story, the structure actually survived a Zeppelin bombing raid back in 1916. An L.20 airship dropped seven high explosives in the area one of which exploded just to the north of the viaduct. Later during the same raid the L.20 dropped 15 bombs onto the nearby Stanton Ironworks.

Awsworth Quirk Alert: Black Pigs, an Owd Oss, Battledore and Shuttlecocks

In the *Awsworth Pub* section, it was mentioned that The Gate Inn is the venue for Morris dancing. This is usually provided by the local Black Pig Border Morris Dancers – who practise at the pub on Wednesday evenings. Formed in 1986 in Eastwood, the Black Pig Border perform Morris dancing from the English/Welsh border, while the former part of their name is taken from the pirate ship from the 1970s children's programme, Captain Pugwash! Morris dancers with a difference, they wear largely black, and also wear spooky black face paint. Meanwhile, amongst their repertoire is the short play known as *The Company of Owd Oss* (that's an "old horse" for those not speaking the lingo), a traditional Christmas play originating from nearby Kimberley. In the play, the horse gets generally abused by the blacksmith, and culminates in the audience being invited to make a charitable donation to "poor owd oss"!

Meanwhile, back in 1744, a certain Mr Smedley set up an institution at Awsworth for the teaching of poor children, but with the curious stipulation that "none should benefit thereby who were unable to play battledore and shuttlecock". For those not in the know, battledore and shuttlecock – or *jeu de volant* as it is also known – is a very old game that is similar to modern badminton. The game is played by two people, with small rackets (battledores) made of parchment or rows of gut stretched across wooden frames, and shuttlecocks, made of a base of some light material, like cork, with trimmed feathers fixed round the top. Like badminton, the object of the game is to bat the shuttlecock to and fro without allowing it to fall to the ground. A little later in 1878 a more conventional boarding school was built on Awsworth's Main Street, and which still stands today, as does the nearby 19th century infant school. Around the same time in 1894, Awsworth was made a civil parish, thus severing long ties with Nuthall – by which time children were presumably allowed to attend school in the area regardless of whether or not they could hit cork and feathers with stretched gut!

A nod to Awsworth's mining past on the approach to the village.

Awsworth Boarding School was opened in 1878. It didn't list battledore and shuttlecock skills as a pre-requisite for entry!

Threes-Up!

	ASKHAM	BECKINGHAM	BEVERCOTES
STATUS:	Village	Village	Hamlet
POPULATION:	193	1,168	28
DISTRICT:	Bassetlaw	Bassetlaw	Bassetlaw
EARLIEST RECORD:	*Ascam*, 1086 (Domesday Book)	*Bechingeham*, 1086 (Domesday Book)	*Beurecote*, 1165
MEANING:	Homestead or enclosure where ash-trees grow	Homestead or enclosure of the family or followers of a man called *Becca* or *Beohha*	Place where beavers have built their nests/lodges
DERIVATION:	From the Old English word *æsc* (ash-tree), replaced by the Old Scandinavian *askr* (also ash-tree) and the Old English *hām* or *hamm* (homestead or enclosure)	From the Old English personal name Becca or Beohha and the Old English word *hām* or *hamm* (homestead or enclosure)	From the Old English words *beofor* (beaver) and *cot* (normally cottage, hut or shelter; here, shelter refers to the beavers nest)

Threes Up Trivia!

The small village of **Askham** is located around five miles south-east of Retford. It has one picturesque pub known as The Duke William and a rather splendid part-Norman church called St Nicholas's. The church today, however, is an amalgam of 12th to 15th century builds, with the nave dating from the 12th century, the chancel from the 13th, the east window from the 14th and the tower from the 15th while the church was also restored and re-roofed in 1863, and further restored in 1906-07. Three almshouses can also be found alongside the churchyard and which were rebuilt in the 19th century from foundations dating back to 1658.

Several miles to the north-east, the Grade II listed parish church of All Saints at **Beckingham** dates mostly from medieval times, while its font is Norman. Specifically, the nave arcades are from the 13th and 14th centuries, the lower parts of the tower are 14th century, while its buttresses, battlements and clerestory are 15th. Three 13th century seats and a piscina also remain while an ancient bracket in the south aisle is carved with the figure of a little man armed with a sword, and with his crowned head stuck onto his body at a right-angle!

All Saints' church is also home to a brass plaque engraved with the sinking troopship *Birkenhead* along with three or four boats taking women and children from the ship, while rows of doomed soldiers line the *Birkenhead's* deck. The plaque is in memory of Marion Parkinson of Beckingham, one of 193 who survived the wreck off the Cape of Good Hope in 1852, but who had to watch around 500 soldiers and sailors perish – and hence the phrase "the Birkenhead drill", made famous by Rudyard Kipling's poem describing courage in the face of hopelessness.

Today, Beckingham Marshes is a RSPB nature reserve, but has also been the site of 104 fracking operations, with the last exercise taking place in 1992. However, this was fracking for oil, and used the less controversial method, requiring less liquid and a lower pressure than that required for shale gas.

As for **Bevercotes**, the place is located around five miles south of Retford, and is effectively a hamlet consisting of a farm, a few houses and Bevercotes Farm Cottages. The hamlet also lies just to the north of a serene forested area known as Bevercotes Park, a Site of Special Scientific Interest and which comprises one of the best examples of semi-natural mixed ash woodland in Nottinghamshire. Much of the park, which is managed by the Forestry Commission, is also land reclaimed from the former Bevercotes Colliery, which opened in the 1960s as the first fully automated colliery in the world. Also one of the deepest mines in Britain, Bevercotes Colliery once featured in a poignant episode of the television programme *Man Alive* in 1967. Called

The Duke William, Askham.

St Nicholas's church, Askham.

Packing Up and Moving Out, the episode told the story of two coal miners from Ashington in Northumberland, a traditionally close-knit mining village and home to generations of mining families dating back to the 19th century. However, the local pits are due for closure, and the National Coal Board is keen to relocate its work-force over 100 miles further south. The programme therefore follows the miners and their families as they leave the depressed North East and start again in "the brash new housing estates of the Nottinghamshire coal-fields". Bevercotes Colliery is shown at length, in all of its shiny new glory. As for the migration south, the move also inspired pit poet Jock Purdon to write the poem *Farewell to 'Cotia*, and which contains this verse:

But leave your picks behind you
You'll not need them again
Off you go to Nottingham
To join Robin's Merry Men

Alas, little did they know that only 26 years later, history would repeat itself when Bevercotes Colliery was also closed in 1993! Another 19 years on, and the former colliery site was also the location of an infamous rave in September 2012 which attracted between 1,000 and 2,000 people!

Heading into Bevercotes Park, a Site of Special Scientific Interest managed by the Forestry Commission on land reclaimed from the former Bevercotes Colliery. Inset: *Beckingham All Saints' church.*

NAME (STATUS):	**BOLE** (Village)
POPULATION:	140
DISTRICT:	Bassetlaw
EARLIEST RECORD:	(*Bolun*, DB, 1086)
MEANING:	Place at the tree-trunks
DERIVATION:	From either the Old English word *bola* or the Old Scandinavian word *bolr* (*bolum* in dative plural form)
FAMOUS RESIDENTS:	**Henrietta Stockdale** (1847-1911), nursing pioneer

Bole Geographic Trivia: Energised

Bole is a village and civil parish in north-east Nottinghamshire, and is located a couple of miles south of Beckingham, close to the River Trent and the Lincolnshire border. It is dominated by the nearby West Burton power stations which, in turn, were built on the site of the deserted medieval village of West Burton. One of the West Burton power stations is a coal-fired power station commissioned in 1968 and provides electricity for around two million people, and the other is a much newer combined cycle gas turbine power station providing electricity for around 1.5 million homes. Both stations are owned and operated by EDF Energy.

Bole Church: St Martin's

The parish church of St Martin is Grade II listed and dates from the 13th century, although a predecessor church is mentioned in the Domesday Book of 1086; its tower and pinnacles are more recent – 14th and 15th century. The church is also home to a large eight-sided Norman font and a pulpit which contains four interesting carved panels of Elizabethan ladies and gentlemen. The church was extensively restored in 1866.

Bole Historic Trivia: The Remarkable Sister Henrietta

Henrietta Stockdale was a former teenage resident of Bole, and was later to become distinguished as a pioneer of nursing in South Africa. Her father became vicar of Bole parish in 1858, establishing the parochial school and also building the old vicarage (now known as Bole House), where the family lived from 1864. Then in 1870, Bishop Allan Becher Webb was made Bishop of Bloemfontein, but before he went out to South Africa he

St Martin's church, Bole.

visited the Stockdales in Bole. A year later, Henrietta responded to a call by Webb for teachers and nurses. She received some training as a nurse at the Clewer Hospital and at the Children's Hospital in Great Ormond Street and then sailed for Port Elizabeth in March 1874. Her party then travelled to Bloemfontein, where they founded the Community of St Michael and All Angels. Soon afterwards, she took her vows as a member of the Anglican Community, and was henceforth known as Sister Henrietta.

Two years later in 1876, Henrietta moved to none other than Kimberley – not the subject of the Nottinghamshire Shire-Ode, of course, but the Kimberley in the Northern Cape Province of South Africa. And it was here that she began to make her mark. Initially employed as district nurse in the mining camps, and then at Kimberley's new Carnarvon Hospital, she eventually established Southern Africa's first training school for nurses at Carnarvon Hospital. Kimberley nurses then moved out to wherever they were needed, providing nursing care, establishing hospitals and starting further training schools for nurses. As for Sister Henrietta, she spent a year as Matron at the St George's Hospital in Bloemfontein in 1877, while during the First Boer War of 1880-1881, she took charge of the military hospital at Newcastle. Later, Henrietta's influence and pressure also led to the first state registration of nurses and midwives in the world when the Cape of Good Hope Medical and Pharmacy Act of 1891 was passed. She eventually died in Kimberley in 1911, and soon after, a stained glass window was installed in her memory at the city's St Cyprian's Cathedral. Then in 1970, a statue of Sister Henrietta was erected in the cathedral grounds and unveiled by Bishop Philip Wheeldon, while a bust, based on the same statue, is located in the north transept of the Anglican Cathedral in Bloemfontein, where the Community of St Michael and All Angels was founded. Finally in 1984, her remains were reinterred at St Cyprian's Cathedral and her grave placed within a commemorative garden, alongside her statue.

But that's not all! For this remarkable woman who built the foundation for professional nursing in South Africa is regarded as a saint by many, and she is therefore remembered annually in Kimberley. The St Cyprian's Guild at the cathedral, in association with the Historical Society of Kimberley and the Northern Cape, organise services led by cathedral clergy and choir at the Sister Henrietta Stockdale Chapel (now a Provincial Heritage Site) on 6th October each year, while the anniversary of her death is fixed in the Lectionary of the Anglican Church of Southern Africa. The centenary of her death in 2011 was also marked with a Health and Wellness Day and a Thanksgiving Mass in the cathedral. And then there are the awards. The Henrietta Stockdale Training College for nurses in Kimberley was named in her honour while The South African Nursing Association established a prize, the Henrietta Stockdale Floating Trophy at the University of the Witwatersrand, which is awarded to students achieving the highest level of professional maturity during the four year nursing degree at the university.

Bole Quirk Alert: Martins' Bells

So this isn't the former war reporter and former independent politician with a penchant for white suits who displaced Neil Hamilton as M.P. for Tatton in 1997, nor is it the former downhill skier … nor, for that matter, is it the American film director or the British poet! These are the bells of St Martin's church in Bole. There are three of them and they hang in a wooden frame … but sadly, they are unable to ring due to the frame and fittings! In terms of specification, the treble (1st bell) is 4 cwt and was cast by Henry II Oldfield in 1611, the second bell is 4.5 cwt and was cast by John Seliok in 1500, while the tenor (3rd bell) is 5 cwt and was also cast by Henry II Oldfield in 1611. But alas, today, Bole's bells are just silent shells!

West Burton power stations.

NAME (STATUS):	**BOUGHTON** (Village)
POPULATION:	c.500
DISTRICT:	Newark and Sherwood
EARLIEST RECORD:	*Buchetone*, 1086 (Domesday); *Bughton*, 14th century
MEANING:	Either "farmstead of a man called Bucca", or "place where bucks are kept"
DERIVATION:	From either the Old English personal name, *Bucca*, or the Old English word *bucca* (buck or male deer), plus the Old English word *tūn* (farmstead)

Boughton Church: St Matthew's

Boughton is attached to the north-eastern tip of Ollerton, with the pair forming the recently-created (1987) civil parish of Ollerton and Boughton. Boughton's church is known as St Matthew's and dates from 1868, replacing a much older chapel of indeterminate age; some historic reports record a late 13th century window, others a beautiful Norman chancel arch. Around 1200, though, the church was given to the priory at Blyth which lasted until around 1403 when the benefice was united with the vicarage of Kneesall as a chapelry. This state of play lasted until 1866, when Boughton was separated from Kneesall and made a perpetual curacy and an independent benefice. By this stage, though, the chapel had fallen into a state of disrepair, and the foundation stone for its replacement was laid in 1867 with the new church consecrated in 1868 having been built in the style of the early 14th century.

Boughton Historic Trivia: Stations

Boughton was also once on the Lancashire, Derbyshire and East Coast Railway. The line was intended to link Warrington on the Manchester Ship Canal to Sutton-on-Sea on the Lincolnshire coast and was financed by a group of coal owners, led by William Arkwright, a descendant of Richard Arkwright. It was the largest railway scheme ever approved by Parliament in a single session with 170 miles of line, including a branch line from Shirebrook to Sheffield, and including dock facilities at each end. The line from Chesterfield to Lincoln was opened in 1897, including Boughton Station which sat on the line between Ollerton and Tuxford Central. However, this proved to be the only part of the railway actually completed and the line never made it into Lancashire. The railway was then bought by the Great Central Railway in 1907 and subsequently became part of the London and North Eastern Railway (LNER) in 1923, and then British Railways on nationalisation in 1948. However, passenger services on the line finished in 1955 and Boughton Station was closed the same year.

On the north-western outskirts of Boughton is the Grade II listed Boughton Pumping Station, now known as Blackburn House, a popular restaurant and venue for wedding receptions. The station was opened in 1905 together with an associated Superintendent's house and five workers cottages, while the Blackburn Engine House, designed by W B Starr, included a huge brick chimney which can be seen for miles around. The Pumphouse was commissioned by the Nottingham Corporation Water Department and was capable of pumping 20 million imperial gallons per day through nearly 16 miles of 30 inch pipe, drawn from an underground aquifer. The station later passed into the hands of Severn Trent Water, but by 1980 it was obsolete and in need of major repair, then in 1988 it suffered further from mining subsidence. However, the Boughton Pumping Station Partnership Trust then secured funding to restore the buildings and by 1998 the works were complete. Finally, in April 2010 the building was purchased by Horizon Investments and re-launched as Blackburn House, named after the original Blackburn Engines which enabled it to pump water from its well to homes in Nottingham.

The Harrow Inn, Boughton.

St Matthew's church, Boughton.

Sculpture of a bull goring an imaginary well at Bulwell Bogs. See Historic Trivia for background.

NAME (STATUS):	**BULWELL** (Town, Suburb)
POPULATION:	22,405
DISTRICT:	City of Nottingham
EARLIEST RECORD:	*Buleuuelle,* 1086 (Domesday Book)
MEANING:	Either "spring or stream of a man called Bula or Bulla", or "place where bulls drink
DERIVATION:	From either the Old English personal name, *Bula* or *Bulla,* or the Old English word bula (bull), plus the Old English word *wella,* (spring or stream)
FAMOUS RESIDENTS:	**John Bird** (b.1936), satirist, actor and comedian; **Jason Booth** (b.1977) and **Nicky Booth** (b.1980), boxers, and holders of concurrent British and Commonwealth titles; **Dr Sir Neil Cossons** (b.1939), former Director of the National Museum of Science and Industry and chairman of English Heritage; **Patrick Doyle** (b.1948), musician and songwriter; **Les Leston** (1920-2012), Grand Prix-winning Formula 1 driver; **Bertie Mee** (1918-2001), Arsenal double-winning manager; **Stanley Middleton** (1818-2009), Booker prize-winning author; **Wilfrid Reid** (1884-1973) professional golfer and golf course designer

Bulwell Pub: The Horseshoe Inn

Bulwell is home to a number of pubs, and was home to the now-closed Scots' Grey (see *Quirk Alert* for more), which had a boxing ring upstairs and a football team that won the FA Sunday Cup in 2009 at Anfield. However, the pub photographed here is The Horseshoe Inn which can be found on Station Road.

The Horseshoe Inn, Bulwell.

Bulwell Church: St Mary the Virgin and All Souls

Bulwell's parish church is one of a handful in the UK dedicated to All Souls rather than All Saints. The current Grade II listed church was built between 1849 and 1850 by the Derby architect, H.I. Stevens, and replaced a much older version that dated from around 1134. However, the old church was badly damaged by a storm in 1843 and had to be demolished. Its replacement was built in the Old English style some sixty yards further south than its predecessor, cost £3,000 and was consecrated by the Bishop of Lincoln. Bulwell is also home to the church of St John the Divine, another Grade II listed church, designed by architect William Knight and built between 1884 and 1885 at a cost of £5,000.

Bulwell Historic Trivia: Bula's Well and Luddism

Regarding Bulwell's place-name origin, Robert Mellors' 1914 version of *Old Nottingham suburbs: then and now* offers similar reasoning to *The Oxford Dictionary of British Place-Names*. However, Mellors suggests that "*the name is usually supposed to have been derived from the spring which runs out of the Bunter Sandstone over a bed of clay, near to the northern end of the Forest, called 'Bull Well'. Dr. Mutschmann, in 'The Place Names of Notts.,' suggests that the first part of the name may stand for a person – Bulla, or a bull, or it may*

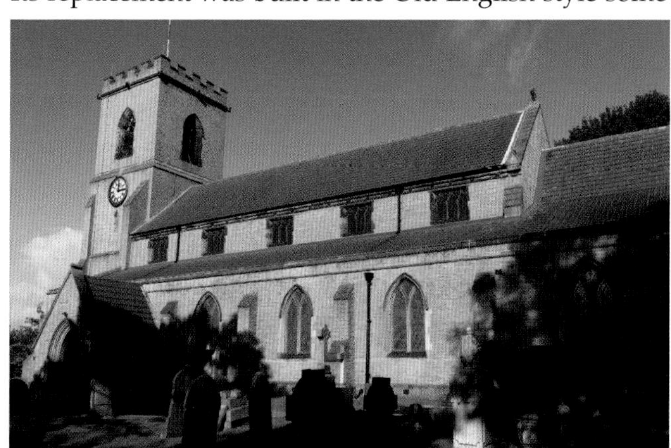

St Mary the Virgin and All Souls' church, Bulwell.

St John the Divine, Bulwell.

The William Peverel, named after the Norman Lord of the Manor who replaced the Anglo-Saxon Godric following the Norman Conquest.

The 18th century Old Town Hall was effectively rendered useless when Bulwell was incorporated into Nottingham in the 1890s!

describe the bubbling sound produced by the flowing water of the spring." Mellors also goes onto state that *"The architect of the National Schools, having a sense of humour, embodied on a stone on the building the pretty legend of once upon a time a bull digging his horns into the rock, and the water gushing out."* And this latter legend is certainly one that the locals will happily bandy about; the local church also has illustrations of this tale carved into sandstone blocks, while a statue of a bull goring a well has recently appeared in the marketplace, too. As for the place-name pronunciation today, it is delivered by the locals in monosyllabic fashion, a phrasing which has gradually formed over the years from "Bulwell" to "Bulwull" to "Buwull", and finally to "Bool".

It was probably around the time that Bulwell was named that the first bridge was built across the River Leen thus supplying access to Nottingham from the north-west, and by the time of its Domesday Book mention the place had become established as a small trading post for all sorts of goods. By this stage, the manor had passed from the unfortunate Anglo-Saxon Godric to William Peverel, lord of Nottingham Castle, while one of his successors, Philip Marc, gained a terrible reputation for extortion, allegedly carried out on behalf of King John.

As Bulwell's popularity as a trading post grew, it encouraged roaming salesmen to flood into the area, undercutting those with established businesses. A local law was therefore passed in c.1320 forbidding anyone without fixed and at least part-covered premises from selling goods or services close to the original businesses ... to which the travelling salesmen responded by simply fixing posts into the ground and applying an appropriate cover over their wares when selling!

It was also at this time that local sandstone quarrying commenced and which went onto be used in many local buildings including sections of the wall surrounding Wollaton Hall built in the late 16th century; much later, Bulwell stone was also used to repair damage caused to the palaces of Westminster during World War II. Inevitably, coal was also mined in the area, commencing in around 1500. As for Bulwell pit itself, this was opened in the 1860s but was a relatively small mine reaching depths of only 546ft; other mines were opened on the fringes of the Bulwell parish at Cinderhill and Bestwood.

On the 11th March 1811, violence exploded in Nottingham leading to the destruction of around sixty textile machines, with similar violence erupting in Bulwell the following week. Indeed, Luddite John Westley from Arnold was the first to die when shot dead whilst breaking into the house of a master weaver at Bulwell, while the last ever reported instance of Luddism in the county also occurred at Bulwell on 2nd November 1816. A year later, saw the Pentrich Revolution in neighbouring Derbyshire, led by an unemployed stockinger called Jeremiah Brandreth. Disaffected by the economic climate, Brandreth led an "army" of around three hundred local workers in a march on Nottingham. Unfortunately, his band of revolutionaries had been infiltrated by Lord Sidmouth's informers and they were intercepted by a small force of the Home Secretary's soldiers at Giltbrook. Brandreth managed to escape and took refuge in Bulwell, but with a £50 reward on his head he was soon betrayed and ultimately convicted of high treason and sentenced to death by public hanging and beheading.

In the 19th century, Bulwell was a town in its own right, but it was absorbed into the city of Nottingham in the 1890s, thus rendering its 18th century Town Hall somewhat redundant! Finally, by the 1960s, demand for housing in the area was so acute that ancient Royal Forest Warrants were flouted and houses were built on Snape Wood and Sellars Wood to the west and Hempshill Vale to the south-west.

Bulwell Quirk Alert: The Hardest Pub in Britain, Bulwell-on-Sea and Bad Stocks

Bulwell was once home to a pub called The Scots' Grey, and latterly The Venue. For many years it ran a successful boxing club, producing a number of champions, but its reputation for toughness came as much from fights *outside* the ring as in it! This was because fights were regularly held on a Saturday night in the nearby Market Place after closing time, with old scores settled as well as plenty of money changing hands! Spectators would form a ring and the bare-knuckle pugilists would fight to the knock out … with additional bouts offered for the Challenger (he who could knock down "the hero"). Remarkably, this "practise" continued until as recently as the 1990s. Small wonder, then, that the Scots' Grey was featured in a television programme, entitled *The Ten Hardest Pubs in Britain*. Since then, the pub has been closed down because it was deemed to be too rough to control. Add in a few recent high profile murders, a number of other shootings, gangland culture and the odd riot and, well, I'm probably doing the good people of Bulwell a severe disservice here … but anyway, it was into this hard and fiercely partisan, Nottingham Forest-supported hotbed of discontent that my wife and I naïvely drove, hoping to get a snap of a "Welcome to Bulwell" sign! And so we get to these traffic lights, and my wife turns to me and says: "What is wrong with these people? That's the third bloke who's given me either a mouthful or an obscene gesture"… or words to that effect! At which point, the penny dropped. We'd only got Rammie sat in the back of our car – Rammie being Derby County's mascot, sitting under a sticker screaming "Up The Rams!" We didn't stop for a coffee!

The centre of Bulwell is located in a valley next to the banks of the River Leen, and a particular area here has been known as "Bulwell Bogs" for over nine hundred years; an area where children can play, paddle and fish. However, in 1872 the local Lord of the Manor attempted to enclose the land around the bogs, an act which led to the people of Bulwell staging a peaceful protest – and eventually winning, with the land officially designated "for the pleasure and leisure of the people of Bulwell". Much later, in 2002, the area was set to be demolished and replaced by a large road bridge plus a transport interchange for buses, trams, taxis, etc … until the locals once again successfully campaigned to prevent the work. The result was an overhaul of the facilities there, resulting in a Green Flag award in 2004 for regeneration. As well as the Bogs, there is also an area about a mile upstream which has always attracted children from miles around to play in the water, leading to the local nickname of "Bulwell-on-Sea".

Finally, Bulwell's historic stocks are located at Bulwell Bogs alongside the River Leen. Originally located in the market place, they had become obsolete by 1911 – although, officially, some offences were still deemed to be punishable by a session in the stocks! Anyway, a wheelwright known as Bob Piggin made the last known stocks in 1825 – and then somewhat ironically went onto become their first ever occupant!

Bulwell Bogs – "for the pleasure and leisure of the people of Bulwell".
Inset: *The old stocks alongside the River Leen at Bulwell Bogs.*

NAME (STATUS):	**BUNNY** (Village)
POPULATION:	c689
DISTRICT:	Rushcliffe
EARLIEST RECORD:	*Bune*, early 11th century; *Bonei*, 1086 (Domesday Book)
MEANING:	Island or dry ground in marsh, where reeds grow
DERIVATION:	From the Old English words *bune* (reed) and *ēg* (island, land partly surrounded by water, dry ground in marsh, well-watered land, or promontory)
FAMOUS RESIDENTS:	**Thomas Parkyns** (1662-1741), architect and wrestling baronet

The church of St Mary the Virgin, Bunny.

The Rancliffe Arms, Bunny.

Bunny Pub: The Rancliffe Arms

The Rancliffe Arms is located on the A60 in between Church Lane and Main Street, the only two access points into the village of Bunny. The pub was originally a coaching inn, parts of which date back to the early 17th century and which stood on the main Nottingham to London turnpike road. It also stands between Bunny Moor to the north and Bunny Hill to the south, with the former a fen-like area of land that gave Bunny its name. The inn is thought to have been designed by and built for Sir Thomas Parkyns (1663-1741) of Bunny Hall – although that association may simply be because it stood next to a patch of ground where Sir Thomas's annual wrestling matches took place on Midsummer's Day. This strictly amateur competition saw the victor win a gold-laced hat, worth 22 shillings. The match was held for 99 years, from 1712-1811, at which point it was stopped because it was deemed to be attracting noisy and unruly crowds!

Bunny Church: St Mary the Virgin

Bunny's church is generally shortened to just St Mary's, and largely dates back to the 14th century. However, there was a predecessor church on the same spot, given records show rectors dating back to 1228 when Robert de Glamorgan was incumbent, and this probably dated from c.1000. It is thought that the 14th century construction was hit by the Black Death which claimed the lives of around a third of the population and took out many skilled artisans and stonemasons; this probably accounts for the different workmanship that is still evident today. The Black Death probably also accounts for why the south-west corner of the graveyard lay undisturbed for centuries, due to the fear of unleashing the disease. This insight also leads onto a further one: that when corpses decay over the centuries, new ones are laid on top. It is estimated that around 8,000 corpses lie in the graveyard from around 800 years of burials, but today, only 390 memorials are visible!

The church is also home to a 14th century oak screen and many monuments to the Parkyns family, including one of Dame Ann Parkyns, and a sculpture of her son, Thomas Parkyns. An impressive church, St Mary's is the largest in South Nottinghamshire and is known as the Cathedral of the Wolds. The vicar of Bunny was also the vicar of nearby Bradmore until 1770 when each village became part of a separate parish.

Bunny Historic Trivia: Bunny Hall

Bunny Hall (not to be confused with its namesake refuge for rabbits, just up the road in Ruddington) was built in the 1570s in the Elizabethan style of the day with an 80ft high tower bearing an enormous stone coat of arms. It was built by Richard Parkyns who had just married Elizabeth, the widow of Humphrey Barlowe, a marriage which saw the manor pass to the Parkyns family and which they retained for almost 300 years. Richard's son, George, inherited the manor next and he was knighted by James I in 1603, passing on the manor to his eldest son, Irsham, when he died. In 1642, the now knighted Sir Irsham Parkyns gave his immediate support to the Royalists during the English Civil War, and within days,

The tower at Bunny Hall.

Prince Rupert along with an escort of cavalry stayed overnight in the village, while in July 1643, Queen Henrietta Maria was entertained at Bunny Hall as she passed through with a 4,000-strong army. Many years after the English Civil War in 1681, Sir Irsham's son, Thomas Parkyns, was elevated to the baronetage in recognition of the family's royalist support during the war. However, it was his son, Thomas Parkyns the second baronet, who is the most notable of the long line of Parkyns. In 1700, he provided the money for a new school. Sir Thomas designed the building himself in an Italian style, and it also included four adjoining rooms for four poor widows of the parish, while he also declared its objective, which is carved in Latin along the string course on the exterior of the building. Somewhat bizarrely, forty shillings per annum were also to be used to purchase gowns and petticoats for each widow along with instructions that the coat of arms belonging to Lady Ann Parkyns (Sir Thomas's mother) was to be embroidered onto the sleeve of the gowns. If a widow did not agree to this homage to her benefactress, then she did not get the gown and the money "saved" was to be distributed amongst the widows who were prepared to wear the dresses!

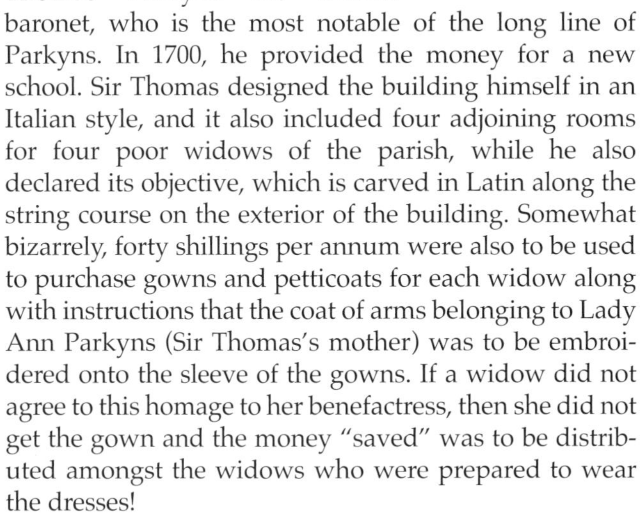

It was also the second baronet who in 1723-25 built what is currently the north wing of the Hall, again to his own design, while he was also responsible for the design and building of numerous other buildings in the village. Add to that the building of a new chancel roof for St Mary's, a new vicarage, the hunting tower on Bunny Hill and the planting of new woods, and he has certainly left his mark on the village and surrounding area. As well as being an architect, Sir Thomas was also a magistrate, author, scholar … and accomplished wrestler (see *Bunny Quirk Alert* for more on the latter).

The third baronet was also a Thomas Parkyns, a child of his father's second marriage, and only 13 years old when he inherited the manor. His only claim to fame appears to be the fact that his second marriage was rather shockingly to a housemaid at Bunny Hall, while under his 59 year reign, the state of the Hall began to decline. However, his son, Thomas Boothby Parkyns, was M.P. for Nottingham, and on elevation to the House of Lords, he was awarded the Barony of Rancliffe in the Irish Peerage in 1795. Meanwhile, the Second Baron Rancliffe, George Augustus Parkyns, was godson to the Prince of Wales and a prominent Whig politician, but despite marrying Elizabeth Forbes in 1807, their marriage was beset by scandal. Unable to obtain a divorce, he was unable to re-marry, didn't produce an heir and therefore caused the failure of both the Parkyns lineage and the hereditary title of Baron Rancliffe when he passed away in 1850.

A kind of scandal followed his passing too, as he left the Hall to his housekeeper, Mrs Burt, thus leaving his brother-in-law, Sir Richard Levinge, extremely aggrieved. However, although Mrs Burt continued to live as Lady of the Manor and the house passed on her death in 1875 to her niece, Arabella Hawksley, the Levinge's eventually claimed the Hall in 1909. Not that this inheritance helped the inhabitants of Bunny. Sir Richard Levinge of Knockdrin Castle, Ireland, promptly gave his tenants notice and set about arranging for the sale of the Hall and its contents along with the estates of Bunny and neighbouring Bradmore, including the farmhouses, land, houses and cottages. As a result, the Mayor of Nottingham, Albert Ball, bought the lot in 1910, but sold the Hall, its park, and Bunny and Rancliffe Woods to a Dr Cordeux. He did at least then offer all of the other tenants on the estate the chance to buy their rented properties, but of course, only some could afford that; the others had to move away. As for Dr Cordeux, he only survived for another five years, whilst his only son was tragically killed at

View down Main Street, Bunny, with a typical early Sir Thomas Parkyns house of red brick on the left, with the original stone-mullioned windows intact.

The Grammar School built by Sir Thomas Parkyns in 1700.

Three for the price of one! Another angle on Thomas Parkyns' Grammar School built in 1700, St Mary the Virgin church, and the Church Hall.

Ypres shortly afterwards.

On the death of Mrs Cordeux, the Hall was bought by the Edwards family who eventually put the house, barns and park up for sale in the early 1990s. It was at this time that the barns were converted into six separate award-winning homes, but the fate of the Hall remained uncertain until bought by Ilkeston-born property developer Chek Whyte in 2000. A remarkable man, he spent his childhood moving in and out of foster care before entering the business world as a dyslexic, colour blind and hardly able to read or write. Nevertheless, he went onto make his fortune in property development, became Chairman of Ilkeston Town F.C. in 2008, and also appeared on an episode of *The Secret Millionaire* in 2007. From 2000, he embarked upon a £1.8m restoration of Bunny Hall under the guidance of English Heritage, and therefore retaining many of its original features, including a coach house, a cheese press and its distinctive 80ft tower. Alas, Whyte was declared bankrupt in 2009 with debts of more than £30m, and had to put Bunny Hall up for sale at £3.75m.

The White House on Church Street, Bunny.

Bunny Quirk Alert: The Wrestling Baronet, Inebriated Ghostly Butlers and Pineapples

Sir Thomas Parkyns (1662-1741) of Bunny Hall was also known as the Wrestling Baronet because of his devotion to the sport. There is a life-size effigy of him in the north aisle of St Mary's church at Bunny, designed by the man himself before his death. The effigy appears in the left-hand panel of the memorial, with Sir Thomas standing ready for a wrestling bout, while the right-hand side shows him stretched out on the floor, having been defeated – or rather thrown – by Father Time! Part of his epitaph contains the words: *That Time at length did throw him it is plain, Who lived in hope that he should rise again.*

Sir Thomas lies in the vault he built, somewhat macabrely in one of the stone coffins that he used to collect when he was alive! Local legend therefore has it that the architect's fascination for coffins led to the hall becoming a haven for ghosts. Indeed, in 2002 the Nottingham Post reported how a medium from Mansfield had found 14 spirits in Bunny Hall — including seven children, a nanny, a horse groom, a cook ... and an inebriated butler! Meanwhile, the Parkyns' also had a penchant for pineapples, with the fruit appearing in the village on top of the Hall's stone and wrought-iron gates, while they also form the main part of the Bunny emblem (*shown left*).

Finally, back in 2011, we genuinely spotted an advertisement in Bunny stating "Giant rabbits for sale". Yes, that's right: bunnies for sale in Bunny! We also found ourselves wondering if Bunny Hall sees strange goings on every full moon! Confused? Try googling Tottington Hall!

NAME (STATUS):	**CHILWELL** (Suburb)
POPULATION:	7,298 (Toton and Chilwell ward)
DISTRICT:	Broxtowe
EARLIEST RECORD:	*Chideuuelle*, 1086 (Domesday Book)
MEANING:	Spring or stream where young people assemble
DERIVATION:	From the Old English words *cild* (child) and *wella* (spring or stream)

Chilwell Pubs: The Cadland and The Charlton Arms

Chilwell has a number of pubs straddling its borders with Toton, Attenborough and Beeston and, as all four Nottingham suburbs are fairly seamless, it makes the pinpointing of location open to debate; indeed in the early 20th century, certain houses on Attenborough Lane were deemed to be in Toton, but their front gardens in Chilwell! However, two pubs that definitely *are* in Chilwell, are The Cadland and The Charlton Arms, both on High Road. The Charlton Arms is named after the local landowning family who once lived in the now-demolished Chilwell Hall while The Cadland, is named after a locally trained racehorse that won The Derby in 1828. He didn't win it easily though, having tied in a dead heat with the 7/2 favourite, The Colonel, and only taking the crown after a deciding run-off which he won by a neck. *Sporting Magazine* commented that *"Such a Derby was never before seen and possibly never will again"*, while racing historian John Orton claimed that *"Two finer races were never seen before"*. Cadland ran 25 times in all between 1828 and 1831, winning 15 of his races.

The Cadland, Chilwell.

The Charlton Arms, Chilwell.

Christ Church, Chilwell.

Chilwell Church: Christ Church

The Anglican church in Chilwell is known as Christ Church, but wasn't founded until 1903, although Chilwell didn't actually become a separate ecclesiastical parish from Attenborough until 1975. Pre-dating Christ Church by some time is the Chilwell Methodist church, which was founded in 1798 as the Methodist First Connection Chapel on Hallams Lane. Then in 1819, Henry Kirkland, a local lace manufacturer and Wesleyan Methodist preacher, formed the Wesleyan Methodist group which took over the chapel later that year. Increased numbers enabled the group to build a larger chapel for 300 people on Chapel Street in 1825, but by 1830, numbers had swelled so much that another chapel was built on the same site, this time for 450 people. By 1866, a Wesleyan Day School had been added, while 1902 saw the building of the current church on Chilwell Road, Beeston. Much larger than its predecessors, this building held up to 750 people and still boasts the tallest building in Beeston today, courtesy of its spire.

Chilwell Historic Trivia: Charlton's and Explosions

Undoubtedly part of the great sprawl of Greater Nottingham today, Chilwell was originally a hamlet on the road from Nottingham to Ashby-de-la-Zouch. For centuries, the Lords of the Manor were the Charlton's who were descended from John de Charlton who was M.P. for the city of London in 1318. A later Sir Thomas Charlton was Speaker of the House of Commons in 1453, while Sir Richard Charlton was slain at the Battle of Bosworth Field in 1485 and his lands confiscated. The Chilwell estate is said to have been purchased in 1572 by a later Thomas Charlton, of Sandiacre, and in 1620 Chilwell became the home of the family and continued to be so until well into the 20th century. Other notable Charltons include Edward Charlton who was a Parliamentary commissioner for raising troops, while William Charlton was High Sheriff of Nottinghamshire in 1824, as was T.B. Charlton in 1879. In between those two dates, the year 1831 saw Nottingham Castle and Beeston Silk Mill destroyed by a disorderly rabble, who then threatened to burn down Chilwell Hall ... until they allegedly found the dead body of the Lord of the Manor, at which point they abandoned their plans! Meanwhile, Chilwell Hall was eventually demolished in the 1930s and modern houses built in its place.

When Thomas Barton developed the first bus routes in the Nottingham area at the start of the 20th century, he was asked during World War I, by contract, to extend the south-western route to Chilwell. This was in order to transport workers from Nottingham to the National Shell Filling Factory No. 6 at Chilwell, and which occupied most of the level ground between Toton and Chilwell. It was the factory which saw Chilwell's population increase rapidly at this time, while the original road between the two villages became a gated military road that is now known as Chetwynd Road, named after the Chetwynd Army Barracks that occupy the site today, and which are also Nottingham's Regimental Headquarters. As for the shell factory, it was the scene of a disastrous explosion in July 1918, with 134 people killed and over 250 more injured. This tragedy remains the largest number of deaths caused by a single explosion in Britain. The factory later became a major depot site for the Royal Army Ordnance Corps, and more recently for the Royal Electrical and Mechanical Engineers.

Chilwell Road Methodist church, Beeston.

Chilwell Quirk Alert: Badders, a bit of Horseplay and The Chilwell Ghost

In 1969 five members of the Chilwell Road Methodist Church broke the world record for continuous badminton by playing non-stop for over 120 hours – this to raise money for Christian Aid. Meanwhile, in the 19th century, a certain John Pearson, who was then in the hosiery trade, was also a very keen amateur florist. One day, whilst visiting a flower show in Derby, he purchased a pair of carnations in large pots, thus delivering himself a dilemma as to how he should get them home in one piece along with his horse! Doubting the integrity of the florists from whom he had bought them – he appears to have convinced himself that they would be changed if he left them – he left his horse at Derby, walked the 11 miles back to Chilwell carrying a large pot under each arm, and then walked back to Derby to fetch his horse. One wonders if the florists changed his horse, just for a laugh! That said, Mr Pearson had the last laugh, as he went on to take up horticulture as a business and became very successful, particularly with his tulips which were hugely popular at that time. Pearson also raised an apple called Pearson's Plate, while he went on to inherit the old Chilwell Manor House, with an orchard attached before planting a further one hundred acres of orchard.

However, we're not finished with John Pearson, just yet. His horticulture business became a significant employer in Chilwell, and he was a well-respected man, therefore his account of the Chilwell Ghost deserves an airing. Located alongside one of Pearson's orchards was a cottage which had for a number of years been occupied by a workman and his family. About 1843 strange noises began to be heard at night, with a regular banging on the shutters which sometimes shook the glass out of the leaded window, but no trace of any missile could ever be found, nor was anyone ever discovered in the vicinity. Determined to clear up the mystery, John Pearson concocted a number of plans to ensnare the perpetrator, but to no avail. One plan involved a replacement frame covered with brown paper coated with lamp black and oil which, at a few yards was impossible to tell from the wooden shutter. As was the norm, the missile hit its target, and the window panes rattled, but nothing came inside, nor could a mark be found on the brown paper. Mr Pearson, being also an amateur chemist, attempted to trace the source to some form of explosive, but again, no evidence was turned up. In the end, the only response he could offer was: *"I have given you the facts; you must draw your own conclusions."*

Such was the fame of the Chilwell Ghost that on Sunday's the village swarmed with sightseers and special extra trains were put on; indeed, two publicans of the aforementioned Charlton Arms and The Cadland, retired with fortunes – having no doubt cranked up the interest with ever-wilder stories as to the "true" nature of The Chilwell Ghost! Eventually, the house was abandoned for many years until a poor cobbler moved in. Despite the villagers' warnings, he stated that he had no fear of ghosts, and that *"the Lord will take care of me"*. He lived in the house for twelve months before leaving, stating that *"while I don't believe in ghosts, it kept knocking, and knocking, and knocking, till I got tired!"* The house was never inhabited again after that, although what did surface over the years were a number of rumours about a missing pedlar, about the original owner of the cottage doing some unexplained digging in his garden at five in the morning, and about public statements from his wife that she could *"hang him any day!"* To quote John Pearson: *"You must draw your own conclusions!"*

NAME (STATUS):	**COATES** (Hamlet)
POPULATION:	c.20
DISTRICT:	Bassetlaw
EARLIEST RECORD:	*Cotes,* 1200
MEANING:	The cottages or huts
DERIVATION:	From the Old English word *cot* (cottage, hut or shelter)

Coates/Cottam General Trivia

Coates is a tiny hamlet situated in north-eastern Nottinghamshire, and is part of the civil parish of North Leverton with Habblesthorpe. A mile to the south is the larger settlement of Cottam, which includes The Moth and Lantern pub. Cottam is also home to the eight cooling towers of Cottam Power Station, a coal-fired station built between 1964 and 1968. Owned by EDF Energy, it is capable of generating 2,000 megawatts, while the neighbouring Cottam Development Centre is owned by E.ON and is a combined cycle gas turbine plant commissioned in 1999, with a generating capacity of 400 mw.

The Moth and Lantern, Cottam, is located a mile south of Coates.

Coates Historic Trivia: Graves and Groups

At the end of the 19th century, two 5½ inch thick fragments of a carved Anglo-Saxon grave cover were discovered at a farm at Coates. One was being used as a coping stone for a wall, the other as a flagstone in the farmyard causeway. However, its discovery here is a mystery as there is no record of any church or chapel having existed at Coates during Anglo-Saxon times, so the grave cover presumably originated from elsewhere. One explanation is that Coates lies less than a mile south of Littleborough and this former Roman posting station known as *Segelocum* was built at the crossing point over the Trent on the Roman Road known as Tillbridge Lane. It was likely, therefore, to have retained its importance through to Anglo-Saxon times, so maybe the grave in question was originally located there.

Some of the cooling towers of Cottam Power Station, rearing up behind buildings in Cottam.

Meanwhile, Coates is also the location of a group of warehouses and a farm. This is the HQ of the Highfields Group, a supplier of wholesome fresh, and prepared domestic and imported pre-packed produce. The company was originally founded by Joseph Stanley Highfield (known as Stan) in 1954 when he purchased a 35 acre smallholding and small dairy herd at Coates. Then in 1965, Stan incorporated a haulage business, J S Highfield Limited. Both businesses are still going today, and the fresh produce business – now known as J S Highfield & Sons – use traditional farming methods, including careful selection of seed varieties and crop rotations that are complemented with modern methods that minimise environmental impact, but still produce natural food to the highest standard.

The main road through Coates.

NAME (STATUS):	**COLSTON BASSETT** (Village)
POPULATION:	225
DISTRICT:	Rushcliffe
EARLIEST RECORD:	*Coletone*, 1086 (Domesday Book); *Coleston Bassett*, 1228
MEANING:	Farmstead of a man called Kolr
DERIVATION:	From the Old Scandinavian personal name, *Kolr* plus the Old English word *tūn* (farmstead). The Bassett affix was a manorial addition relating to the Basset family.

Colston Bassett Etymological Trivia: Affixated

Colston Bassett is an affluent little village in the Vale of Belvoir in the south-eastern part of Nottinghamshire. The Bassett affix was a manorial addition relating to the Basset family, a powerful and influential Norman family who were given the estate in around 1120 by Henry I. The beneficiary, Ralph Basset, also happened to be Lord Chief Justice of England, and it is likely that the parish became known as Colston Bassett shortly after Ralph's death in 1127. Having said that, the affix is also thought to have been applied to distinguish it from nearby Car Colston. As for the Basset family, it is thought that they were largely non-resident landlords, and were more likely to reside at their main possession of Drayton, in Staffordshire; a place which also received the same affix. However, the Basset's had owned Drayton since the 11th century when the same Ralph Basset was Lord of the Manor, and they held both Drayton Bassett and Colston Bassett until 1390 when the last Lord Bassett – also a Ralph Bassett – died without an heir.

Colston Bassett Pub: The Martin's Arms

One of the prettiest country pubs you're likely to see, The Martin's Arms is located in the centre of Colston Bassett, and has also been voted Nottinghamshire Dining Pub of the Year for the last three years (2012-2014). A Grade II listed building, the Martin's Arms takes its name from the 18th and 19th century Lords of the Manor.

The Martin's Arms, Colston Bassett.

Colston Bassett Church: St Mary's and St John the Divine

The church of St John the Divine in Colston Bassett is yet another Grade II-listed Nottinghamshire church, although the listing is not due to its age; the church was only built in 1892 when it replaced the defunct and derelict 13th century St Mary's church. The reason behind this decision was not just because St Mary's was in need of drastic restoration, but because it was set apart from the current village location. The most touted reason for this "setting apart" is because Colston Bassett was subject to a disastrous outbreak of the plague which claimed 83 victims between July 1604 and March 1605. However, the Reverend Evelyn Young in his *History of Colston Bassett* states that although it is likely that the medieval village once clustered around the now-ruined St Mary's church, it had moved well before 1604 – probably due to a much earlier outbreak of the plague, and probably at the time of the Black Death in 1349; certainly a map of 1600 doesn't show any buildings around the old church.

The architect for the new church in 1892 was Arthur W. Brewill of Nottingham who had been commissioned

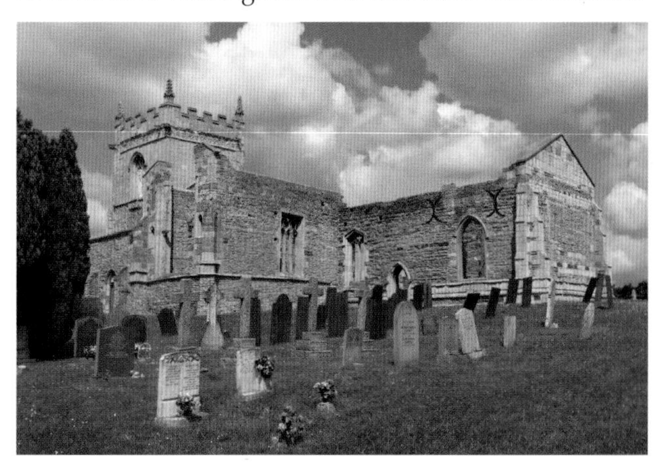

The now-abandoned St Mary's church. Built in the 13th century, it was never restored due to it being set apart from the modern village of Colston Bassett, and was replaced in 1892 by the church of St John the Divine.

by Robert Millington Knowles, High Sheriff of Nottinghamshire, to build a church in memory of his wife and of his son John Knowles, who had drowned, aged only 21. Brewill designed the new church on a grand scale in white stone in the early perpendicular style, and it has been described by Nikolaus Pevsner (1902-1983), the renowned scholar of historical architecture, as one of the most beautiful village churches in England. The building work was carried out by Messrs Bell and Sons, and was consecrated on the 2nd August 1892 by the Bishop of Southwell. However, the construction was initially deemed to be of poor quality and the church underwent a significant restoration programme in 1934 by Charles Marriott Oldrid Scott. A later Bishop of Southwell, the Rt Revd Henry Mosley, then re-opened the repaired building on the 12th August 1936.

The church of St John the Divine, Colston Bassett.

Colston Bassett Historical Trivia: All Sorts of Bassett's

Back when the village of *Coletone* was being recorded in Domesday Book (1086), there were two parishes of Colston and Kinoulton, while prior to the Norman Conquest, both were included in the wider area of the Anglo-Saxon manor of Newbold. Following the Conquest, Newbold disappeared from the map, and the Bassett affix was applied a few decades later. The village then remained in the Basset family for eight generations until the last Lord Ralph Basset died in 1390, at which point the entire estate passed to his nephew Sir Hugh Shirley. However, this inheritance was successfully contested and the estate eventually passed to the Stafford family who then retained ownership until 1521 when the surviving Stafford heir, the Duke of Buckingham, was executed for high treason. Buckingham was tried before a panel of 17 peers, accused of "listening to prophecies of the King's death and intending to kill the King". The estate then passed to Sir Thomas Kitson, who became Sheriff of London in 1533, but on the death of his son (also Thomas) in 1574, the estate passed to his godson, Edward Golding, who held the estate until his death in 1584. His son (also called Edward Golding) acquired the estate and actually lived in the village in the newly built manor house on the site of the current Colston Bassett Hall, while in 1610, he was made a baronet.

The shaft of the Grade II listed market cross in Colston Bassett, dates from 1831, and commemorates the coronation of William IV. It stands on a 15th century sandstone base. Colston Bassett was originally granted a market charter in 1257 by Henry III, allowing Ralph Basset and his heirs a weekly Wednesday market. Here, the cross is shown in front of the old Telegraph Office.

During the English Civil War, Edward Golding was a dedicated Royalist while Colonel Francis Hacker, who lived in Hall House, was a staunch Parliamentarian. He was thought to have been heavily influenced by his friend Colonel Hutchinson of neighbouring Owthorpe Hall, who was the foremost Parliamentarian commander in Nottinghamshire. However, Thomas Hacker, Francis Hacker's younger brother, was a Royalist, and he was killed in a skirmish at Colston

Colston Bassett Hall. This incarnation of the house was built by Sir Edward Golding between 1704 and 1710.

Bassett in May 1643. As for Francis, he actually supervised arrangements for the execution of King Charles I, so it was little surprise that when Charles II was restored to the throne in 1660, Colonel Hacker was hung drawn and quartered for treason. As for the Goldings, they lasted another generation, with the next Sir Edward Golding rebuilding the Hall and carrying out extensive tree planting between 1704 and 1710. The estate then passed to the Martin family, with Henry Martin responsible for the construction of several of Colston Bassett's larger properties such as the Rectory and the Yews (or Colston Bassett House as it is now known). The next owner was George Thomas Davy who bought the manor in 1864, and who was responsible for landscaping the village to the design and layout that can be seen today. He then sold to Robert Millington Knowles in 1876 whose main legacy was the building of the church of St John the Divine. When he died in 1924, the estate passed to his daughter and son in law, Sir Edward and Lady Le Marchant and the estate remains with the Le Marchant family to this day.

Colston Bassett Quirk Alert: No Connection and One of Six

George Bassett & Co. Ltd, the world-famous sweet factory famed for its Liquorice Allsorts, was established in Sheffield in 1842, while the nearby Nottinghamshire town of Worksop was famous for the growth of liquorice, and today still has a public house called The Liquorice Gardens. Given that Worksop is also located in the Bassetlaw local government district of Nottinghamshire, you'd think there might be a connection to Colston Bassett somewhere. Alas, though, not via Bassetlaw (*Bernesedelaue*, 1086), as the name is

Colston Bassett Dairy, winner of many awards over the years for their Stilton and Shropshire Blue.

Anglo-Saxon and therefore pre-dates the Norman *Basset* family. Of course, it is possible that a connection between the Basset's of Colston Bassett, and George Bassett of Liquorice Allsorts fame does exist somewhere in the Bassett/Basset ancestry, but no confectionary connection can be confirmed in this book!

That said, the village of Colston Bassett does possess a famous dairy which opened in 1913 following the vision of a local doctor, Dr William Windley. Using milk from local farms within a 1.5 mile radius, Colston Bassett Dairy is one of only six dairies that are permitted to make Stilton cheese, plus it also manufactures small quantities of white Stilton and Shropshire Blue. The dairy has won many awards over the years, while Colston Bassett Stilton was named Best British Cheese at the 2013 World Cheese Awards. Shropshire Blue was also recognised – winning a coveted gold award and adds to the accolades the dairy picked up in 2012, including a gold three-star and gold two-star at the Great Taste Awards 2013.

Looking towards the church of St John the Divine.

Threes-Up!

	COMMONSIDE	KERSALL	LITTLE GREEN
Status:	Suburb	Village	Hamlet
Population:	c.2,000	83	c.20
District:	Ashfield	Newark and Sherwood	Rushcliffe
Earliest Record:	Unknown	*Cherueshale*, 1086 (Domesday Book); *Kyrneshale*, 1196	Unknown
Meaning:	On the side of the village where the common is	Nook of land of a man called Cynehere	Place with a little green
Derivation:	A modern derivation	From the Old English personal name *Cynehere* plus the Old English word *halh* (nook or corner of land)	Probably a modern derivation

Threes Up Trivia!

Commonside is a housing estate and a large industrial estate in the south-western part of Huthwaite. The estate is wedged in between the B6026 to the north, the B6027 (also known as Common Road) to the east, and Nuns Brook Road which encloses the suburb to the west and the south. A few yards to the west of Nuns Brook Road is a brook that marks the boundary with Derbyshire while at the top of Common Road is a pair of former pit winding wheels (*shown top left*) that once used to haul cages up and down at Huthwaite's New Hucknall Colliery. They were unveiled and dedicated in October 1995 as a memorial to the loyal service given by generations of Huthwaite mineworkers. Although coal was mined in Huthwaite from at least the 16th century, large scale production only began in 1876 after sinking New Hucknall Colliery off Common Road. However, despite producing nearly 12 million tonnes of coal since nationalisation to the National Coal Board in 1947, the pit was closed in 1982. Meanwhile, All Saint's church, which is also located at the top of Common Road, is constructed from stone hewn from New Hucknall Colliery, and was built between 1902 and 1903.

All Saints' church, Commonside, Huthwaite.

Meanwhile, **Kersall** is a tiny village located just off the A616 between Newark and Ollerton. Just to the north-west of the village is Kersall Lodge, a Grade II listed farmhouse dating from the 18th century, while to the south is Maplebeck where you will find The Beehive, the smallest pub in Nottinghamshire and the unusually named St Radegund's church which dates from the 13th century. As for The Beehive, we are fortunate that it still survives, as last century an American visitor was so taken with it that he tried to buy it, intending to ship it back to America, brick by brick!

Finally, **Little Green** (*top right*) is an area located on Spring Lane at the northernmost tip of Car Colston and just south-west of Screveton. A number of attractive homes grace Little Green, while "The Old Hall" now doubles up as Southfields Pre-School. All of these properties face an area of open greenery, which perhaps gives Little Green its name, perhaps because this ample sized green pales into insignificance compared with the 29 acres of village green in Car Colston which is believed to be the largest rural common in England.

St Radegund's church, Maplebeck, is located just south of Kersall.

The Beehive, Maplebeck – the smallest pub in Nottinghamshire.

NAME (STATUS):	**COLWICK** (Suburb and Village)
POPULATION:	2,829
DISTRICT:	Gedling
EARLIEST RECORD:	*Over Colwick*, 1086 (Domesday Book)
MEANING:	Probably works where charcoal is made or stored
DERIVATION:	From the Old English words *col* (coal) and *wīc* (earlier Romano-British settlement, specialised farm or building, or trading/industrial settlement)

St John the Baptist church in the grounds of Colwick Hall has been derelict since 1933.

Colwick Church: St John the Baptist

There are two churches of the same name in Colwick. The one in use as a place of worship today on Vale Road is much the younger of the two, built in 1951, and dedicated to St John the Baptist. However, there is a much older church in the grounds of Colwick Hall, this one Grade II listed and also named after St John the Baptist. It was built by Sir John Byron in the 16th century incorporating 14th and 15th century sections from an earlier church. Then in 1648, the church was repaired and a chancel and steeple built by Sir John Musters while in 1684, he rebuilt the tower and chancel, and added battlements to the nave to make it match up with the rest of the building. Much later, in 1885, a vestry and an organ chamber were added on the north wall of the church. However, by the early 20th century, the church was in a poor state, particularly the roof, and although repairs were continually made, the condition of the church continued to deteriorate. By 1920 some of the services were being held in the Schoolrooms in wintertime and later in a newly built Parish Hall, which also began to cater for marriages, too. By 1933 the church was abandoned as dangerous and was finally closed as unsafe in March 1936 – which was pretty timely, as in November 1936, a principal beam gave way, bringing down most of the nave roof! Fortunately, the Byron family monuments had already been removed to the crypt of Newstead Abbey, while the Musters family monuments had been re-housed at All Saints' church, Annesley. The church remained derelict and therefore in 1949, the Planning Department of Nottingham City Council served notice that the church would be demol-

The new St John the Baptist church on Vale Road was built in 1951 as a replacement for its much older namesake.

ished. However, this move was met with resistance from the Rector and churchwardens who pointed out that the church was not officially closed and they hoped to restore it at some time in the future. Alas, this was never to be. The new church of St John the Baptist was built in 1951 on Vale Road, and in 1976 the old church graveyard was closed and the church made officially redundant. In 1979, the old church was taken over by Nottingham City Council and they approved a £150,000 scheme to make the ruins safe, clear the headstones, and lay out the grounds as a quiet sitting area.

Colwick Historic Trivia: Colwick Hall

Today, the former village of Colwick is seen as a south-eastern suburb of Greater Nottingham, although it actually lies just outside the Nottingham unitary authority area. However, despite its absorption into the urban sprawl of Greater Nottingham, Colwick has recently won the right to be recognised as a village again following a campaign by members of Colwick Parish Council. The place was originally a village back in 1086, when the Domesday Book recorded Colwick as *two* villages: *Over Colwick* and *Nether Colwick*. At that time, the manor was owned by William Peverel and Over Colwick comprised the manor house, the church, a water mill, 30 acres of meadow and 15 acres of wood, and Nether Colwick comprised the village. However, the former eventually became known as simply Colwick while the latter became known as Netherfield.

On the death of William de Colwick in 1362, the estate passed by the marriage of his daughter Joan to Sir Richard Byron. The Byrons then lived at Colwick for around 180 years with Sir John Byron rebuilding Colwick church in the 16th century. It was also Sir John Byron who was granted Newstead Abbey by Henry VIII following the Dissolution of the Monasteries. The two parts of Colwick were then briefly united under one owner when Sir James Stonehouse acquired Over Colwick from Sir John Byron and Nether Colwick from the Wood family. A later Sir James Stonehouse then sold Colwick to Sir John Musters in 1675, a wealthy merchant from London who began the restoration of the church in 1684. Colwick Hall remained under the

The Toby Carvery Colwick Park, one of two Colwick pubs, the other being The Starting Gate, located over the road and so-named due to its proximity to Nottingham Racecourse and dog track.

Colwick Hall, built for the Musters family between 1775 and 1776.

Warm-down after the 15:45 at Colwick Park on Sunday 1 June, 2014.

control of the Musters family for another 200 years, and the present Hall was funded by another John Musters between 1775 and 1776. Designed by John Carr and built by local builder, Samuel Stretton, it was constructed of red brick, with ashlar dressings and

The winners cross the finish line at the 15:45 at Colwick Park on Sunday 1 June, 2014.

hipped slate roofs with a two storey central block and single storey wings, while the frontage saw four Ionic pillars surmounted by a pediment. A few decades later, in 1805, John Musters' son, Jack, married Mary Chaworth, and the name Chaworth-Musters appeared for the first time. Jack inherited the Hall from his father in 1827, but four years later, the Hall was sacked and partly burned by rioters who were protesting at the Second Reform Bill. Mary Chaworth-Musters was said to have spent the night in pouring rain with her daughter Sophia, crouched beneath the shrubbery, and died at Wiverton Hall some four months later, allegedly from the shock. The last Chaworth-Musters owner was John Patricius Chaworth-Musters who inherited the Colwick estate in 1888. However, he only held it for a year before selling it to Colonel Horatio Davies who, in turn, sold it to the Nottingham Racecourse Company. The Hall thus became a public house and the rest of the buildings were used to accommodate grooms and jockeys. Finally, whizzing forward to 1965, the Hall was acquired from the Racecourse Company by Nottingham Corporation, who then allowed the building to fall into disrepair until it was saved by local businessman Chek Whyte, who eventually sold Colwick Hall to current owners, Pearl Hotels and Restaurants.

As for the Nottingham Racecourse Company, they staged both forms of racing at Colwick Park until the mid-1990s, when it abandoned National Hunt racing to become a flat-only course. The course hosts two early-season "listed" races – the Kilvington Stakes for fillies over 6 furlongs, and the Further Flight Stakes over 1 mile 6 furlongs.

Colwick Quirk Alert: Banned Cheese and The Gruesome Murders at Saville's Spinney

In the 17th century, Colwick was the birthplace of Colwick cheese, a soft and creamy curd cheese. By the 18th century, it was already being made at a number of other locations, and survived up until the late 20th century when it was banned under new health and safety regulations as it was made from unpasteurised milk.

Meanwhile, Colwick was also the site of the gruesome murders at Saville's Spinney in 1844. William Saville cut the throats of his wife and three children in Colwick Woods where they then lay for three days before being discovered. The murders created such uproar, that his hanging at County Hall attracted record crowds. Alas, further tragedy ensued. It was said that every available space was occupied long before the appointed time. Numerous folk fainted and the lucky ones were lifted up and passed by the crowd to safety. But after the execution at three minutes past eight, folk immediately attempted to get away from the suffocating mass, but most of the doors along the Pavement were closed. Many were crushed against the walls while others were trampled upon in the blind panic that ensued. The rest were conveyed towards an outlet at Garner's Hill, where many more fell down the steps there, and within seconds the steps and narrow thoroughfare was completely blocked. In all, seventeen were crushed to death and more than a hundred received serious injuries, with many of them suffering dislocations or broken limbs. William Saville had unwittingly claimed many more victims!

NAME (STATUS):	**CROMWELL** (Village)
POPULATION:	232
DISTRICT:	Newark and Sherwood
EARLIEST RECORD:	*Crunwelle*, 1086 (Domesday Book)
MEANING:	Crooked stream
DERIVATION:	From the Old English words *crumb* (crooked) and *wella* (spring or stream)

Cromwell Geographic Trivia: The Tidal Trent

Cromwell Lock lies just to the east of the village of Cromwell, and is the official point where the non-tidal River Trent ends. From here, commercial traffic and pleasure craft can navigate their way north towards Torksey and Gainsborough and ultimately the River Humber. However, navigators on the Trent must wait till the tide is ebbing in their favour to ensure a safe passage.

Cromwell Church: St Giles

St Giles' church is Grade I listed and dates from the 13th century with the south doorway, the nave arcade and some lancet windows surviving from this time. From the 14th century are two medieval windows in the chancel along with an arcade of two bays which was opened up into the chancel in the 19th century, while the tower dates from around 1427.

St Giles' church, Cromwell.

Cromwell Historic Trivia: The Cromwell's of Cromwell

Cromwell was situated between Newark and Retford on the old Great North Road, a coaching route used by

The old Cromwell sign on the now-bypassed part of original Great North Road.

Cromwell Lock on the River Trent.

mail coaches between London, York and Edinburgh – and indeed, the portion of road that runs through Cromwell today alongside the A1 is still known as Great North Road. However, much earlier than that, the Romans built a villa at Cromwell, presumably because the place was close to the Fosse Way, and only around three miles north-west of their posting station that was known as *Crococolana*. In 1882 workmen involved in improving the navigation on the River Trent also found remains of what they thought to be a Roman bridge at Cromwell, but which archaeologists now believe is 8th century Mercian.

Somewhat appropriately, the village was owned in medieval times by the Cromwell family. Their seat eventually became Tattershall Castle, over the border in Lincolnshire, and the first Baron Cromwell (from the second creation) was Ralph Cromwell who was elevated to Lord Cromwell in 1375. The first prominent Cromwell of the second creation was also a Ralph Cromwell, the 3rd Lord Cromwell, who served as Lord Treasurer under Henry VI from 1433-1443. However, the more famous Cromwells came from later branches of the barony. The fourth creation in 1536 of the Barons Cromwell of Wimbledon included Henry VIIIs famous chief minister from 1532-1540, Thomas Cromwell, the 1st Earl of Essex, and destined to be executed for treason in 1540, while the fifth creation of the Barons Cromwell (of Oakham, this time) included the most famous of all, Oliver Cromwell (1599-1658), the Parliamentarian leader who overthrew the monarchy during the English Civil War.

Finally, Cromwell is one of the four "Thankful Villages" in Nottinghamshire – those rare places that suffered no fatalities during World War I.

Cromwell Quirk Alert: Vina's Dolls and Mrs Clarke's Fancy

The Old Rectory at Cromwell was built in around 1680, but today, it hosts Vina's Doll Gallery, formerly the Vina Cooke Museum of Dolls and Bygone Childhood. The Gallery includes a large collection of dolls dating from the 18th century to the present day, as well as Vina Cooke's own handmade portrait dolls. As well as many more besides, these include Robin Hood, The Beatles, Cliff Richard, Audrey Hepburn, Dr. Zhivago, the Tudor and Stuart Kings and Queens, characters from Alice in Wonderland and the Wizard of Oz, plus local heroes Torvill & Dean in their famous Bolero costumes.

Meanwhile, the curator of the gallery also happens to be a member of the local Rattlejag Morris. Formed in 2002, Rattlejag Morris is a mixed dance side who specifically aim to revive and develop dance tradition from the Nottinghamshire, Lincolnshire and East Yorkshire areas. They perform broom dances, bacca pipe dances and sword dances, along with other dances which are unique to their group, while they use a variety of rattles, shakers, castanets and bellsticks to give each dance its own distinctive sound. Although their signature dance is *The Holderness Rattle*, the Rattlejag Morris also uses many obscure Nottinghamshire-based tunes, too. Examples include *The Wanderer*, named after the River Trent, *King Lud's Dance* which is all about the Nottinghamshire Luddites, *Mrs Clarke's Fancy* which is about a lady from Ranby near Retford, *The Golden Ball* which is about a 19th century pub in Worksop, *Castle Hill* which is about an annual Morris dance at sunrise on May 1st at Laxton, and finally, *Rufford Park*, which is all about a mass brawl with tragic consequences between poachers and gamekeepers at Rufford Park in 1851!

The Old Rectory, Cromwell, today home to Vina's Doll Gallery.

Name (Status):	**DUNHAM-ON-TRENT** (Village)
Population:	351
District:	Bassetlaw
Earliest Record:	*Duneham*, 1086 (Domesday Book)
Meaning:	Homestead or village on a hill
Derivation:	From the Old English words *dūn* (hill) and *hām* (homestead)

The White Swan, Dunham-on-Trent.

The Bridge Inn, Dunham-on-Trent.

Dunham-on-Trent Pubs: The White Swan and The Bridge Inn

Dunham is home to two very handsome white washed pubs, the White Swan and the Grade II-listed Bridge Inn. They are located within a few yards of each other on the A57, just before it heads over the Trent into Lincolnshire – and where you also have to pay an astronomical toll of 40p to cross the Trent!

Dunham-on-Trent Church: St Oswald's and Brother Grim

St Oswald's is another Grade I listed church, while three headstones in the churchyard are Grade II listed (dated 1729, 1731 and 1738), as are two gateways into the churchyard. As for the church itself, the tower is its oldest part and dates from the 15th century along with its strikingly large Perpendicular windows and five bells, while the south nave wall was constructed much later in 1802. The rest of the church is Victorian, built between 1861 and 1862 by T.C. Hine. Happily, at the end of the 18th century, the Archdeacon of Nottingham, Sir Richard Kaye, employed a water-colour painter named Samuel Hieronymus Grim to make drawings of several churches, and his drawing of the pre-Victorian St Oswald's can still be found in no less than the British Museum.

St Oswald's church, Dunham-on-Trent.

Dunham-on-Trent Historic Trivia: Dunham Bridge

The toll bridge mentioned above is known as Dunham Bridge and was built and opened in 1832 – thanks to the

Dunham Bridge with the pipe bridge in the foreground obscuring the road toll bridge behind it.

Dunham Bridge Act 1830. Prior to this point, the only way to cross the river was by the Dunham Ferry – and which in 1814 would have cost you half a crown! As for the 1832 bridge, this was a four-span cast-iron structure built by the civil engineer, George Leather. The superstructure was then rebuilt on its original piers between 1975 and 1977 to trunk road standards, while a new toll plaza was opened in 1994, doubling the number of lanes through the booths from two to four. However, passage is free on Christmas Day and Boxing Day, while three-wheeled invalid carriages are exempt from tolls all year round!

One of St Oswald's two Grade II listed churchyard archways.

NAME (STATUS):	**EATON** (Village)
POPULATION:	233
DISTRICT:	Bassetlaw
EARLIEST RECORD:	*Etune*, 1086 (Domesday Book)
MEANING:	Farmstead or estate on a river
DERIVATION:	From the Old English words *ēēa* (river) and *tūn* (farmstead)

Eaton Church: All Saints

All Saints' church at Eaton is Grade II listed, but relatively modern, having been rebuilt in 1860, but with the south chancel wall retaining a 15th century piscina. The church was rebuilt in Steetley stone by G. Shaw of Manchester for H. Bridgeman Simpson of Babworth Hall. Today, there is just the one bell – hung for swing chiming in the bell cote!

Whitehouses, a Grade II listed pub just north of Eaton.

The banks of the River Idle, seen from Eaton, and possible site of an ancient and important battle in 616.

Eaton Historic Trivia: Bretwalda

It is thought that the village of Eaton pinpoints the site of a famous battle in 616 that was known as the Battle of the River Idle. The battle was fought between the East Angles under Rædwald and the Northumbrians under Æthelfrith. The East Anglian's won the battle and Æthelfrith was killed, this leading to the establishment of Edwin as king of Northumbria. As for Rædwald, he was the most powerful of the English kings south of the River Humber and was referred to in the Anglo-Saxon Chronicle, written centuries after his death, as *Bretwalda* – an Old English term meaning "Britain-ruler". He is considered by historians to be the most likely occupant of the famous Sutton Hoo ship-burial, and therefore the owner of the famous Anglo-Saxon helmet discovered there.

Eaton Quirk Alert: Quintessentially Islamic

Intriguingly for a quintessential English village, Eaton is home to the Al Karam Secondary School, a Muslim boarding school and Islamic Studies College. Based at Eaton Hall, a former teacher training college, this independent school was founded by Mohammed Pirzada in 1995 when he bought it for £910,000, thanks to funds raised from Muslim donors around the country. Many of its pupils are from inner-city Britain, thanks to annual fees that are kept deliberately low due to ongoing generous fund-raising. Explaining the aims of the school, Pirzada states: *"Not only do we need Imam training, we need Muslims in this country who are civilised, who understand this country, but also understand their faith. We need a school to train our younger generation not just to be Muslims, but to be decent British citizens."* Ever since their first batch of students completed their GCSE's in 1998, the school has consistently appeared near the top of the Nottinghamshire league tables.

All Saints' church, Eaton.

Eaton village.

NAME (STATUS):	**EDINGLEY** (Village)
POPULATION:	443
DISTRICT:	Newark and Sherwood
EARLIEST RECORD:	*Eddyngleia*, c.1180
MEANING:	Woodland clearing associated with a man called Eddi
DERIVATION:	From the Old English personal name, *Eddi*, plus the Old English words *ing* (associated with) and *lēah* (woodland clearing)

Edingley Church: St Giles

The small church of St Giles at Edingley dates from the 12th century and is Grade II listed – as are a couple of late 17th century headstones in the churchyard. St Giles has a slightly squat appearance thanks to its lack of a tower, although it's rather quaint bellcote somewhat compensates. In terms of old features, the west doorway is Norman with its chevron and cable moulding while the north wall also includes a narrow Norman window. However, the church was heavily restored during the 19th century with the chancel rebuilt by Henry Machon in 1844 and further restored by Charles Hodgson Fowler in around 1890.

Edingley Historic Trivia: Old Allotments and Old Schools

Edingley's allotments are historic and the current plots still align to the same land laid out in the enclosure act of 1781. More recently, the village hasn't had much luck with schools. The village school was built in 1911-12 but closed in the 1960's, while the private Edgehill School took over the building and extended northwards with a series of temporary buildings ... but then, itself, closed in 1996. The same building is now known as the Old Schoolroom, and today it serves as the village community hall.

The Old Reindeer, Edingley, parts of which date back to the middle of the 17th century.

The Norman-style west doorway of St Giles.

Edingley Quirk Alert: Oh Deer!

Today, Edingley is home to Forrest Feeds, an animal feed specialist that was established in the village in 1982. As well as its animal feed products, though, it also produces accessories for birds, cats, dogs, horses, poultry, farm animals and all manner of other small animals ... plus offers elements of giftware, too. One element of giftware that caught my eye was the animal-related coasters and place-mats: "Fowl Play" for a couple of hens, "Great Scott" for a pair of Scottie dogs ... and guess what caption for an upside-down deer?

St Giles' church, Edingley.

The lychgate, St Giles' church.

NAME (STATUS):	**ELTON** (Village)
POPULATION:	c.75
DISTRICT:	Rushcliffe
EARLIEST RECORD:	*Ailetone*, 1086 (Domesday Book); *Elleton*, 1088
MEANING:	Farmstead of a man called Ella
DERIVATION:	From the Old English personal name, *Ella*, plus the Old English word *tūn* (enclosure, farmstead, village, manor or estate)
FAMOUS RESIDENTS:	**Don Masson**, former Notts County, QPR and Derby County midfielder, and capped 17 times by Scotland

Elton Geographical and Etymological Trivia

Elton is a small village located on the A52 in the Vale of Belvoir, roughly half way between Nottingham and Grantham. It actually lies along a country lane that bisects the A52 and, as is demonstrated by the above photograph, the signs at either end of that country lane actually call the place Elton-On-The-Hill. However, most maps represent it as simply "Elton" and when I drove through recently it didn't feel much like a hill, either; indeed, physical maps place the village at a soaring altitude of 22-37 metres above sea level! However, on digging a little deeper, it would appear that until recently, Elton-on-the-Hill was the name of the ecclesiastical parish and Elton the name of the *civil* parish. Furthermore, the 1825 volume called *A Topographical Dictionary of the United Kingdom* lists the place as *Elton-super-montem* – suggesting that the place has been associated with a hill for some time! Finally, the village also went by the nickname of "The Magpie Village" in the early 20th century when buildings belonging to Elton Manor and the Rectory were white-washed and the timber painted black.

Elton Pub: The Manor Arms and Little India

The Manor Arms lies on the A52 at the crossroads with Station Road and Sutton Lane, and now has an Indian restaurant attached known as Little India. Back in the 1920s, three royal princes were once photographed outside the Manor Arms at a meet of the Belvoir Hunt, the princes being the Prince of Wales, the Duke of Kent and the Duke of York – the latter going onto become George VI in 1936!

Elton Church: St Michael and All Angels

The Grade II listed St Michael and All Angels' church dates possibly from the late Norman period, with a single Norman-looking corbel head surviving, along with three round medieval arches on the south side of the nave suggesting a former aisle from that period, but which was demolished in 1786. Dating from slightly later, a 20th century porch shelters a 14th century doorway. However, the church was heavily restored between 1855 and 1857 and given stucco rendering in imitation of ashlar. The tower was also rebuilt in brick at this time, and has two bells (dated 1702 and 1856), plus a relatively modern clock installed in 1969. Meanwhile back in 1780, the verger dug up around 200 silver coins from the reign of Henry II ... and received a £10 reward for his trouble from the Lady of the Manor, Mrs Collin!

Elton Historic Trivia: Ex-Manor

Elton-on-the-Hill was once home to an early 19th-century manor house with extensive grounds, but this was demolished in 1933 by its last owner, W. Noël Parr, a Nottingham solicitor who lived in the Old Rectory until 1957. All that remains of the manor house and its grounds are the 18th-century gateway into Sutton Lane, the 19th century lodge, the red brick walls of the kitchen gardens with a late 18th century fort-like Grade II listed gazebo, and a grey brick brew house, now converted into a home and enlarged. The Old Rectory in Station Road is also contemporary with these buildings, dating from the early 19th century.

The Manor Arms and Little India, Elton-on-the-Hill.

St Michael and All Angels' church, Elton-on-the-Hill.

Left: *The gateway to the former Elton Manor, which was demolished in 1933.* Above: *Also surviving is this perimeter wall with a Grade II-listed brick gazebo built in.*

Elton Quirk Alert: Gryffindor Gravestone and a Blasphemous Paultry Scrub!

A family tomb dedicated to the Launder family and dating from 1780, along with a group of headstones in the graveyard of Elton's parish church of St Michael and All Angels are all Grade II listed. However, since around the turn of the 21st century, those gravestones attract considerably less attention than another, purely because this other is dedicated to a certain William Harry Potter!

The Rev. William Selby was inducted into Elton parish church in 1686, but appears not to have been the most Godly of men. Bingham court records of 1709, report that "*John Trinbury, in justification of his assault upon the Rector of Elton complained that at the funeral of Ellen Ragsdale three or four years earlier, the said Rector was so drunk that he could not say the usual prayers for the dead but fell asleep at the reading desk and had to be disturbed by the Parish Clerk, and then he went to the grave with the corpse and bid them put her in saying 'God help thee poor Nell' without any other prayers or ceremony and afterwards was led home by the Clerk. On the following day the Rector answered in a similar sworn statement that he was abused by the said John Trinbury in a very scandalous manner being called a knave, a rascal and a 'paultry scrub' and having his clothes pulled off his back by the said John and his wife and daughter.*" Apparently, the Rector had already been charged the previous year for blasphemy, having asked the following question: "Was God Almighty a drone? If not what was he doing before he made the Earth?"

I wonder if he knows the answer to his question now...

The Grange, Elton-on-the-Hill, and today a very attractive B&B.

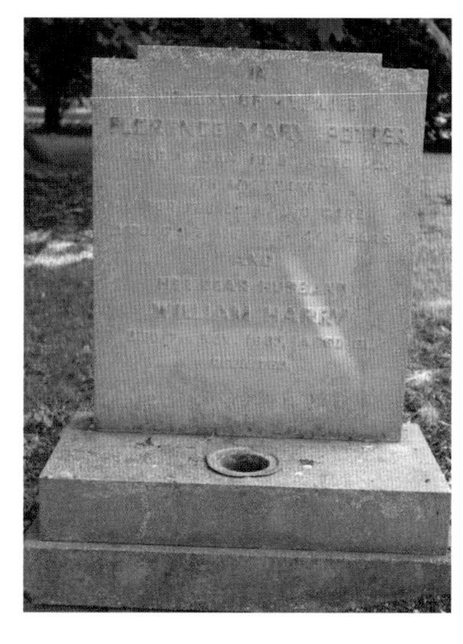

Gravestone of William Harry Potter in the graveyard at St Michael and All Angels' church, Elton-on-the-Hill.

NAME (STATUS):	**EVERTON (Village)**
POPULATION:	591
DISTRICT:	Bassetlaw
EARLIEST RECORD:	*Evretone*, 1086 (Domesday Book)
MEANING:	Farmstead where wild boars are seen
DERIVATION:	From the Old English words *eofor* (wild boar) and *tūn* (enclosure, farmstead, village, manor or estate).

Everton Pubs: The Blacksmith's Arms and The Sun Inn

Everton is a village and civil parish located on the A631 between Gainsborough and Bawtry – and it is on the A631 where you will find The Sun Inn, a self-styled "country pub and restaurant". Meanwhile, in the centre of the village is The Blacksmiths Arms, a genuine 17th century freehouse. The pub has also been a venue in the past for the aforementioned Rattlejag Morris (see *Cromwell Quirk Alert*).

The Sun Inn, Everton.

Everton Church: Holy Trinity

Another Grade II listed church, Holy Trinity dates back to the late 11th century, although its ancient tympanum over the south doorway, crudely engraved with the heads of two dragons facing each other with tongues outstretched, may even be Saxon in origin. The church is one of several built by the Normans shortly after 1066 along the route of the Roman Road that connected Lincoln and York via Littleborough and Doncaster. There were a number of additions to Holy

The Blacksmiths Arms, Everton.

Holy Trinity church, Everton.

Trinity between the 11th and 16th centuries, including a late 12th century arcade which divides the nave and aisle while the clerestory and the windows of the nave and aisle are 15th century. However, the Norman arch in the chancel and another little horseshoe arch in the tower survive from the 11th century – although the tower is largely 15th century. The church was then partly restored in 1841, and two years later, the chancel was extended eastward and finished with an octagonal apse, while a southern annex was also added. The 19th century also saw the creation of a replica of the original Norman font.

Everton's nod to its Anglo-Saxon origins.

Everton Historic Trivia: Mills and Drainage

Everton Mill was a four-storey brick tower windmill built around 1820. However, the sails were removed in 1930, as the mill had been worked since 1898 by steam engines. The mill was still working in the 1940s but was closed in 1950 and the machinery dismantled, although the mill tower still stands today.

If you climb to the top of Holy Trinity church tower, you get an extensive view over the flat country that surrounds it, particularly to the north and the area that is known as "The Carrs". In turn, the whole area of The Carrs was once the southern part of a vast 70,000 acre tract of flat marsh land, known as the "Levels of Hatfield Chase." The Nottinghamshire portion of The Carrs extends for around 10,000 acres from the border with South Yorkshire near Bawtry to the border with Lincolnshire near Gainsborough. For many centuries, the River Idle and its artificial deviation, the Bycar Dyke, were ineffectual in draining this district, so in 1650, the famous Dutch engineer, Cornelius Vermuyden, was consulted. This led to the construction of sluices and banks at great expense ... but which also proved to be ineffective; a rare failure for the great man. Subsequent Acts of Parliament enabled further works to be carried out, and this included the Inclosure & Drainage Act (24 July 1833). The Act finally led to an improvement in drainage off The Carrs, meaning that today, the soil in the district is much improved, while the area is also a haven for birdwatchers.

The Norman chancel arch in Holy Trinity church.

Everton Quirk Alert: A Dangerous Enemy

Everton was the burial place in 1682 for Anthony Gilby, an active Royalist and mid-17th century M.P. He hailed from Lincolnshire but became very wealthy after marrying a Nottinghamshire heiress. During the English Civil War, he joined the Newark garrison under Lord Belasyse, was fined £25 in 1650 for being, according to the local major-general, "a dangerous enemy", and in 1655 was imprisoned for his collaboration in a failed rising. Nevertheless, on release from prison he became an M.P. and by 1675, Gilby had helped pass several Parliamentary Acts and Bills while he also received the government whip. However, when he later put himself forward to represent Hull, he was rejected following the revelation that he had embezzled £650 worth of lead and 12,000 bricks, belonging to the Hull garrison! He rather fortuitously escaped justice, though, thanks to "the consideration of his loyal and eminent services"!

The tympanum above the south doorway at Holy Trinity church, and which possibly dates back to Saxon times.

NAME:	**FRIEZELAND**
POPULATION:	Unknown
DISTRICT:	Unknown
EARLIEST RECORD:	Unknown
MEANING:	Unknown
DERIVATION:	Unknown

Friezeland Trivia: Friezadoon

According to the Ordnance Survey, and the AA Close-Up Britain Road Atlas, Friezeland is an area just to the north-east of the village of Underwood. Research tells me that Friezeland Grassland is the site of a former sand and gravel quarry, and which is now a Site of Special Scientific Interest (SSSI) containing species-rich pools, flushes and grassland; certainly no evidence of a local branch of Iceland, anyway! Neither is there anything else to identify the place or indicate where the name derives from. I visited the area and asked a few of the locals – but they actually knew less than me! So there isn't a Friezeland sign, a Friezeland Road, a Friezeland Farm or a Friezeland pub; a modern-day Brigadoon, perhaps, that only appears when temperatures drop below a certain threshold? Anyway, it would appear that the grassland is the sum total of whatever Friezeland amounts to – and this is located in between the woods off Felley Mill Lane North (*top left*) and Felley Priory, while at the western edge of the alleged site is the Dog and Quayle pub (*top right*) and Bracken Park, home to Underwood Villa Football Club.

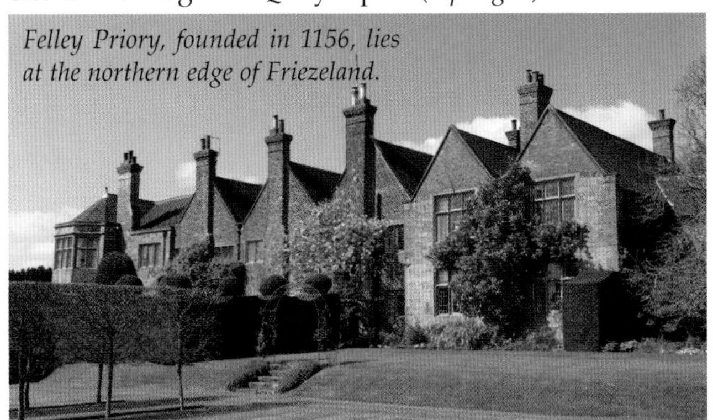

Felley Priory, founded in 1156, lies at the northern edge of Friezeland.

As for Felley Priory, it was founded in 1156 as an Augustinian establishment, and originally consisted of 12 canons. Thankfully, not all of the Priory was completely destroyed following the 1535 Dissolution of the Monasteries, and parts were used elsewhere in the construction of the subsequent house and gardens that appeared in its place; for example, the pillars at the entrance to the garden were originally part of the Priory church and date from the late 12th century, while the high garden wall to the south-west is believed to be part of the priory boundary wall. However, the central part of the house was constructed in the 16th and 17th centuries, although it was also plundered during the English Civil War and became an army garrison and Royalist stronghold. The house eventually came into the ownership of the Chaworth-Musters family in 1822, although they did not live there for many years until Major Robert Chaworth-Musters moved to Felley in 1973, having sold the family home at nearby Annesley Hall. Today, the beautiful gardens are open to the public for much of the year, with specially organised highlights including Daffodil Sunday in April and Bluebell Woodland Walk in May. As chance had it, I visited in between the two events and managed to capture both in almost their full glory.

NAME (STATUS):	**GOTHAM** (Village)
POPULATION:	1,563
DISTRICT:	Rushcliffe
EARLIEST RECORD:	*Gatham*, 1086 (Domesday Book)
MEANING:	Homestead or enclosure where goats are kept
DERIVATION:	From the Old English words *gāt* (goat) and *hām* (homestead) or *hamm* (enclosure)

Gotham Pub: The Cuckoo Bush Inn

Gotham is home to three pubs, all of which are on the main road through the village. At the northern end of the village is The Star Inn, which originally started as a beer house with horses stabled there together with other small farm animals to the rear, while framework knitters worked upstairs. Opposite the church towards the southern end of the village is The Sun Inn. Originally built in 1840 and called the Peel Inn (after the incumbent Prime Minister), it was an old coaching inn and was a popular weekend venue for Nottingham gentry in their horse drawn coaches. In 1849 the Nottingham Ancient Imperial Order of Oddfellows opened the Prince Albert Lodge at The Sun Inn, while later it became a very popular place for honeymooners. Finally, in between The Star Inn and The Sun Inn is The Cuckoo Bush Inn, and which is named after the antics of the Wise Men of Gotham (see *Gotham Quirk Alert*). The Cuckoo Bush Inn was built in 1858 on the site of an earlier same-named place. A fourth pub, The Windmill, was demolished in 2007 and was named after the local windmill (also now deceased) that dated back to at least 1296.

The Cuckoo Bush Inn, Gotham.

Gotham Church: St Lawrence

St Lawrence's church is Grade I listed, and its oldest parts date from the 13th century. This includes its unusual broached spire which is one of the oldest stone spires in the country and the only one in Nottinghamshire to follow the design of the ancient *wooden* broached spires. Inside, the arcades and the nave date from the 13th and 14th century while the clerestory is 15th century. The church also includes numerous monuments to the St Andrew family who were Lords of the Manor from the 13th to the 17th century. The church was restored in 1789 and repaired in 1869.

Gotham Historic Trivia: Moots, Gypsum and a Tornado

On a hillside alongside Gotham is a place where the Saxons, the Danes and their medieval ancestors assembled for a session that was known as the Hundred Moot. It was here that justice was dispensed and local affairs were presided over for the 30 or so villages of the Hundred of Rushcliffe. Below this point is the alleged site of Rushcliffe Hall, seat of the St Andrew family from the 13th to the 17th century. As for the Manor House, that is thought to date back to 1210 and was probably built by the monks of Lenton Priory. It is also alleged to have had an underground passage to the church with the entrance located behind a fireplace, while the Old Curate House, built in 1863 by the Reverend John Vaughan, had a similar secret passage.

Gotham village water pump, with the Sun Inn in the background.

St Lawrence's, Gotham.

During the mid-19th century, framework knitting reached its peak in Gotham, with 87 knitters recorded in 27 workshops around the village. However, towards the end of the 19th century, the industry was replaced by the mining of gypsum with three drift mines having been dug into the hills on the outskirts of the village. At their peak, some 400,000 tons of rock and plaster products were being exported annually and the Gotham mines were supplying one third of the country's requirements. The industry also resulted in an influx of labour from other areas and ancillary trades developed alongside. This industrial growth eventually led to a two-mile railway branch line being introduced in 1899 from the Great Central main line at Ruddington. The branch line was closed in 1965, but the part adjacent to the village has been converted to a relief road and the remainder retained as a nature trail. As for the gypsum mines, they gradually became exhausted and two were closed in 1960 with the final one closing in 1990.

Dropping back into the 19th century, the village water pump was built in 1832 in The Square by Earl Howe, piping water from the nearby Weldon Spring. When that spring dried up in 1885, he linked the pump to another local spring – and which today lies alongside the 14th green on Rushcliffe Golf Course! This was also the point that the pleasant hexagonal tiled shelter was built over it. Slightly earlier, the 1870s also saw the building of a Primitive Methodist Chapel at The Gas, and which became Gotham's *third* chapel following the building of the Wesleyan chapel in 1836 on Curzon Street and the Band of Hope and Primitive Methodist Chapel built in 1849 on Moor Lane. All three chapels were popular among the expanding population of the village, while today, all three have been converted into private homes, as has the former Malt Street bakery building, too. As for the aforementioned street called The Gas, this was the name given to a narrow footpath that provided a shortcut through the village avoiding the main road. The name either originated from its gas tarmacadam surface or perhaps from a Second World War soldier returning home using the German words *die Gasse* which translate into "narrow passage". It is believed to be the only alleyway with this name in the country.

die Gasse

Gotham Legends – including the cuckoo bush crew!

Finally, in August 1984, Gotham was hit by a tornado which uprooted trees, blew garden sheds onto power cables, destroyed greenhouses and severely damaged houses, roofs and chimneys. Thankfully, no one was injured.

Gotham Quirk Alert: The Wise Men of Gotham and a Genuine Batman Connection

Gotham is most famed for the stories of the "Wise Men of Gotham", which depict the villagers of Gotham as idiots. However, there was very much a method in their madness, as it was allegedly feigned in order to avoid a Royal Highway being built through the village – as they would then be expected to build and maintain the route. This was the time of King John, and madness was deemed to be highly contagious – so when the King's knights saw the villagers behaving as if insane, they swiftly withdrew and the King's road was re-routed to avoid the village! Another similar story suggests that King John actually intended building a hunting lodge at Gotham, and this was deemed a bad thing because of the superstition that the ground passed over by a king had to subsequently become a public highway ... and thus, again, the concern over future maintenance. As for their acts of feigned insanity, these included raking the moon out of the pond, attempting to drown an eel in a pond, burning down a forge to get rid of a wasps nest, rolling cheeses downhill to help them find their own way to Nottingham, putting cows on thatched roofs to eat the straw...and most famously of all, building a hedge around a cuckoo to keep it captive and then blaming themselves for its escape for not building the hedge high enough! A variation on the latter theme suggests that they fenced off a small tree in order to keep a cuckoo captive from the sheriff of Nottingham, while yet another suggests that the Wise Men thought that the cuckoo was the harbinger of spring and summer, a time of plenty, and what better way to bring on good weather and good crops all year round than to keep the cuckoo captive ... but captive with a very low fence! Whatever their motivation, their antics certainly convinced the King's men to steer clear. As for today, what is known as the Cuckoo Bush Mound is situated at the top of Court Hill to the south of the village and is the alleged site of the Wise Men's cuckoo pen! As it happens, though, the mound in question is also a 3,000 year-old Neolithic burial mound. When excavated in 1847, it was found to contain two graves, one of which contained a flint spearhead and a bronze pin.

Finally, at the beginning of this section, the derivation of the place-name Gotham is confirmed as "homestead or enclosure where goats are kept". And alas, this also explains the place-name pronunciation, which is "Goat-um" and not the same as its Batman equivalent! However, there is a genuine connection to the American superhero. Firstly, reminded of the foolish ingenuity of the Nottinghamshire Gotham's residents, the 19th century author Washington Irving gave the name "Gotham" to New York City in his satirical periodical called *The Salmagundi Papers* (1807). In turn, the American comic book artist Bob Kane named the New York home of his DC Comics superhero, Batman, as Gotham City. Furthermore, the existence of the Nottinghamshire Gotham was recently acknowledged in the DC Universe in an issue of *Batman: Legends of the Dark Knight*, although the connection between the two names within the DC Universe has not been fully explained. However, in a story entitled *Cityscape* in an issue of *Batman Chronicles*, it is revealed that Gotham was initially built for the purpose of housing the criminally insane. Robin then quotes: "*I even have a name for it. We could call it 'Gotham' after a village in England – where, according to common belief, all are bereft of their wits.*" Responding to the connection between the Nottinghamshire Gotham and the New York City Gotham, former New York mayor Rudolph Giuliani wrote that it was "*a pleasure to have this opportunity to acknowledge the cultural and historical link between the two places.*"

Below: *Above the front door of this house at the end of Monks Lane, is the name "G. Hives, 1831". He was a builder and beer seller and his home was once reputed to be known as the Poachers Pub!*

Cuckoo Bush Mound, a 3,000 year-old Neolithic burial mound, but which is also deemed to be the site of the famous Wise Men of Gotham's cuckoo pen – and which was recently decorated with a mock fence in honour of the legend!

NAME (STATUS):	**GROVE** (Village)
POPULATION:	105
DISTRICT:	Bassetlaw
EARLIEST RECORD:	*Grava*, 1086 (Domesday Book)
MEANING:	Place at the grove or coppiced wood
DERIVATION:	From the Old English word *grāf(a)*, meaning "grove, copse or coppiced wood"

Grove Church: St Helen's

St Helen's church is relatively recent, dating from 1882, when it was built in 13th century style by C. Hodgson Fowler on the site of, and using the foundations of its medieval predecessor. Indeed, two of the original floor-stones survive in the tower, one showing a chalice by the stem of a cross, and the other carrying portraits of Hugh Hercy of 1455 and his wife, Elizabeth. Restored by a Hercy descendant, Hugh is portrayed as a knight in armour with sword and dagger and his feet on a dog, while Elizabeth has a long pleated gown and head-dress. As for the construction of the original church, historians are unsure although there was clearly a church and a priest here in 1086 when Domesday Book recorded such. It was also a double rectory that was consolidated in May 1227 by Walter de Grey, Archbishop of York, by which stage the village was already under the influence of the ancient de Hercy family.

Grove Historic Trivia: Grove's Lords and Grove Hall

After the Norman Conquest, William I granted the barony of Grove along with the manor of West Retford to Roger de Busli, although by the mid-12th century, it was owned by Gilbert de Arches. It then passed to the Hercy family in the 13th century via Gilbert's great grand-daughter, Theophania. Two hundred years later, during the Wars of the Roses (1455-1487), the Hercy family, along with their neighbours the Stanhope's, of Rampton, were active supporters of the House of Lancaster. The manor remained with the Hercy family through fourteen generations until Sir John de Hercy died in 1570. Childless, he bequeathed the manor to Barbara, one of his eight sisters and co-heiress who had married George Nevile of Ragnall. The manor then remained with the Nevile's until the end of the 17th century, when Sir Edward Nevile sold it to Sir Creswell Levinz, a Judge of the Common Pleas. Sir Creswell's son, William, became M.P. for East Retford and was High Sheriff of Nottinghamshire from 1707 to 1708, but his son (also William), sold the manor and estate of Grove in 1762 to Anthony Eyre of Rampton and Adwick-le-Street. Anthony Eyre's son, Anthony Hardolph Eyre, died in 1836 leaving two daughters, one of which, Frances, inherited Grove. As she married Granville Harcourt Vernon, son of the Archbishop of York, the property and manor then passed down the Harcourt-Vernon family to Lieutenant-Colonel Granville Charles FitzHerbert Harcourt-Vernon, who sold the house in 1946.

The original Grove Hall was built by the Hercy family, but it was succeeded by a large brick house in the old English style, with gable ends and mullion windows. Both the Levinz's and the Eyre's made alterations with Anthony Eyre making wholesale changes after engaging the talents of 18th century architect John Carr of York. The gardens were added in 1798 and at that time, were amongst the finest in the county, while Grove Hall was widely recognised as the most elevated and picturesque stately home in Nottinghamshire. However, it was demolished in 1952, and today, 51 properties stand on what is known as Grove Hall Gardens.

Just to the north-west of Grove is Castle Hill Wood, where there once stood a castle on a mount which appears to have been surrounded by a double trench with an entrance to the south-east. The fortification was either Roman, or perhaps pre-Roman, but nothing of it remains today. Certainly there were many Roman coins found in this area in 1684, together with numerous other Roman artefacts, while in 1718, two impressive moulded altars were unearthed.

St Helen's church, Grove.

Name (Status):	**HAYTON** (Village)
Population:	385
District:	Bassetlaw
Earliest Record:	*Heiton*, 1175
Meaning:	Farmstead where hay is made
Derivation:	From the Old English words *hēg* (hay) and *tūn* (farmstead)

Hayton Pub: The Boat Inn

The picturesque Boat Inn is located on the B1403 just before the bridge takes the road over the Chesterfield Canal. The canal's history has already appeared in the *Conventional Nottinghamshire* section, but it doesn't mention that the Chesterfield Canal is widely recognised as one of the most beautiful and varied waterways in England and that every yard of its 46 miles can be walked on the towpath known as The Cuckoo Way – and that includes the stretch on the other side of the bridge from The Boat Inn.

The Boat Inn, Hayton.

Hayton Church: St Peter's

The Norman church of St Peter's at Hayton is Grade I listed and dates from the 12th century. The original nave arcade still survives along with its round arches and pillars and one capital carved with foliage, as does the round-arched south doorway and further Norman masonry in the nave. The window tracery and the ashlar-faced west tower are a little later, mostly early 14th century, as is the octagonal font, while the south porch with a stone roof on transverse ribs was built around 1400. The latter is also decorated externally with intricate pinnacles with the crockets at the foot of each pinnacle subject to tiny sculptured heads of men and animals. The embattled west tower contains a 16th century bell while the majority of the glass is 19th century including the east window which dates from 1877. The church was restored in 1885 by the architect Somers Clarke.

The original 12th-century south doorway at St Peter's church, Hayton.

Hayton Historic Trivia: Hayton Castle

Hayton Castle has been described as a "probable fortified manor house, founded by the de Hayton family", and although there are only earthwork remains, the site is a scheduled monument. Certainly today, the rectangular platform is surrounded by a shallow medieval moat while the road to the private Hayton Castle Farm House cuts through the site. This mid-18th century building along with Hayton Castle Cottage are both Grade II listed and are located around 300 yards from the ancient site. As for Hayton Castle, this was also the seat of the Hartshorn family during the 17th and 18th centuries.

Hayton Quirk Alert: Hayton Shooters

The above-mentioned Hayton Castle Farm is today home to Hayton Castle Clay Shoot. Established nearly 20 years ago, the shoot has grown from holding small competitions to running large charity events, and also offers both corporate entertainment and one to one coaching.

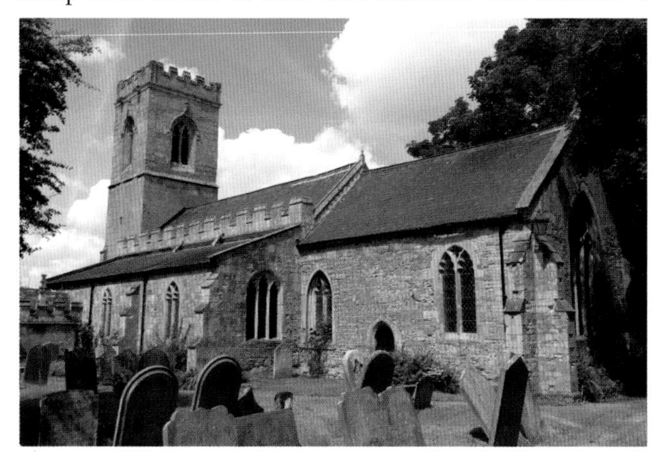

St Peter's church, Hayton.

The Chesterfield Canal at Hayton.

NAME (STATUS):	**HEADON** (Village)
POPULATION:	253 (parish of Headon cum Upton)
DISTRICT:	Bassetlaw
EARLIEST RECORD:	*Hedune*, 1086 (Domesday Book)
MEANING:	Probably "high hill"
DERIVATION:	From the Old English words *hēah* (high) and *dūn* (hill); alternatively, it may be related to the Old English word *hath*, meaning "heath, heather or uncultivated land"

St Peter's church, Headon.

Headon Church: St Peter's

Like nearby Hayton, the church at Headon is also Grade I listed, is also known as St Peter's, and is also medieval, dating from the 12th century – although much of what remains dates from the 14th century. The church also contains a remarkable Jacobean pulpit with a canopy, and an Elizabethan oak chest. Located at the top of the hill in the centre of Headon, the building was once much larger than it is now, suggesting both wealth and a larger community than at present. It also has an unusually low tower, theorised to be because the Black Death put a stop to its build before a spire could be added – and hence just the embattled parapet was added.

Headon Historic Trivia: Headon Park and Microlighting

In the early 16th century, a certain George Wasteneys created Headon Park to the west of the village and it was probably here that a house of some consequence existed – probably known as Headon Hall – although there is no trace of the hall now, nor is there of its successor. A little later in the 17th and 18th centuries, Headon became the seat of the Wasteneys Baronetcy. It was created on 18 December 1622 for Sir Hardolph Wasteneys who also served as Sheriff of Nottinghamshire from 1635-1636. When he died in 1649, his son, also Sir Hardolph Wasteneys, became the second Baronet, with Sir Edmund Wasteneys the third Baronet in 1673 and yet another Sir Hardolph Wasteneys, the fourth Baronet in 1678. During a large part of this baronetcy period, the Wasteneys made neighbouring Grove Hall their principal residence, and before it was demolished in 1952, it was home to a striking portrait of the fourth Baronet. The fourth Baronet also went on to become Member of Parliament for East Retford, but the Wasteneys Baronetcy became extinct on his death in 1742 as he died without an heir. He had, however, built Headon Manor, rebuilding the former manor house as a mansion in 1710. When he died, Headon Park, as it was then known, passed to his great-niece Judith Laetitia Bury, and thence to her husband Anthony Eyre of Grove. Anthony Hardolph Eyre (1757-1836), resident at the much grander Grove Hall, demolished the house at Headon in the early 1790s and ploughed up the parkland and thus little remains today. There were, however, seven fine avenues converging on the Hall and of these, one or two may still be traced.

A much more recent piece of history saw the Microflight Aviation School being set up in Headon in 2000. A Civil Aviation Authority approved flight training centre, the school specialises in microlight tuition and pilot training. The last fourteen years have seen the main runway widened and extended to 600 metres and a second runway added. Apparently, your microlight can either be Flex Wing (that's the one with the hang-glider type wings with the trike unit, engine, seats and landing gear suspended below) or Fixed Wing (more closely resembles a light aircraft and has a closed cockpit). For those interested, the school offers half hour and one hour trial flights, with the latter taking in parts of the Peak District, including Chatsworth House and the Derwent Valley.

Headon Quirk Alert: Two for the Price of One

It was mentioned above that St Peter's church was once much larger than it is today. This sort of explains an unusual feature, in that St Peter's had both a vicarage and a rectory, so until both were united in 1881, the church had been home to both a rector and a vicar since the earliest known records! I wonder if they always got on…

NAME (STATUS):	**HOLME** (Village)
POPULATION:	165
DISTRICT:	Newark and Sherwood
EARLIEST RECORD:	*Holme*, 1203
MEANING:	Island, dry ground in marsh, or water-meadow
DERIVATION:	From the Old Scandinavian word *holmr*, meaning "island, promontory, raised ground in marsh, or river-meadow"

Holme Church: St Giles

The original St Giles' church was built in the late 12th century, but the current incarnation was almost completely rebuilt in around 1485 by John Barton, including its distinctive low broach spire and two-tiered porch. Barton's rebus (a heraldic expression to denote surnames) of a tun (a medieval barrel) with a bar through it (and hence Bar-ton) is in evidence all over the church. Barton's other additions included a south aisle and chantry chapel, while over the church entrance is a fine band of seven shields carved with heraldry; the inevitable Barton rebus, and the merchant's mark – bales of wool and the Staple of Calais with sheep below. Barton died in 1491 and is buried in the chancel with his wife, Isabella, in a tomb that Barton commissioned during his lifetime. The tomb bears the recumbent effigies of Barton and his wife, with John clothed as a merchant of the 15th century, with his feet resting on a barrel, and those of Isabella on a dog.

The Muskham Ferry in North Muskham, taken from the Holme (eastern) side of the Trent. Up until the late 16th century, both villages were on the western bank!

Other points of interest in the church are the widely-acclaimed early Tudor carved poppy heads of birds, animals and angels, while the room over the porch is the eponymous subject of the local legend of "Nan Scott's Chamber" (see *Holme Quirk Alert* for more). Then there are the three ancient bells, one dating from the 15th century, the other two from 1592 and 1657. The church was restored by Nevile Truman in the mid-20th century.

Holme Historic Trivia: The Old Hall and the New Hall

Located at the southern end of the village, today Holme Old Hall is a farmhouse known as Old Hall Farm, but the site was for many centuries the home of the aforementioned Barton family. The farmhouse was built at the end of the 19th century, with the Barton family's former Holme Old Hall having been demolished to make way for it. An account from 1905 describing the "modern farmhouse", states that the demolished predecessor had included a chimney-piece bearing the Barton arms, while a "posy" was built into the fabric of the stables. Having made his fortune out of the wool trade, it is also said that John Barton had a window installed in Holme Old Hall and which contained the words: *I thanke God, and ever shall. It is the shepe hath payed for all*. Meanwhile, what is today known as Holme Hall is a completely different Grade II listed *Georgian* country home located in the centre of the village, and was built in 1796 by Abigail Gawthern with money left to her by her uncle, the Archbishop of Canterbury, Thomas Secker. A few years later, the house regularly played host to Lord Byron who was a close family friend. Later, it became a girl's school and also housed prisoners of war during World War II, while more

St Giles' church, Holme.

Holme village is defined by its 12th century church.

recently it was converted into a Boutique Bed and Breakfast offering beauty treatments, private yoga sessions and afternoon tea!

Holme Hall, built in 1796 by Abigail Gawthern.

Holme Quirk Alert: A Dramatic Reconfiguration and Nan Scott's Chamber

Today, Holme is on the eastern bank of the River Trent. Remarkably, though, it wasn't always there; up until the late 16th century, it was situated on the western bank! The reconfiguration occurred following catastrophic floods sometime during the second half of the 16th century; in fact, the twin settlements of Holme and North Muskham were both on the western side of the Trent, but the new course split them asunder. In terms of pinpointing the date, a number of texts suggest around 1600. However, Saxton's 1576 map of Nottinghamshire places Holme on the eastern bank of the Trent, so the reconfiguration must have occurred before then. As for the inhabitants of Holme and North Muskham, what had for centuries been a short walk between the two suddenly turned into a costly ferry crossing!

Finally, Holme's legend of Nan Scott's Chamber suggests that Nan left her house in Holme for several weeks during the great plague of 1666 and lived in the room above the church porch to escape infection. Stocked up with food, she is said to have observed from the window, villager after villager being carried into the burial ground. When she eventually emerged from her refuge for further supplies, she found the parish deserted apart from one woman, and was so horrified that she returned to the chamber and lived there for the rest of her life.

The two-tier porch at the front of St Giles' church, and also known as Nan Scott's Chamber.

Holme Village.

NAME (STATUS): **HUCKNALL** (Town)
POPULATION: 32,099
DISTRICT: Ashfield
EARLIEST RECORD: *Hochenale*, 1086 (Domesday Book)
MEANING: Nook of land of a man called Hucca
DERIVATION: From the Old English personal name, *Hucca*, plus the Old English word *halh* (nook or corner of land)
FAMOUS RESIDENTS: **Robin Bailey** (1919-1999), actor; **Steve Blatherwick** (b.1973), footballer; **Lord Byron** (d.1824), poet, philosopher, revolutionary; **Ben Caunt** (1815-1861), bare-knuckle boxer; **Eric Coates** (1886-1957), composer; **Zechariah Green** (1817-1897), philanthropist; **Jack Hall** (1883-1938), footballer; **Thomas Cecil Howitt** (1889-1968), architect; **Ada Lovelace** (1815-1852), mathematician; **Enoch "Knocker" West** (1886-1965), footballer; **Sam Weller-Widdowson** (1851-1927), footballer, cricketer

Hucknall Etymology: Nooks, Knolls and Normans

Quite apart from the dubious usage of Huck 'n' all in *Arnold's Daughter*, the place-name hasn't had straightforward usage over the centuries, either! For starters, the place had an affix apportioned during the middle ages in order to represent a noble Norman family, and so from 1295 until 1915, the town was known as *Hucknall Torkard*, taken from the local 13th century landowning Torcard family. Indeed, the former town name can still be seen on some of Hucknall's older buildings. Before the "Torkard" affix was applied, though, the town was recorded in Domesday Book (1086) as simply *Hochenale*. The name probably means "nook of land of a man called Hucca", but other theories offer "nook of land of the *Hōcanere*", based on even earlier place-names of *Hokeuhale* and *Hokenale*. Other alternatives are *Occa's Knoll*, based on the Saxon word for "place", thus meaning "Occa's place", and *Oak-en-hale*, meaning "place of the oak".

Hucknall Pub: The Red Lion

The Red Lion is Hucknall's oldest pub. It was kept by churchwarden Theophilus Allcock in 1749, and is also allegedly an old haunt of Lord Byron. The story goes that the Byron tenants were feasted at The Red Lion on their annual rent day and there is a plaque in the pub to commemorate this. It is also said that the bare-knuckle prize-fighter, Ben Caunt, acted as candlesnuffer at The Red Lion when a youth.

The Red Lion, Hucknall, an old haunt of Lord Byron.

Hucknall Church: St Mary Magdalene

The church of St Mary Magdalene is Grade II listed and is located in the centre of Hucknall alongside the market place. Large parts of the church are medieval, although the current incarnation was built on the site of an even older Anglo-Saxon predecessor that is thought to have dated from the 8th century, this theory having solidified following the discovery of original Saxon stonework in 1938. The tower was constructed in stages between the 12th and 14th centuries, with the porch added in 1320.

The medieval church consisted only of a chancel, nave, north aisle and tower, with the aisle windows and clerestory added in the 14th century, but it was considerably enlarged in the Victorian period, with work commencing in 1872. The south aisle was added by Evans and Jolly between 1872 and 1874, and the unusually long transepts by R. C. Clarke in 1887 and 1888. Much later, in 2004, a carved Armenian stone cross known as a *Khatchkar* was given to the church in memory of the work that the rector and the British people had done for Armenia following the catastrophic earthquake of 1988.

However, the greatest attraction of St Mary Magdalene is the fact that the famous poet, the 6th Lord

St Mary Magdalene church, Hucknall.

Byron is buried here and the church thus attracts visitors from all over the world. Also buried alongside him in the family vault below the chancel is his daughter, the famous mathematician, Ada Lovelace, who is widely acknowledged as the world's first computer programmer. The graveyard is also home to the tombstone of Ben Caunt, bare-knuckle fist-fighting legend and Boxing Champion of all England 1841-45. Caunt was also known as "The Torkard Giant" (he was 6ft 2in and weighed 18 stone) and it is contested that the Westminster hour-bell, Big Ben, is named after him. In his final fight in September 1857, Caunt fought Nat Langham at Home Circuit where after 60 rounds both men were too exhausted to continue and a draw was declared.

This statue stands on Station Street as a memorial to the mining industry in Hucknall.

St Mary Magdalene contains the largest collection of stained glass windows by the Victorian artist C.E. Kempe – 25 in all, mostly added in the 1880s. The church is also home to some rare wall paintings, beautiful carvings and wall mosaics while there is also a sensory garden and a memorial garden to Lord Byron. Byron repaid the favour during his lifetime, donating what is known as the Angelus bell, which dates from the 14th century. Its weight is unknown because it is so old and the ringers are therefore afraid of it breaking if it were to be moved from the tower – where it sits alongside a ring of eight bells installed in 1958. Meanwhile, the four-faced clock dates from 1882, having replaced the one installed by Richard Roe in 1685.

Hucknall Town Football Club, originally a colliery team founded in 1945.

Hucknall Historic Trivia: Three Stations, Hucknall FC and RAF Hucknall

Hucknall was historically a centre for framework knitting, after which coal mining led to a rapid expansion of the town and its population during the 19th century; indeed it grew from a village into a town in under a hundred years. Hucknall was therefore essentially a colliery town from 1861 to 1986 following the formation of the Hucknall Colliery Company in 1861. Two shafts were sunk, Hucknall No. 1 colliery (known as "Top Pit") in 1861, and Hucknall No. 2 colliery (known as "Bottom Pit") in 1866. However, Top Pit had closed by 1943, with Bottom Pit lasting much longer, before closing in 1986.

Inevitably, the coal mining industry brought the railways to the town in the 19th century in the form of three railway lines. The first was the Midland Railway line from Nottingham to Mansfield and Worksop, the second was the Great Northern Railway route up the Leen Valley and onto Shirebrook, and the third was the Great Central Railway, the last main line ever built from the north of England to London, and which opened 15th March 1899. The first of these lines was eventually closed to passengers in 1964, although it continued as a freight route serving collieries at Hucknall, Linby and Annesley – with the Hucknall station on this line known as "Hucknall Byron". However, in the 1990s the line was reopened to passengers in stages as the Robin Hood Line.

Meanwhile, the second line was closed to passengers much earlier, in 1931, but remained in use for freight until 1968 (this station was called "Hucknall Town"), while the third line was closed in 1966, although the Hucknall station here (known as "Hucknall Central"), had closed earlier, on 4 March 1963. Finally with respect to coal mining, the industry has left its legacy in the form of the town's senior football team, Hucknall Town F.C. This is because the team were originally founded as a colliery team in 1945 and went by the name of Hucknall Colliery Welfare F.C. The name-change to Hucknall Town occurred in 1987 after closure of the local pit and, under their new name, they steadily worked their way upwards through the leagues from the Notts Alliance, through the Central Midlands League, the Northern Counties East League, until they finally arrived in the Northern Premier League in 1999. Better still, they actually won the NPL in the 2003/04 season, but were unable to secure promotion to the Football Conference as their Watnall Road ground didn't meet the appropriate specifications.

In 1916, Hucknall Airfield was built to the south-west of the town, and soon became home to a number of RAF squadrons, although the site didn't become known as RAF Hucknall until 1928. From the early 1930s, Rolls-Royce also began to share the airfield with the RAF in order to test and validate new engine designs and modifications. During World War II, the aerodrome was the location of the first flight of a P-51 Mustang, fitted with a Rolls-Royce Merlin engine; the Merlin eventually enabled the Mustang to reach its full

The Station Hotel on Station Terrace, a relic of Hucknall's railway past.

Hucknall Station, formerly Hucknall Byron on the 19th century Midland Railway line, but now part of the Robin Hood Line and northern terminus for the Nottingham tram network.

potential and achieve spectacular high altitude performance. Then in 1953, the site developed the world's first vertical take-off jet "aircraft" known as The Flying Bedstead (see *Hucknall Quirk Alert* for more). The flight test centre closed in 1971, although engines continued to be tested there until late 2008; today, only components are manufactured there.

Hucknall Quirk Alert: The One That Got Away, The Flying Bedstead and Byron's Right Foot

In September 1940, German pilot Franz von Werra was shot down over Kent. As a prisoner of war, he escaped twice before being transferred to Camp No. 10 at Swanwick in Derbyshire. Here, von Werra joined a group who called themselves the *Swanwick Tiefbau*, and who were digging an escape tunnel. On the 20th December 1940, and armed with forged money and fake identity papers, von Werra and four others slipped out of the tunnel under the cover of anti-aircraft fire and the singing of the camp choir. The others were recaptured quickly, but von Werra, clad in his flying suit, managed to avoid capture, masquerading as Captain Van Lott, a Dutch Royal Netherlands Air Force pilot. He claimed to a friendly locomotive driver that he was a downed bomber pilot trying to reach his unit, and asked to be taken to the nearest RAF base – which happened to be the aerodrome at RAF Hucknall. At Hucknall, Squadron Leader Boniface asked for his credentials, and von Werra claimed to be based at Dyce near Aberdeen. While Boniface went to check this, von Werra sloped off to the nearest hangar, telling a mechanic that he was cleared for a test flight. Boniface arrived in time to arrest him at gunpoint, as he sat in the cockpit, trying to learn the controls. Von Werra was later transferred to Canada, where he became the only German to escape and succeed in returning to Germany. He managed to escape from a prison train in January 1941 from where he crossed the frozen St Lawrence River, gained entry to the United States (which was still neutral in 1941), and then managed to cross over to Mexico with the help of the German Consul. From there he made it back to Germany on 18th April 1941 by way of Rio de Janeiro, Barcelona and Rome. His exploits can be seen in the 1957 film *The One That Got Away*.

In 1952-53, the Rolls-Royce flight test site at Hucknall researched and tested the prototype of the first Jet-powered Vertical Take-off and Landing Plane. Its maiden flight took place on 3 July 1953, and due to its resemblance to a four-poster bed, it soon earned its nickname of The Flying Bedstead. The first untethered flight was piloted by Captain Ron Shepherd on the 3 August 1954. According to distinguished witnesses, The Flying Bedstead rose slowly into the air and hovered steadily. It then moved forward, made a circuit of the area, then demonstrated sideways and backwards movements before making a successful landing. The flight was a tremendous success and during the next four months a number of Flying Bedstead flights were made, up to a height of 50ft.

Finally, it was also mentioned earlier that the 6th Lord Byron and famous 19th century poet, was buried in the family vault below the chancel. Now in 1938, a theory was doing the rounds that there was an ancient crypt under the chancel, but to carry out excavations meant opening the Byron vault. This duly happened on 15th June and, as the lid of Byron's coffin was not fastened down, the excavators were able to take a peek at the poet – who, by all accounts, was in a perfect state of preservation … and thus they were able to confirm that Byron was indeed lame in the right foot!

NAME (STATUS):	**IDLE** (River)
DISTRICT:	Bassetlaw
LENGTH:	26 miles (42 km)
SOURCE:	Confluence of the River Maun and the River Meden
SOURCE ELEVATION:	59ft (18m)
MOUTH:	River Trent at West Stockwith
MOUTH ELEVATION:	0ft (0m)

River Idle at Eaton

River Idle Geographic Trivia: From the Maun to the Trent

The River Idle is contained completely in Nottinghamshire, running for 26 miles from its source – which is at the confluence of the River Maun and River Meden, near Markham Moor – to its terminus which is at the point that it flows into the River Trent at West Stockwith. Its course takes it due north from Markham Moor to Retford, having been joined by the River Poulter in between. After Retford, the Idle turns north-west at Mattersey where it is joined by its second tributary, the River Ryton, before heading onto the South Yorkshire border at Bawtry. It then briefly forms the border between Nottinghamshire and South Yorkshire before heading north-eastwards from Newington across Nottinghamshire to eventually form the border with Lincolnshire for a short distance too – a stretch which includes a place known as Idle Stop. After leaving the Lincolnshire border, it flows roughly south-eastwards before arriving at West Stockwith and the River Trent.

Interestingly, the Idle originally flowed northwards from Idle Stop to meet the River Don on Hatfield Chase, but it was diverted onto its current eastward trajectory by drainage engineers in 1628. As for navigation rights, these were removed from the River Idle in 1972, although it actually remains navigable for the 11 miles from its mouth on the Trent up to Bawtry. However, it can only be accessed through sluice gates for which the Environment Agency requires a 48 hour notice period; they also impose a high toll, too! Furthermore, entrance through the first sluice is only possible for an hour either side of high tide while the EA also require all boaters to sign an indemnity form, which absolves them of any responsibility for loss or damage to boats!

Most of the land surrounding the river's 26-mile stretch is classed as a flood-plain, while the stretch between Retford and Bawtry is partly occupied by a number of sand and gravel pits. Beyond Bawtry the river is constrained by high flood banks, to allow the low lying areas to be drained for agriculture. It is also important for conservation, with the Idle Washlands and some of the sand and gravel pits of the Idle Valley being designated Sites of Special Scientific Interest. The River Idle also has a catchment area of around 280 square miles and which has an average annual rainfall of around 24 inches with about a third of this finding its way into the river. However, this is countered by the fact that there are significant discharges from sewage treatment works into the Idle's tributaries, as they pass through more urban areas. For this reason, the General Quality Assessment level apportioned to the River Idle by the Environments Agency is a "C" (on a scale of "A" to "F").

River Idle Historic Trivia: Engineering Genius and the Wars of the Idle

As stated above, the River Idle was diverted eastwards towards the Trent in 1628. Prior to that, it had flowed northwards from Idle Stop, eventually joining the River Don just north-west of Sandtoft. However, in 1626 the Dutch drainage engineer Cornelius Vermuyden was appointed by King Charles I to drain Hatfield Chase. Part of this work saw the Idle blocked by a dam

The River Idle, upstream (left) and downstream at Mattersey Thorpe.

The River Idle as it flows through Kings Park at Retford.

The River Idle, where it divides the counties of Nottinghamshire and South Yorkshire, just east of Bawtry.

constructed at Idle Stop, and its waters were diverted along the Bycarrs Dyke, a Roman navigation channel, which joined the River Trent at West Stockwith. In order to isolate the river from Hatfield Chase, a barrier bank was constructed along the northern edge of this channel, for five miles from the dam to Stockwith. Meanwhile a navigable sluice was built about one mile west of the river mouth at Misterton Soss between 1629 and 1630, to prevent water from the Trent flooding the land to the south of Bycarrs Dyke, particularly the villages of Misterton and Haxey Commons.

In addition to this work, a drainage channel called the New Idle River was constructed in a straight line from Idle Stop to Dirtness, before being routed east to join the Trent at Althorpe. However, the whole drainage scheme caused a great deal of anger from affected parties and successful court cases were brought to bear. In order to relieve the Idle, the Commission of Sewers ordered a new cut, to carry water from Misterton, Gringley and Everton to the Trent, but this scheme was beset by further landowner objections and then the outbreak of the English Civil War. Vermuyden's partners (known as the Participants) supported the King, while commoners on the Isle of Axholme supported the Parliamentarians. Alleging that the Royalists would invade Axholme from the south, they broke down Misterton sluice and the Snow Sewer flood gates in 1642, causing widespread flooding and damage estimated at £20,000. The Sheriff of Lincoln repaired both structures, but a band of 400 villagers destroyed them again. Trouble continued for many years and in 1656, the Participants actually raised an "army" and fought a total of 31 pitched battles, including several against the men of Misterton and Gringley. It was not until 1719 that the issues were finally settled and peace returned to the area! As for the New Idle River, its course is now followed by Idle Bank, a road that runs in a dead straight line for around nine miles between Idle Stop and Dirtness Bridge. A final configuration change came in the 1770s when a feeder was constructed from the River Idle to the Chesterfield Canal, around two miles above the Retford aqueduct, so that water could flow by gravity to the canal.

As mentioned earlier, the River Idle was navigable by shallow-drafted boats up as far as Bawtry until 1972, which is why the latter became a key inland port for several centuries for the export of Derbyshire coal, lead and iron along with Sheffield steel. Interestingly, a 1720 Act of Parliament actually cleared the way for making the Idle navigable to Retford, although the plan never materialised. It remained under consideration until 1757, but by this time, much of the river's trade had been lost, with the Derbyshire lead trade using an improved River Derwent, and the Sheffield trade using the River Don Navigation. Bawtry's fortunes were further damaged by the opening of the Chesterfield

The River Idle, upstream (left) and downstream at Misson.

Canal in 1777 which provided a more convenient outlet for most goods, and by 1828 commercial traffic had ceased to use the River Idle. General navigation rights on the river finally ceased, when the Trent River Authority (General Powers) Act of 1972 was passed.

River Idle Drainage: The Taming of Nature and Kate and Ada

Downstream of Bawtry, the banks of the River Idle have been raised so that the river acts as a high level carrier for the drainage of the surrounding land. Meanwhile, the area between the river and the Chesterfield Canal to the south, and around the Warping Drain to the north, is drained by a network of drainage ditches, which are connected to the river by a number of sluices and pumping stations. Ordinarily, water is pumped *from* the ditches to avoid flooding of the surrounding land, but the pumping station at Gringley can also operate in reverse, supplying water *to* the ditches for irrigation purposes when required. The outflow into the River Trent is also controlled by a pumping station and two sluices, and when the water level in the Trent is low, the sluice gates allow water to leave the Idle by gravity, while at high tide, four electric pumps are used to pump the outflow into the space between the sluice gates until it can again discharge by gravity. The pumping station was commissioned in 1981, and was the largest all-electric pumping station in Britain at the time. When all four pumps are operating, it can discharge 2,124 tons per minute.

If you study the map between Misson and West Stockwith, you will notice that for around ten miles, two water courses run alongside each other. One is obviously the River Idle (the northernmost water course), but the other is known as the Mother Drain, a large drainage ditch that was constructed between 1796 and 1801 by Thomas Dyson to collect water from the low-lying land to the south of the river. The Mother Drain was then pumped into the river by two pumping stations at Misterton Soss, the first example of steam engines being used for land drainage outside of the Fens. The first station, called Kate, was built in 1828, and the second, called Ada, in 1839, with both stations using a beam engine to drive a 34ft scoop wheel. By 1910, a bridge had also been constructed with tide gates which were designed to shut as the level in the River Trent rose. However, both Kate and Ada became redundant in 1941, when the drainage system was re-organised to feed excess water to a diesel pumping station at Gringley, while the tide gates have also now been replaced by the vertical sluice at the entrance to the river. Today, both 19th century pumping stations carry Grade II listing status, while the Gringley pumping station was upgraded again in 2005 when electric pumps were installed.

As for the 34 miles of watercourse in the low-lying region to the south of the Mother Drain, this is managed by the Everton Internal Drainage Board, pumping into the Idle at Scaftworth and Gringley. The Board was founded in 1945, but is actually the successor to a similar organisation established in 1796. Meanwhile the 24.7 miles of drains and ditches on the north side of the river is managed by the Finningley Internal Drainage Board, and includes the pumping station at Idle Stop. And above Idle Stop, the river flows through an area where the drainage of 53 miles of watercourse is the responsibility of the Rivers Idle and Ryton Internal Drainage Board, formed in 1987. In general, though, areas to the west of the Idle drain into the river by gravity at a number of locations, but the region to the east of the river and to the north of Retford drains to a single outfall at Wiseton, where a pumping station pumps the water into the river when river levels are too high for gravity flow.

The confluence of the River Idle with the River Trent.

River Idle Conservation: SSSI's

The lower River Idle is home to four areas of grassland which are subject to periodic flooding, and which provide habitat for wintering and breeding birds. Collectively, they form the Idle Washlands Site of Special Scientific Interest (SSSI). Historically, this sort of territory comprised a much greater area of around 250 hectares, but much of it is now cut off from the river by high flood defence banks while the 1980s saw further flood defence work and land drainage reduce this area to 88 hectares. Meanwhile, further up-river, the Sutton and Lound gravel pits are still part of an active quarrying operation which is run by the construction group Tarmac. However, some 316 hectares have been designated as another SSSI which provides an important wetland habitat for 172 different species of birds, including a number of birds which normally occupy the coastal fringes rather than inland sites such as the ringed plover and oystercatchers. The Nottinghamshire Wildlife Trust have also been active in planting reeds to improve the habitat, which are grown at Langford Quarry in a joint venture between Tarmac and the RSPB.

NAME (STATUS):	**KIMBERLEY** (Town)
POPULATION:	6,053
DISTRICT:	Broxtowe
EARLIEST RECORD:	*Chinemarleie*, 1086 (Domesday Book)
MEANING:	Woodland clearing of a man called Cynemær
DERIVATION:	From the Old English personal name Cynemær and the Old English word *lēah* (woodland clearing or glade)
FAMOUS RESIDENTS:	**John Reynolds** (b.1963), British Superbike Champion 1992, 2001 & 2004

Kimberley Pub: The Stag Inn

Kimberley is home to many pubs, most of which were tied to the local brewery (see *Kimberley Historic Trivia*). Of these, The Stag Inn dates from the early 18th century when it was part of a row of four cottages before it became a farmhouse, coaching inn and blacksmiths. It was also known as The Reindeer during the 1860s.

Kimberley Church: Holy Trinity

Holy Trinity church can be found on Church Hill, and which is also locally known as Kettle Bank – probably named after the 11th century landowner, Grimketel. However, there are no remains of the original Norman church with the present one built in 1847 – and which only became a parish church the following year when Kimberley was detached from its parent parish of Greasley.

Kimberley Historic Trivia: Martyrs and Ale

Kimberley was given to William Peverel after the Norman Conquest, but the Peverel's relinquished control when they chose the wrong side during the Anarchy (1135-54). The estate was thus acquired by Henry II. King John then granted land in the area to Ralph de Greasley in 1212 who took up residence at nearby Greasley Castle, with Kimberley then being part of the parish of Greasley. The land then passed by

Kimberley's Stag Inn dates back to the 18th century.

The Nelson & Railway dates back to the 17th century when it was known as The Pelican before becoming The Lord Nelson, Railway Hotel in the 19th century.

Holy Trinity church, Kimberley.

The Chapel of Rest on top of Knowle Hill.

inheritance and marriage to Nicholas de Cantelupe who in 1343 founded Beauvale Priory, a Carthusian monastery just to the north of Kimberley, but which was eventually dissolved by King Henry VIII in 1535. However, the Carthusians refused to accept Henry's supremacy over the church and Robert Lawrence, Prior of Beauvale, travelled to London to see Thomas Cromwell in the hope of stopping the dissolution of his priory. Alas, both Lawrence and two other Carthusian Priors were imprisoned in the Tower of London as traitors. All three were tried on April 28th 1535 and charged with "verbal treason" for claiming Henry was not the supreme head of the Church of England. The jury refused to find the men guilty as they felt they did not act maliciously; Cromwell, however, threatened the jury until they returned a guilty verdict. Lawrence therefore became one of the so-called Carthusian Martyrs who were hung, drawn and quartered on May 4th 1535. The execution was deliberately gory in order to deter others and demonstrate the King's power. Lawrence was hung by a rope long enough to avoid fatally strangling him, thus ensuring he was still alive when butchered, mutilated and ultimately quartered. Over 400 years later, Robert Lawrence was sanctified by Pope Paul VI in 1970. Today the remains of the Priory are designated as a scheduled ancient monument (see p29 for photo).

Moving onto 1627 and the Priory's land came into the possession of Arthur Capell, 1st Baron Capell of Hadham; alas, Arthur was beheaded in 1649 having fought for the Royalists in the English Civil War. By 1753 the land had been purchased by Sir Matthew Lamb whose grandson William Lamb (Lord Melbourne) became Prime Minister in 1834. The Lamb's Kimberley estates then passed by marriage to the 5th Earl Cowper in 1805 and on the death of the 7th Earl in 1913 were sold off in pieces. As for the part of Kimberley retained by the de Cantelupe's, this passed first to John Zouch – who then died at the Battle of Bosworth Field in 1485. He was posthumously found guilty of high treason with his property forfeited to Henry VII who awarded it to John Savage. The Savage family sold the land to the Earl of Rutland in the early 17th century whose successors sold off the Kimberley estate in parcels in the early 19th century.

Sticking with the 19th century and Kimberley Brewery was established in 1832, making it the oldest independent brewery in Nottinghamshire. It was Samuel Robinson who opened the first commercial brewery in a rented bake-house using water from the Alley Spring in what is now called Hardy Street, while Stephen Hanson built Hanson's Limited on Brewery Street in 1847, also using water from the Alley Spring. By 1857, William and Thomas Hardy, successful beer merchants from Heanor, had bought Samuel Robinsons brewery and by 1861 they had moved out of the bake-house and into new premises which make up a large proportion of today's former brewery site. Meanwhile, also in 1861,

Inset: *Hardy's and Hanson's buildings on Nine Corners, Kimberley.*
Looking towards more brewery buildings from the Nelson & Railway. Notice the Greene King emblem at the top of the pub sign, the company who in 2006, brought an end to over 170 years of brewing in Kimberley.

Stephen Hanson died and the business was carried on by his wife Mary and son Robert Hanson. There was much friendly rivalry between the two brewing companies who proceeded to buy pubs throughout the area to supply with their own ales. Having both been attracted by the supply of excellent brewing water from the local Holly Well spring, both breweries thrived independently until 1930, when under increasing pressure from larger brewing companies, the two companies combined. As Hardy's & Hanson's Kimberley Brewery, the company survived until a multi-million pound takeover by Greene King in 2005. By 2006, the inevitable sale and closure had followed with Greene King bringing an end to over 170 years of brewing in Kimberley – and which pretty much sent the brewery industry the same way as the town's coal mining and hosiery industries, decades earlier.

Kimberley Quirk Alert: Off the Rails and Quirky Seating

The Midland Railway line that ran through the breweries enabled both the Hardy's and the Hanson's to construct sidings. The station was opened in 1880 but the line closed in 1916 when ten miles of double track was taken up as part of the war effort in the battle for the Dardanelles. It was never re-laid.

More recently, Chapel Street was converted into a cul-de-sac, and its former bottom end was developed into Toll Bar Square where small events and markets are now held. The square is also home to some clever seating, fashioned as beer barrels, and some impressive mosaics, all of which tip their hat to the village's former industries, including brewing, hosiery and coal, plus a couple of mosaics depicting the Old Mill and Forty Bridges.

Kimberley's public benches in Toll Bar Square!

Kimberley's striking war memorial that was unveiled in September 1921.

NAME (STATUS):	**KIRTON** (Village)
POPULATION:	261
DISTRICT:	Newark and Sherwood
EARLIEST RECORD:	*Circeton*, 1086 (Domesday Book); *Kirketon*, end of 12th century
MEANING:	Village with a church
DERIVATION:	From the Old Scandinavian word *kirkja* (church), plus the Old English word *tūn* (village or farmstead)

The Fox is Kirton's only pub.

Holy Trinity church, Kirton.

Kirton Church: Holy Trinity

Kirton's Grade II listed parish church of Holy Trinity dates from the 13th century, although the tower was built in around 1425. Surviving from the 13th century is the Early English chancel arch, the nave arcade of three bays, the north doorway with two worn heads, and a window to the west, while the font is slightly older and almost certainly Norman. Also Grade II listed is the churchyard wall and the beautiful lychgate which, with the church, provide a striking view when you hit a distinctive 90 degree turn on the A6705, with the church rising high above the lychgate on a little knoll that is reached by 40 steps and surrounded by beautiful trees. The church was repaired in around 1835 when its old fittings were removed, and it was thoroughly restored in 1865, while in 1891 an ancient doorway in the aisle was unblocked when traces of a medieval mural painting were found.

Kirton Historic Trivia: From Tochi to Henry Gaily Knight

In 1943, Romano-British earthworks were found between Kirton and Tuxford and which appear to have been made up of irregular enclosures surrounded by a ditch and sometimes by a rampart. The settlements aren't straightforward to classify, with some probably having contained hutted homes, banked and ditched for protective purposes and placed on hilltops, possibly for drainage purposes. Other discoveries include sunken streets, rectangular huts or houses, and round foundations – perhaps for dovecotes – making these mounds and banks the best Romano-British earthworks in the county. Roman pottery dating from the 1st to the 3rd century was also found along with Roman roof-tiles and numerous fragments of querns or millstones used for grinding corn into flour.

As for the village of Kirton, its name strongly suggests that it was formed by the Saxons – thanks to the Saxon *tūn* in its name – and then developed by the Danes, since the forepart of the name preserves the Danish word for a church. This latter fact also suggests that the invading 9th century Vikings found an existing Saxon church in situ – which they possibly didn't destroy! Of course, the Saxon's eventually wrested back control, but the last Saxon owner of the Kirton manor, Tochi, lost his lands to Geoffrey Alselin after the Norman Conquest of 1066. A short time later, the lands were owned by Gilbert de Gant whose grandson founded the nearby and now-ruined 12th century Rufford Abbey, but which also included a grange at Kirton. Meanwhile in 1191, the future King John (then Earl of Mortain), gave the church at Kirton to the Archbishop of Rouen. At that time the church was a chapel affiliated to West Markham and formed part of the royal chapelry of Blyth and Tickhill, but upon the outbreak of war with France, the chapelry reverted to the Crown; the Knights Templar also obtained lands and rents in Kirton at this time, too.

Moving onto 1316, and Thomas, Earl of Lancaster became Lord of Kirton … only to be beheaded in 1322 for leading the baronial rebellion against his nephew Edward II. A later Lord, Sir Robert Markham, took an active part in the Wars of the Roses, but after serving Richard III, he turned against him, and in 1487 led out his retainers to fight for Henry VII at East Stoke. Then in 1537, Rufford Abbey, along with its possessions that included Kirton, were granted by Henry VIII to George Talbot, the Earl of Shrewsbury who, in turn, bestowed "lands in Kyrketon" to his son, then aged about 12, but already betrothed to the daughter of the Earl of Rutland!

By exchange of lands in 1591, Sir William Holles of Haughton became one of Kirton's owners, while the Clerksons were prominent landowners in the village during the reign of Charles I. Clerksons and Knights (by marriage) then held the village from the 17th to the 19th century, including the well-known Henry Gaily Knight who was the principal owner at Kirton until his death in 1846.

Kirton Quirk Alert: Unnaturally Scottish, Unnaturally Wed, and Natural Justice

In 1600, when the rector of Kirton sued John Clerkson for tithes, it was found that Clerkson was an unnaturalised Scotsman and therefore incapable of holding an English living! Having said that, the Scot held the benefice until his death in 1603 – although there is no information as to how old he was or how he died – naturally or otherwise! The Clerksons prevailed after his death, though, holding land in Kirton throughout the reign of Charles II (1660-1685) including a period when another John Clerkson wedded Esther Knight and Mary Clerkson was married to John Knight. The Knights were the children of Sir Ralph of Firbeck, Langold and Warsop who, after fighting against Charles I in the English Civil War, later switched allegiance and played an important role in the Restoration, for which he received a knighthood!

Anyway, John Knight's ten year-old daughter was apparently married under false pretences to the son of the scheming family lawyer. But when the lawyer was pressed to account for himself in front of a judge, Knight's daughter miraculously disappeared. This caused a local outcry, and thankfully the daughter was found, whilst a special Act of Parliament was required in order to nullify the marriage!

Finally, hop-growing was commonplace in Kirton in the 18th and 19th centuries. Alas for one hop-grower, it is recorded that he "turned out" his wife who thus became the responsibility of the parish ... at which point, the Justices seized the hop-growers' product to the value of 60s, and used the money to pay the ousted wife's maintenance!

Hall Farm, Kirton, was built by the Clerkson family in the 1630s.

Kirton's Holy Trinity church rises high above the A6705. The church is Grade II listed, as is the lychgate in the foreground.

NAME (STATUS):	**LENTON** (Ex-Village, Suburb)
POPULATION:	11,143
DISTRICT:	City of Nottingham
EARLIEST RECORD:	*Lentune*, 1086 (Domesday Book)
MEANING:	Farmstead by the River Leen
DERIVATION:	From the River Leen plus the Old English word *tūn* (village or farmstead)
FAMOUS RESIDENTS:	**Albert Ball**, RAF Captain, VC, the UK's leading flying ace at the time of his death (May 1917) with 44 victories

Lenton Pub: The Three Wheatsheaves and The White Hart

The Three Wheatsheaves on Derby Road is possibly the oldest pub in Lenton and, like The White Hart, on Gregory Street, was initially built as a farmhouse. The White Hart is thought to have been built between 1660 and 1680, but no one is certain of a build date for The Three Wheatsheaves. In fact, even the current owners, Shipstones, have no idea as to its build date, they having acquired the pub in 1938 from Philip John Pearson-Gregory. Prior to this, the pub had always belonged to the Gregory family, Lords of the Manor since way back in the 1630s when William Gregory bought the manor of Lenton for £2,500 from the Crown who, in turn, had claimed the lands following the dissolution of Lenton Priory. As for the Gregorys, it was they who supplied the pub with its name, since their arms, granted in 1662, include three stooks of corn.

A recent inspection of The Three Wheatsheaves by an architectural specialist dated an internal staircase to the late 17th century, so the two pubs might be of a similar age. As for the earliest reference to the pub, that comes from an advert placed in the Nottingham Journal in 1810 by Landlady Mary Hopkins who (minus a guitar) informs her friends and the public that she has "fitted up THE THREE WHEATSHEAVES INN in a genteel Style", hoping to merit their patronage, having "laid in an assortment of Spirituous Liquors and Wines of the very first Quality". Certainly, as well as picking up local patronage, the pub was well positioned for traders on the main road from Derby to Nottingham, while the arrival of the railway in 1848 with its nearby Lenton Station would have added many more punters. As for Mary's husband, Humphrey Hopkins, he was registered from 1812 until 1841 as both innkeeper and farmer, while Thomas Highfield, landlord from 1912 to 1947, owned a tame fox which he used to take for regular walks on a lead! He also kept a donkey for which he charged a penny a ride for children, thus earning his pub the nickname of The Donkey Pub.

Built during the reign of Charles II, the White Hart eventually became a coffee house, and very popular with the locals because of its bowling greens. The establishment became the White Hart in 1804, although it was also known as Peverel Prison thanks to an area built into the property that housed non-serious offenders – mainly debtors. They weren't treated that harshly, though, as it is alleged they were allowed out in the afternoons to act as waiters – presumably to assist in repaying their debts! The White Hart also played host to the future King Edward VIII in the late 1920s, when he was still Prince of Wales (he held farm holdings in Lenton). More recently it has been a haunt of bikers while it has also hosted gay speed-dating, too!

Lenton Church: Holy Trinity and The Priory Church of St Anthony

Holy Trinity, Lenton, is a Grade II listed church that dates from relatively recent times. It was designed in the Early English style by the prolific architect, H.I.

The Three Wheatsheaves, Lenton, dates back to the 17th century and is named after the arms of the Gregorys who owned the manor of Lenton back then.

The White Hart, Lenton, and which used to double up as a prison in the 19th century!

Stevens of Derby and opened in 1842. Initially, it only had one bell, but five more were added in 1856 and another two were donated by Albert and Frederick Ball in 1902. However, the church's most prized possession is the mid-12th century font that was originally built for Lenton Priory. One of only five rectangular narrative fonts, it is recognised as one of the most interesting in the country, particularly since its style of carvings is unparalleled in England. Measuring 34in by 28in by 30in, its sides are carved with scenes of Jesus' Baptism, Crucifixion and Resurrection. Also depicted is the Dome of St Sophia in Istanbul and the three Mary's at the Sepulchre.

Prior to the construction of Holy Trinity church, the parish church for Lenton was The Priory Church of St Anthony. It was originally associated with a chapel in the hospital at Lenton Priory, a Cluniac house founded by William Peverel sometime before 1108 – although there is no reference to a church in the Priory's foundation charter. The church probably dates back to the early days of the Priory, though, as one reference refers to Henry II granting 80 acres of land and a mill to the "church" of Lenton. Another record of 1291 states that Lenton Priory was valued at £13 6s 8d with a vicarage valued at £4 13s 4d, while further valuations are recorded in 1341 and 1428. The final valuation in 1534 – four years prior to Lenton Priory's dissolution – is recorded by *Valor Ecclesiasticus* as £54 10s while the church of Lenton, appropriated to the Priory, was valued at £9 2s 6d.

Holy Trinity church, Lenton.

The Priory Church of St Anthony, Lenton, with the original chancel nearside.

The church either survived the priory's dissolution fate or was re-built, since a parson's 1603 reference states that his flock included 47 persons who were "not of our parish but doe come to our church", suggesting that the legacy of the Priory still had some local allure. This version of the church was still in full use at the turn of the 19th century, although Archdeacon Eyre visited in 1811 and prescribed various repairs to the roof, steeple and walls, thus indicating its declining health. He also objected to cattle grazing in the churchyard, as they damaged the graves and stones, and ordered that only sheep were to be allowed in! The steeple was then repaired again in 1829, but by 1844, it was recorded that the church was a "roofless ruin" except for the chancel. A faculty was then obtained for the old parish church to be dismantled except for the chancel and vestry, and it was also at this time that the famous old font described above was transferred to Holy Trinity church.

St Anthony was left partially demolished for nearly 40 years, but then underwent a major restoration programme which commenced in 1883. New windows were inserted into the old walls, and a new nave and aisles were built, while the original chancel survived and was restored. The church was consecrated by the Bishop of Lincoln, and dedicated the following year to the church of St Anthony, commonly known as the Priory Church.

Lenton Historic Trivia: Lenton Priory

Lenton Priory was a Cluniac monastic house founded by William Peverel at the beginning of the 12th century, and dedicated to the Holy Trinity – although Peverel established in the foundation charter that Lenton Priory would be free from the obligation to pay tribute to Cluny Abbey in France, "save the annual payment of a mark of silver as an acknowledgement". The priory was also granted a large endowment of property in Nottinghamshire and Derbyshire, as well as control of the churches of St Mary, St Peter and St Nicholas, all in Nottingham, and other churches in Nottinghamshire, Leicestershire and Northamptonshire. That said, although it is believed that Peverel did indeed grant these gifts to the priory, the charter of foundation which documents them is believed to be a non-contemporary forgery, with the dates implausible. Nevertheless, the priory was given Royal Confirmation Charters by a succession of kings, confirming the priory's earlier endowments as well as a few more besides. Once again, the additions were local churches, tithes, land, and manors, but there were also some special concessions, too. Henry IIs charters granted the priory freedom from taxes, tolls, and customs duties as well as an eight-day fair to celebrate St Martin's Day. Henry IIIs charter extended this fair to twelve days in length while King John's granted the monks game from the royal forests in Nottinghamshire and Derbyshire.

Inset: *The remains of one of Lenton Priory's stone columns.*
Above: *Lenton Boulevard, which was laid out in the 1880s along with Castle Boulevard, Gregory Boulevard and Radford Boulevard to form a big loop around the western part of Nottingham. It was also at 32 Lenton Boulevard that the WWI flying ace Albert Ball VC was born.*

Nevertheless, part of this property became the cause of violent disagreement following the seizure of the Peverel family estates by the crown, during the reign of Henry II, who promptly granted the estates to his son, the future King John of England. On his ascendancy to the throne, John transferred this property to Lichfield Cathedral, thus starting around 300 years of disagreement between Priory and Cathedral about rightful ownership of the property. In the mid-13th century, extreme violence involving sheep broke out (see *Lenton Quirk Alert* for more), while other similar attacks occurred such as the monks using violence to steal geese, hay and oats. As a result, the Bishop of Lichfield appealed to Pope Innocent IV, who thus assembled a commission in 1252 at St. Mary's church in Leicester and which ruled that Lenton Priory be fined 100 marks on top of the £60 they had already paid Lichfield Cathedral in "compensation for the damage". The commission attempted to mitigate by granting the priory a portion of the tithes from some of the disputed parishes. This bought around 23 years of peace until 1275 when the dispute was renewed and which continued to flare up periodically all the way up to the Dissolution in the 1530s.

The priory was home mostly to French monks until the late 14th century when it was freed from the control of its French mother-house, Cluny Abbey. Before that, the poor French monks, unused to the cold, were granted permission by Pope Alexander IV in the winter of 1257/58 to wear caps during church services due to the "vehement cold". From the 13th-century the priory struggled financially and was constantly noted for its poverty, being £1,000 in debt in 1262 – around three times the priory's gross annual income – while in May 1313, Edward II placed the priory under his protection and appointed a keeper to oversee the priory's affairs. Of course, as an institution owing allegiance to a mother-house in France, the priory's income was also seized by the Crown during the incessant wars with France during the 14th century – and this lead to the eventual decoupling from its mother house in 1392.

Despite its poverty, the priory is believed to have had the finest set of guest-chambers around Nottingham, and as such, received a number of royal visits, including: Henry III in 1230, Edward I in 1302 and 1303, Edward II in 1307 and 1323, and Edward III in 1336. Of course, the priory was dissolved in 1538 as part of King Henry VIIIs Dissolution of the Monasteries. Prior Heath was thrown into prison in February 1538, along with many of his monks, all accused of high treason. In March, courtesy of the Verbal Treasons Act of December 1534, the prior with eight of his monks and four labourers of Lenton were indicted for treason and executed, although Thomas Cromwell's private notes reveal that Heath's fate was sealed before he had gone to trial. The executions took place in Nottingham and its surroundings, including in front of the priory itself where some of the quarters of those executed were displayed. Following dissolution the priory was demolished and its lands passed into private hands with William Stretton eventually buying the manor in 1802 and building a large house there called "The Priory". When William died he left the house to his son Sempronius who in 1842 was followed by his brother Severus William Lynam Stretton. Severus sold the house to the Sisters of Nazareth in 1880 who eventually sold the property in the early 21st century and the site was redeveloped for housing.

As for Lenton Fair, that survived the priory's 16th century demise, although its emphasis slowly changed, and in 1584 it was described as a horse-fair when servants of Mary, Queen of Scots attended. By the 17th century the Fair had acquired a reputation as a great fair for all sorts of horses and by the 19th century it was largely frequented by farmers and horse dealers. The Fair finally ceased at the beginning of the 20th century.

Lenton Quirk Alert: Sheep Murderers and Cat Burglars

The disagreements between Lichfield Cathedral and Lenton Priory became violent in 1250-51 when the monks of Lenton armed themselves and attempted to steal wool and lambs from the disputed parish of Tideswell in Derbyshire, which had been controversially granted to Lichfield by King John. Pre-empting the monks' attack the Dean of the cathedral ordered the wool and sheep to be kept within the nave of the village church, not expecting the monks of Lenton to defile the church. However, they did, and a fight ensued in which 18 lambs were killed within the church, either trampled under the horses' hooves or butchered by the attackers. The monks also managed to carry off 14 of the lambs.

From the 13th century, Lenton Priory was known for its poverty, but in the 12th century, it was very wealthy and the fortunes of the rural village of Lenton fell into step with its Priory neighbour. Contrast that to Lenton's nine hundredth anniversary in 2005, when a News of the World article dubbed Kimbolton Avenue in Lenton "the most burgled road in Britain". Those poor monks must have been turning in their graves! Well, those that weren't sheep murderers, anyway! They would also have been astonished to find that their nearby 12th century rural village had been absorbed by a modern metropolis, and not recently either; Lenton became part of Nottingham in 1877, by which stage agriculture had given way to industry, primarily lace.

The war memorial in Albert Ball Memorial Gardens, on the corner of Church Street and Sherwin Road, Lenton. It was erected in 1919 and stands in front of some almshouses dedicated to Captain Albert Ball VC, who died during WWI, an air ace and a national hero; the war memorial is dedicated to 288 men who fell during WWI, including Captain Ball.

Lenton Recreation Ground.

Threes-Up!

	RUFFS	SPION KOP	STANLEY
STATUS:	Suburb	Residential Area	Hamlet
POPULATION:	c.2,000	c.300	c.20
DISTRICT:	Ashfield	Mansfield	Ashfield
EARLIEST RECORD:	Unknown	Early 20th century	Unknown
MEANING:	N/A	See Three's Up Trivia	Probably stony woodland clearing
DERIVATION:	Named after Ruffs Farm		From the Old English words *stān* (stone, rock or boundary stone) and *lēah* (wood, woodland clearing or glade)

Threes Up Trivia!

The area known as **Ruffs**, to the south of Hucknall is a housing estate, and its roots were planted when Ruffs Farm and Nabbs Farm were purchased by Portland Estates in the 1930s. Building of the estate commenced in 1937, taking its name from the first of the two farms – although both farms had long roads named after them, with Ruffs Drive and Nabbs Lane running largely parallel to each other from the B6009. The expansion of the Ruffs estate was curtailed during World War II, but resumed in 1949 when 50 more homes were built, and space earmarked for 600 more. It was also at this time that Holgate Infant School was built at the north-eastern edge of Ruffs on High Leys Road, becoming Hucknall's first new school since the 1870's. Later Ruffs additions included a Co-operative Society branch in 1954 and an Anglican church known as St Peter and St Paul, which was built on Ruffs Drive in 1958, while the two main Ruffs pubs also appeared on the estate's two main roads, with the Masons Arms at the end of Ruffs Drive, and the Nabb Inn at the other end of Nabbs Lane. The Anglican church of St Peter and St Paul was built in a modernist style by the architect Vernon Royle and consists of a hexagonal shape with floor-to-ceiling glass dominating two of the walls, while the roof is adorned with a small fibreglass spire. The building is also connected to the Church Hall next door.

Spion Kop is a small residential and former industrial area on the A60, heading north out of Mansfield Woodhouse and is located about half a mile south of Market Warsop. The place is named after the Battle of Spion Kop which took place during the Second Boer War in Natal, South Africa in January 1900. The battle's precise location was about 24 miles west-south-west of Ladysmith on the hilltop of Spioenkop along the Tugela River, and took place between 23rd and 24th January. It turned out to be a heavy British defeat to the forces of the South African Republic and the Orange Free State during the campaign to relieve Ladysmith.

Stanley is only the tiniest of hamlets, and is located at the merger of Shepherd's Lane and Silverhill Lane, a stone's throw from the Derbyshire border and around a mile or so to the south of the major tourist attraction of Hardwick Hall. The hamlet has neither a church nor a pub, although the Hardwick Inn is located half a mile or so to the north.

The Masons Arms is located at the top of Ruffs Drive.

NAME (STATUS): **MANSFIELD** (Town)
POPULATION: 99,600
DISTRICT: Mansfield
EARLIEST RECORD: *Mamesfelde*, 1086 (Domesday Book); *Maunnesfeld*, 1227; *Mannesfeld*, 1377
MEANING: Open land by the River Maun
DERIVATION: From the river-name which, in turn, is derived from the Celtic word *mamm* (breast-like hill), plus the Old English word *feld* (field or open land)
FAMOUS RESIDENTS: **Rebecca Adlington** (b.1989), swimmer/Olympic gold medallist; **Richard Bacon** (b.1975), TV presenter; **Kris Commons** (b.1983), footballer; **Stephen Critchlow**, actor; **Robert Dodsley** (1704-1764), poet and playwright; **Mark Holmes**, lead singer with Platinum Blonde; **Robert Kozluk** (b.1977), footballer; **Ric Lee** (b.1948), musician; **Leo Lyons** (b.1943), musician; **John Ogdon** (1937-1989), pianist and composer; **Greg Owen** (b.1972), professional golfer; **James Perch** (b.1985), footballer; **Alvin Stardust** (1942-2014), singer; **John Webster** (b.1955), theologian; **Oliver Wilson** (b.1980), professional golfer

Mansfield Pub: Sir John Cockle

A number of Mansfield's many pubs have intriguing names, such as Nell Gwyn, The Widow Frost, The Bold Forester and The Oddfellows! But the best trivia is delivered by Sir John Cockle – a pub on Sutton Road which is named after a character who appears in a folk song written by Malcolm Seymour of Mansfield, and which tells the story of how a lowly miller came by his knighthood. Having taken in a weary traveller one night, John Cockle serves him ale and venison and brags about it being from the King's own deer … at which point the traveller reveals himself as … the King himself! The King explains that, by rights, Cockle should be hanged – but because he took him in and fed him, he knights him instead. It is said the King was Henry II and that Cockle's family was given £300 a year while Sir John was appointed the Overseer to Sherwood Forest. A 17th century manuscript is perhaps the first to record the legend in *A pleasant ballad of King Henry II and the Miller of Mansfield*. Then in the 18th century a satirical play was written by Mansfield-born Robert Dodsley called *The King and the Miller of Mansfield* which was performed at the Theatre Royal on Drury Lane. In fact, the play even spawned a sequel called *Sir John Cockle at Court!* The legend also gave its name to the King's Mill area between Mansfield and Sutton-in-Ashfield, where it is thought the mill was located.

The Sir John Cockle, Mansfield.

Mansfield Church: St Peter and St Paul

The Grade I listed church of St Peter and St Paul is one of those rare British churches that still have some Saxon brickwork intact – in this case, the lower brickwork on the east side of the tower. The early Norman tower was then added to the Saxon church, the lower stages of which survive to this day, as does a wide Norman arch that opens into the 14th century nave – the latter having replaced an early 12th century nave that had been added along with a chancel; indeed, fragments of the 12th century zigzag moulding still survive in the outer wall of the chancel – these having been dated to around 1113. The aisles were then added at the end of the 12th century. Other Norman survivors are the base of a column that supports the westernmost pier of the north

St Peter and St Paul's church, Mansfield.

arcade, and the outline of a Norman window on the west wall. A little later, two chantry chapels were added around 1475 with the battlements and clerestory following in the late 15th or early 16th century. The spire was added to the tower in 1699 and a clock in 1802. As for the eight bells, the oldest dates from 1603 while the earliest reference to an organ at St Peter's was written in 1794. However, the present organ was installed in 1972 and is one of the finest in the Southwell and Nottingham Diocese – although it spent the first 135 years of its life first at the small church of St Wilfrid's in Honington, Lincolnshire, and then from 1868 at Clare College Chapel, Cambridge. The organ was commissioned by the rector of St Wilfrid's, Dr Henry Cole, an organ enthusiast, but was said to have been much too large for Honington, such that the volume frightened the elderly people living in the village while it also vibrated the windows to such an extent that wooden pegs had to be placed in them. Even more bizarre is that the Reverend Cole was buried in the case of his grand piano in the aisle of the church!

Mansfield Historic Trivia: Villas, Palaces, Mansfield Bitter and Giant Headstocks

Settlement in the Mansfield area is known to date back to the Bronze Age with axes from the period discovered, while evidence of an Iron Age "green lane" was discovered at Leeming Lane and which was later used by the Romans to link Mansfield to Worksop. However, a far greater Roman discovery was made by Major Hayman Rooke just to the north of Mansfield in 1786 between Mansfield Woodhouse and Pleasley, when he unearthed Nottinghamshire's best-known Roman villa (see page 14 for more) A cache of denarii (small silver Roman coins) was also found near King's Mill in 1849.

Switching to the 8th century, it is believed that early English royalty stayed in the Mansfield area, with the Mercian Kings using the place as a base for hunting in nearby Sherwood Forest. Spinning forward another four centuries and King John's Palace – a retreat for royal families and dignitaries – was built at Clipstone in the 12th century, just east of Mansfield. Then in 1227, Mansfield was granted a market charter, while in November 1377, King Richard II signed a warrant granting the right for the tenants of Mansfield to hold a fair every year for four days.

Alas, the majority of Mansfield's old buildings date from the 17th century onwards, thanks to the fact that many older buildings were demolished in the early 20th century to make way for new development. Several cruck-framed buildings were demolished in 1929 and another went in 1973 – and which was believed to have dated from around 1400 – while many other classic Tudor houses were demolished before they could be reviewed for listed status.

In 1855, Mansfield Brewery was founded following the formation of a partnership between brewer John Watson of Sheffield, farmer Samuel Hage of Ollerton,

King's Mill Reservoir, with King's Mill Hospital in the background.
Inset: Built in 1875, this is part of the 15-arched viaduct that runs through Mansfield town centre for 240 metres.

and farmer and investor William Baily, of Mansfield, although Watson had sold his £450 share of the business to the other two partners within two years. To support their business, Hage and Baily established a malting facility in 1863 as well as concentrating on beer production. The partners were then joined in 1873 by Addison Titley and in 1885 by Baily's brother-in-law, William Jackson Chadburn, who actually went onto become the dominant owning partner in the early 20th century. The late 19th century saw Mansfield Brewery buying a number of pubs that were to provide an outlet for their beer, and by 1901, the firm was flourishing, leasing 72 licensed premises from public houses to hotels, as well as numerous off licenses. This success resulted in the rebuilding of the main brewery in 1907, and production immediately increased from 17,000 to 20,000 barrels per annum. By 1925 the business had become a private limited liability company known as The Mansfield Brewery Company Ltd, while in 1935 the company became publicly listed on the London Stock Exchange, having acquired Chesterfield Brewery with its own 100 pubs the previous year. Further acquisitions occurred in 1955 (Hornby's soft drink distributors), in 1980 (TW Beac), and in 1985, when North County Breweries of Humberside were acquired for £42m – although the company failed in its attempt to buy Shipstones Brewery in 1978. By 1987, the company was operating a total of 420 licensed premises, and was one of the Mansfield area's largest employers. This was very much the hey-day of Mansfield Brewery, and the main beer brewed was Mansfield Bitter, along with other popular brands including Riding Bitter, Marston Old Baily, and Marksman Lager. Mansfield Bitter was also advertised in 1982 with a photograph of then US president Ronald Reagan and the tagline: *He might be president of the most powerful nation on earth ... but he's never had a pint of Mansfield*. By 1997, profits were *still* increasing and a new beer, 'Redeye' was launched. However, in 1999, the company was taken over by Wolverhampton & Dudley Breweries for £253m, who promptly moved production to Park Brewery in Wolverhampton, and Mansfield Brewery was eventually closed in 2002. Worse still, the distinct flavour of the Mansfield beers was soon lost; the beers had always been enhanced by the local hard water content, but as soon as production switched to Wolverhampton, the distinct flavour was lost and sales soon began to fall. Meanwhile, the brewery's assets were later sold to Pubmaster Ltd and the Mansfield Brewery site was eventually demolished in 2008, bringing an end to over a century and a half of successful brewing in the town. In fact, the brewery chimney which had dominated the Mansfield skyline for more than 150 years disappeared in just three seconds in July 2008 and the famous 'M' sign which heralded the brewery is now located in Mansfield Museum.

There are a couple of sub-stories here, though. Firstly, Mansfield Brewery eventually went the same way as Home Ales of Arnold and Kimberley Ales of Kimberley, but it did last an extra 15 years. Mansfield Brewery also profited from the demise of Home Ales when they were awarded the contract brewing for all Home Brewery products following their take over by Scottish & Newcastle in 1986, and the closure of their Daybrook site. The second sub-story is that an off-shoot of Mansfield Brewery did actually survive a little longer. In 1977, Mansfield Brewery had acquired a soft-drinks manufacturer, R.L. Jones, who retailed the brands Sunecta and Mandora, and these products were produced on Bellamy Road in south-east Mansfield. Mansfield Brewery eventually sold the business to Scottish drinks company A. G. Barr plc in 1988 for £21.5m, A. G. Barr being the producers of Irn-Bru, Tizer and, since 1988, Mandora. At that time the company employed 400 people, but production eventually ceased in January 2011 when A. G. Barr closed the factory and transferred manufacturing to other sites.

Like so many other towns in the surrounding area, Mansfield was once a coal mining town and the largest mine was sunk at Clipstone to the north-east of the town. Originally owned by the Bolsover Colliery Company, it passed to the National Coal Board in 1947 and the shafts were considerably extended in the 1950s to exploit deeper seams. Although closed in 1993, it was re-opened by RJB Mining (now UK Coal) in 1994 and

Clipstone Colliery pit headstocks, the largest in Europe and third largest in the world.

Mansfield's modern King's Mill hospital.

operated until its final closure in 2003. Today, the site is unusual in that its pit headstocks remain – but there is a very good reason for that, as they are the tallest in Europe and the third tallest in the world, not to mention Grade II listed. As a result, there is an on-going battle between those who wish to preserve the historic site and those who wish to demolish the structure and re-develop the area.

The death of brewing and coal mining in Mansfield has obviously lead to the large-scale demolition of former industrial sites and the birth of new developments, to which we can add the reconstruction of the impressive King's Mill Hospital. It was this redevelopment that prompted Nottinghamshire's largest town (Nottingham is a city) to pitch for city status in 2009. The move was unsuccessful, but the Centre for Cities did categorise Mansfield as a "small city" – a categorisation that is helped, size-wise, by the fact that Mansfield is the centre of the Mansfield Urban Area, which also includes the towns of Sutton-in-Ashfield and Kirkby-in-Ashfield along with the large village of Mansfield Woodhouse. Unfortunately, the death of those two great industries, along with the textile industry, means that Mansfield currently has 20.2% (12,890) of its working age population seeking out of work benefits.

Mansfield Quirk Alert: The Largest "Improving Worst Town" without a Station

Today, Mansfield is a stop on the Robin Hood Line which links Nottingham with Worksop. However, from 1964 until the opening of the Robin Hood line in 1995, Mansfield was the largest town in Britain without a railway station! This was a remarkable position for a town with around 100,000 inhabitants, but if any of them needed to hop on a train between those years, they had to find their way to Alfreton, around eight miles to the south-west – a town with a population of only 22,000! Even more ironic, is that between 1916 and 1956, Mansfield actually had *two* stations; one on the Midland Railway line called Mansfield Town and located on Station Road, and the other called Mansfield Central on the local section of the Mansfield Railway that was connected with the Great Central Railway.

Finally, the 2005 and 2007 editions of Channel 4's programme *The Best and Worst Places to Live in the UK* named Mansfield in the latter list in 6th and 9th place, respectively. The placement was largely due to the poor performance of Mansfield schools at that time, but this position has improved to such an extent that it is no longer in the alleged worst 20 places to live, this due to a large reduction in crime, huge improvements in local schools and, apparently, being known for good air quality, too!

The memorial to Lord George Bentinck (1802-1848), located in Mansfield market place. The son of the 4th Duke of Portland, Bentinck was a Conservative MP most noted for his role in the unseating of Sir Robert Peel over the Corn Laws.

The 16th century market cross in Buttercross Market, Mansfield.

NAME (STATUS):	**MAUN** (River)
DISTRICT:	Ashfield, Mansfield, Newark and Sherwood, Bassetlaw
SOURCE:	Kirkby-in-Ashfield
SOURCE ELEVATION:	490ft (150m)
MOUTH:	River Idle
MOUTH ELEVATION:	59ft (18m)
MEANING:	Breast-like hill
DERIVATION:	From the Celtic word *mamm* (breast-like)

River Maun Geographic Trivia: From Kirkby-in-Ashfield to the River Idle

The source of the River Maun is just to the north of Kirkby-in-Ashfield from where it flows north-eastwards under the railway. It is then culverted as it crosses first the B6021 and then the B6022 before emerging in the Maun Valley Industrial Park. It then passes under first the B6139 and then the A617, after which it feeds King's Mill Reservoir. At the exit from the reservoir, the river is crossed by the five-arched King's Mill Viaduct, a Grade II listed structure built around 1819 for the Mansfield and Pinxton Railway, before being crossed by a ten-arched Grade II listed viaduct, built in 1875 and part of the disused Drury Dam railway. In between the two viaducts, the Maun is joined by Cauldwell Water at Bleakhills. As for the second of those two viaducts, part of it spans the Quarry Lane Nature Reserve, on the south bank of the Maun. From here, the river works its way through the centre of Mansfield, albeit culverted in numerous places. One of the places where the river does see daylight is on Bridge Street where the pub now known as Town Mill was originally a mill built in around 1775. From here, the Maun travels underground for around half a mile before emerging on the south side of the B6033. It then heads off out of Mansfield on a north-easterly trajectory, passing a large sewage works, the outflow from which contributes a significant portion of the flow below this point.

The River Maun as it passes under King's Mill Viaduct at Mansfield.

The River Maun at Edwinstowe.

After passing under the A6117, and arriving in Mansfield Woodhouse, the river enters Maun Valley Park, a wetland nature reserve covering 42 acres, before leaving the village after passing under New Mill Lane. For the first time, the Maun now enters open countryside, bearing east to pass to the north of the village of Clipstone. As it does, it flows along the edge of Badger Hill, High Rocks and then Cavendish Wood to the south and a number of large fish ponds to the north, while just north of Kings Clipstone, the Maun is joined by Vicar Water. It is then crossed by a railway at Clipstone Junction before flowing to the south of Edwinstowe, after which it is joined on the western edge of Ollerton by Rainworth Water, flowing northwards from Rufford Abbey. From this latest confluence, the Maun then heads NNE, passing Ollerton and Ollerton Watermill, the latter having been built in 1713 and worked commercially until 1984.

From Ollerton, the Maun enters the latter stages of its journey and which becomes intertwined with the River Meden. The two watercourses actually merge briefly to the north-east of Perlethorpe, before a weir separates the two, directing them both eastwards, with the River Maun the more southerly of the two. They then both turn northwards to the west of Markham Moor Roundabout on the A1, before merging again to form the River Idle.

River Maun Historic Trivia: King's Mill Reservoir and King's Mill Viaduct.

It was mentioned in the previous section that, early in its journey, the River Maun feeds the King's Mill reservoir. However, the reservoir was once a medieval mill pond and there was even a mill situated here back in 1086 when the Domesday Book records one, while there is also mention of a fulling mill there in 1292. Much later, the 1780s saw an explosion of mills in the area, following Sir Richard Arkwright's first ground-breaking water-powered cotton-spinning mill, built in 1771 in neighbouring Derbyshire. William Cavendish-Bentinck, the third Duke of Portland, and latterly Home Secretary, actively encouraged the building of textile mills to relieve unemployment and poverty in the area – ironically, largely caused by the mills in the first place, as they had replaced the town's former main industry of framework knitting. The first Mansfield-based water-powered cotton-spinning mill was Hermitage Mill, built, in 1782 on Hermitage Lane, followed three years later by Little Matlock Mill on Sheepbridge Lane. Both mills still stand today. Field Mill on Nottingham Road was then converted to cotton-spinning in 1785, as was Town Mill, a former cotton-grinding mill originally built in 1744 – although six years later, Field Mill forced the closure of nearby Drury Mill, a corn mill, because the water level in Field Mill Dam had been raised, preventing Drury's wheel from working efficiently. However, Field Mill has not survived; it was demolished in 1925, while Town Mill became Old Town Mill in 1870, when a steam-powered mill was built on the eastern bank of the Maun and which became known as New Town Mill. The philanthropic Bentinck also created a Sunday school in 1786 for the education of his young workers, offering basic reading and maths, as well as moral instruction!

Other mills built were Stanton's Mill (1785), Bath Mill (1792) and Bleakhills Mill (1795). As for King's Mill, the fourth Duke of Portland – also William Bentinck – agreed with the millers who leased mills further down the river that a large head of water was required to maintain the water supply throughout the year. Between 1837 and 1839, he therefore built a dam and flooded 72 acres of farmland to form the King's Mill reservoir – and then proceeded to collect payment from the grateful millers! Before we leave the Mansfield mills, though, it is worth mentioning that one effect of the conversion of mills from corn grinding to cotton spinning was that a number of windmills were built – to mill the corn into flour – and therefore the number of windmills in Mansfield rose from 3 to 13 between 1774 and 1824. As for the textile mills, by 1887 most of them were marked on maps as "cotton doubling mills", thanks to the process of winding multiple strands of cotton together to form thicker threads, but by 1899, only Field Mill and Bath Mill were still marked in this way; most of the rest were marked simply as "Hosiery". The exception was Rock Valley Mill, which was operated by Dickenson Ellis as a mustard mill in the early 19th century. However, in 1873, they started packing the mustard in decorated tin boxes which were made on-site from pre-printed metal sheet. They were soon making tin boxes for other companies, and this led to the formation of Rock Valley Tin Works in 1889. Three years later, a printing works was established, to print the metal sheets, and it became a limited company in 1895. The business still survives today as Carnaud Metal Box Engineering.

When the River Maun exits King's Mill reservoir it is crossed by King's Mill viaduct, which was built around 1819 for the Mansfield and Pinxton Railway by the engineer Josias Jessop. The Mansfield and Pinxton Railway was initially an 8 mile-long horse-drawn railway which ran from Mansfield to Pinxton where it met the Cromford Canal – Jessop's more famous father, William, having been the chief engineer of the Cromford Canal Company during its construction in the late 18th century. The opening ceremony for the Mansfield and Pinxton Railway was held on 13 April 1819, close to the King's Mill viaduct which a local newspaper described as *"the beautiful five-arched bridge, constructed under the direction of Mr. Jessop, the engineer"*. The railway was adapted for locomotive traffic in 1847. Today, the central arch of the Grade II listed structure still carries the date 1817. Restored in 1990, it is now used as a footpath, as the Robin Hood Line has been diverted to avoid it.

The River Maun at Ollerton.

Part of the brief stretch where the River Meden and the River Maun merge, before being split out again by a weir at the far end of this shot.

Name (Status):	**MEADOWS** (Suburb)
Population:	7,870
District:	City of Nottingham
Meaning:	A series of meadows
Derivation:	Named after the large area of wetland or floodplain which extended from the River Leen to the River Trent. After enclosure the area was drained and gradually urbanised.

Meadows Pub: The Vat and Fiddle

Meadows is home to a number of pubs including the Vat and Fiddle, while The Medz on Arkwright Street is named in honour of its suburb location.

The Vat and Fiddle, Meadows.

Meadows Church: St George and St Saviour

There are two Grade II listed churches in Meadows that are known as "St George in the Meadows" and "St Saviour in the Meadows". St Saviour's was built in 1863 on Arkwright Walk and St George's in the 1880s on St George's Drive. Both naves were designed by local architect, Richard Charles Sutton. St Saviour's church actually replaced a small mission chapel which had served the residents of Meadows but which was struggling to accommodate the increasing number of worshippers from the increasing Meadows population. The much larger St Saviour's cost around £3,000 to build, and offered seats for 750 people. Meanwhile, St George's church had its chancel, organ chamber and vestries added in 1897 (designed by George Frederick Bodley) and the Lady Chapel in 1911 (designed by C.G. Hare). The parish of St George was later merged with that of St John the Baptist's church from Leenside, when the latter was demolished following damage incurred during World War II. Today, St George's supports the Forward in Faith movement and is under the control of the Bishop of Beverley.

The church of St George in Meadows is located on St George's Drive.

Meadows Historic Trivia: Nottingham Arkwright Street, the Victoria Embankment and 'Q' Blocks

"Meadows" is the name given to an inner-city area of Nottingham that was originally a large area of wetland or floodplain which extended from the River Leen to the River Trent. After enclosure, though, the area was drained and gradually became urbanised throughout the 19th century, with lots of terraced housing built to house the workers who, in turn, worked on the railways and in the factories and warehouses that were also part of the urbanisation of Meadows. In fact, many of the terraced houses were actually built by the railway companies for their employees such as the Great Central Railway which ran through the area en-route from London to Nottingham and then onto Manchester Piccadilly. Despite the proximity of Nottingham Victoria station, Meadows actually had its own station which was known as Nottingham Arkwright Street. The station was opened in 1899 and a carriage shed and locomotive depot were constructed on the up side, and goods, coal and timber yards on the down side. The goods yard became home to one of the first goliath travelling cranes in England,

The spire of the church of St Saviour's peeping above the trees on Arkwright Walk, Meadows.

electrically driven with a span of 60ft and capable of lifting a full load of 25 tons at a rate of 5ft per minute. However, the engine shed closed in 1909 with locomotives moved to the larger Annesley shed to the north of the city, while the station lasted until the Beeching Report recommended it for closure in 1963 – although it managed to cling on until 1969.

In 1901, two years after Nottingham Arkwright Street was constructed, the famous Victoria Embankment was built. This acknowledged Victorian masterpiece is actually a very attractive flood defence along with a promenade and stretches for 1¼ miles along the north bank of the River Trent and thus marks the southern limits of Meadows. Five years later in 1906, the New Meadows recreation ground was opened immediately to the north of the Embankment while in 1920 Jesse Boot purchased the remainder of the land within the Embankment adjacent to the Trent and then bequeathed it to the citizens of Nottingham in perpetuity for recreational use. This included the memorial gardens, playing fields, war memorial, Grade II listed bandstand and two sports pavilions, all of which survive today, and have played host to around 10,000 runners every September since 1981 at the start and finish of the Robin Hood Marathon.

As for those 19th century terraces built by the railway companies, many of them were demolished in the 1970s and replaced by modern council houses. Also demolished in 1975 was the viaduct carrying the Great Central Railway and Arkwright Street Station, thus leaving little or no trace of Meadows' 19th century past – although St Saviour's Church survived in this area, along with the housing to the south of Wilford Crescent and which abuts onto the recreation ground. The 1970s redevelopment, however, was due to be short-lived, following the introduction of the £200m Meadows Neighbourhood Plan in 2009. The 1970s build had been based on the Radburn model of planning which consisted of segregating traffic and pedestrians by constructing cul-de-sacs, feeder roads and underpasses; the 2009 Plan intended to undo most of that by reintroducing the traditional street layout! This would have been achieved by 'turning around' many houses and demolishing many of the unpopular 'Q' blocks, replacing them with modern energy efficient family homes, while the council also anticipated that the new layout would help reduce crime and anti-social behaviour – but would also provide easy access in and out of the area for the police! Alas, during November 2010, the government announced that the plan had been cancelled as part of austerity measures – although in September 2011, Nottingham City Homes did at least announce that fifteen of the undesirable 'Q' blocks would be demolished and replaced with new family-sized housing. It is also hoped that Meadows will benefit from the construction of the tram extensions and the redevelopment of Nottingham Victoria railway station just to the north of the suburb, as two of the new tram routes (Lines 2 and 3) will pass through Meadows and will include three tram stops in the suburb.

Meadows Quirk Alert: Namedropping

At the south-western end of Meadows, a toll booth used to collect tolls on Wilford Bridge over the Trent. Meanwhile, a little further along the Victoria Embankment nothing now remains of the Toll House Inn, scene of much lunch-time hilarity when I worked at Boots in the late 1990s. However, if you go back another 20 years, I can honestly say that the first time I ever rode across the Victoria Embankment it was in the back of a Mercedes being driven by the great Brian Clough. This was the late 1970s, and I was good friends with his eldest son. Like most people who knew the great man, I have anecdotes. Like the time I went around to his house and asked if he wanted me to take my trainers off. *"Take 'em off; they look like they're going to drop off, son!"*

The Victoria Embankment, just beyond Wilford Bridge at the south-western edge of Meadows. Inset (left): *The War Memorial at the eastern end of the Victoria Embankment and at the south-eastern limit of Meadows.* (right): *The old Toll House that still sits on Wilford Bridge at the south-western extremity of Meadows. Today (2014) the whole area is in upheaval as tram lines are laid to link Meadows to the Nottingham tram system.*

NAME (STATUS):	**MISSON** (Village)
POPULATION:	745
DISTRICT:	Bassetlaw
EARLIEST RECORD:	*Misne*, 1086 (Domesday Book)
MEANING:	Mossy or marshy place
DERIVATION:	From the Old English word *mos* (moss, marsh or bog)

Misson Geographic Trivia: Splendid Isolation

I have read that Misson is unique in Nottinghamshire terms in that it is inaccessible by road from any other part of the county – this being based on the fact that the only route into the village is by one road that turns eastwards towards the village from the A614 in South Yorkshire. However, that isn't quite the case. Because although Misson Springs which lies just to the north of Misson is the northernmost *place* in Nottinghamshire, there is still a road further north that passes through the northernmost tip of Nottinghamshire on an east-to-west bearing. The B1396 is known as Sanderson's Bank on its brief Nottinghamshire sojourn, but it is also met by Springs Road, that heads largely southwards towards Misson Springs, and then becomes Station Road as it heads into Misson. So there are two ways in and out of Misson after all; they're just an awfully long way apart, but the northernmost entry point *is* in Nottinghamshire – just!

As for that junction of Springs Road with the B1396, if you were to go straight across from Springs Road, you would be on Misson Bank, a drainage ditch that heads off in a straight line towards Wroot in Lincolnshire.

The Angel Inn, Misson.

The White Horse Inn, Misson.

Misson Pub: The White Horse Inn and The Angel Inn

Misson has two very attractive pubs. First there is the White Horse Inn, which some websites claim dates back to the 11th century. It certainly has beautiful character with white-washed stone walls and dark external timbers along with internal wooden beams and "original" fireplaces … but 11th century? As for the Angel Inn on Dame Lane, that is around 200 years old and is probably most famous these days for its classic cars events, including classic car displays and an annual 84 mile classic car rally which starts and finishes at the Angel Inn.

Misson Church: St John the Baptist

The Grade I listed St John the Baptist church at Misson was largely of the 14th to 16th century Perpendicular period, but large parts of it had to be rebuilt between 1892 and 1894, when extensive damage was caused following a lightning strike. Then over one hundred years later, in June 2007, the church was also subjected to around £100,000 worth of damage – but this time, not by the elements, but by criminals who had stripped the church roof of its lead and, ironically, its copper lightning conductor, too! However, there is a mildly satisfying outcome – for a milkman on his early morning delivery, spotted the heinous heritage thieves' van and then the ladder propped up against the north side of the church … and then finally spotted the men on the roof – who promptly did a runner and abandoned their priceless loot. Of course, that didn't help the grievously violated church, or the people who run it, who were left to desperately canvas for grants and third-party assistance to fund new roofs for the nave and the north and south aisles. Happily for the church, they succeeded, and by October 2010 the work was complete: new roofs, a new lightning conductor and, most importantly, a new

St John the Baptist church, Misson.

The River Idle at Misson.

beamed roof alarm! Anyway, perhaps the time has come to bring a new rule into play for such odious miscreants as these; violate a medieval masterpiece, and suffer medieval punishment! Luckily for them, large parts of the church had been rebuilt in the early 1890s!

Misson Historic Trivia: The Roman and Dutch Connections

A mile to the south-west of Misson village, and still in the Misson parish, is the tiny settlement of Newington, and here on Hagg Hill it is thought that a Roman encampment was located with the site going on to be further developed by the Danes who arrived in the 8th and 9th century. After the Norman Conquest, most of the land around Misson went to Roger de Busli, while at the same time, a predecessor church to the current one must have existed in Misson, as a church is recorded as being built here in 1150 and attached to the priory at Mattersey in 1185, although the first vicar, John Clarell, is not recorded until 1292.

In 1620, the nearby River Idle provided transportation for the North Nottinghamshire contingent of the Pilgrim Fathers, thereafter travelling down the Trent and sailing from the East Coast to Holland. From there, they made their historic voyage in the Mayflower to settle New England. Meanwhile, the Dutch connection re-surfaced six years later when Cornelius Vermuyden drained Hatfield Chase, thus benefiting Misson (see *Idle* chapter for more). The 17th century also saw other key Misson events, with 48 buildings in Misson completely destroyed by fire on 3rd August 1652 and Misson School built in 1693, one of the very first to be founded in Nottinghamshire. Meanwhile, the 18th century saw 700 cattle die of distemper in 1742, and the common land enclosed between 1760 and 1762 by Jonathan Acklam.

Misson Quirk Alert: Lightning Strikes and Bloodhound Missiles

As mentioned earlier, Misson Church was damaged by a lightning strike in 1892. At the time, the Reverend F.W. Keene was taking a Sunday School class when the bell tower took the brunt of the strike. The effect was so severe that Keene's clothes were charred and his gold watch chain was melted; the good reverend himself had to be taken to hospital for treatment. As for the church, the tower was gutted by the resulting fire and two of the pinnacles collapsed, while the roof of the nave was also set alight, the clock was completely destroyed and the church bells partly melted before crashing to the ground. The repairs cost over £1,000.

St John the Baptist church tower, which was gutted by fire in 1892 following a lightning strike.

Talk of lightning strikes brings us onto the "Misson

Rocket Site" – as it certainly wouldn't have done for this place to be struck by lightning when it was operational. It is located a mile or so to the north-east of Misson, and is the former 65 acre Military Air Defence Bloodhound Missile Site. Here, 94 Squadron reformed on 1st October 1960, as a Bloodhound air defence missile unit for the defence of nearby RAF Finningley. The surrounding area was also a former RAF bombing range and military training area originally acquired by the Ministry of Defence in the 1930s. Covering 850 acres known as Misson Carr, 610 acres were sold by auction in 1969 and returned to agricultural use, while the rest was retained by the Army as a dry training area. The remaining 200 acres was eventually relinquished by the military in 1995 and by 1997, Misson Carr was designated a Site of Special Scientific Interest (SSSI), as 50 years of restricted public access and protection from intensive agriculture had enabled the area to develop into a fascinating wildlife haven – this thanks to a variety of habitats including nationally rare wet woodlands, marsh, and old grazing pastures. The area also boasts the county's largest remaining fragment of fenland not lost to drainage and agriculture over the last three hundred years. The site eventually became known as Misson Carr Nature Reserve, having been acquired by the Nottinghamshire Wildlife Trust in 2001. The site's importance is characterised by the sheer variety of habitats and species that thrive here but it is particularly noted for its populations of moths and birds, including all five native species of owl. As for the former rocket site, this is now a commercial development characterised by large metal storage sheds that accommodate over 1,000 military vehicles. The current occupiers, L. Jackson & Co, work closely with the Ministry of Defence and NATO forces for the disposal of ex-military vehicles, plant and equipment, while they are also one of the largest suppliers of surplus military vehicles and equipment worldwide, with the vehicles supplied to the construction and mining industries, utility companies, as well as public and private sector companies.

High Street, Misson.

NAME (STATUS):	**NORTON** (Village)
POPULATION:	143
DISTRICT:	Bassetlaw
EARLIEST RECORD:	*Nortone*, 1086 (Domesday Book)
MEANING:	North farmstead or village
DERIVATION:	From the Old English words *north* (north or northern) and *tūn* (farmstead or village)

Norton Pub: The Greendale Oak Inn, Cuckney

The Greendale Oak at Norton's neighbour, Cuckney is thought to date back to the 1660s. The story goes that the 1st Duke of Portland told a friend at dinner in 1724 that he had an oak tree so large (allegedly 35ft round) that you could drive a coach and four horses through it. The friend challenged him to bet on it, which he did, at which point the Duke then despatched his woodmen to attend to the matter; apparently, they cut an archway in the tree ten feet high and six feet wide. The very next morning, the Duke's narrowest carriage was driven through the Greendale Oak, and the wager was his. The mutilated tree survived for another 200 years, gradually diminishing in size. And, of course, the pub is named after the famous tree.

The Greendale Oak Inn, Cuckney.

The centre of Norton village.

Meanwhile, for completeness, the 3rd Duke of Portland was William Henry Cavendish-Bentinck, twice British Prime Minister, once in 1783 and again between 1807 and his death in 1809; in fact, to this day, he is the Prime Minister with the longest gap between just two periods of office. He also had the finest park in this area of Nottinghamshire, with many ancient oak trees besides the Greendale Oak, two of which stood guard at the side of the north gate and which were known as Large Porter (98ft) and Little Porter (88ft).

Norton Church: St Mary's, Norton Cuckney

St Mary's church is actually located on Norton Road at the north-eastern edge of Cuckney before the road heads off for Norton – which perhaps explains the fact that the church is named as "St Mary's, Norton Cuckney". The church is Grade I listed and dates from the 12th century while the porch is 13th century although it retains its original Norman ornamentation; the doorway into the church is also Norman, with its zigzag mouldings. The nave of c.1200 is unusually long and is divided from its aisle by an arcade of six round arches supported by pillars of varying shapes; circular, quatrefoil and octagonal. Meanwhile, the base of the tower is 13th century and the top is 15th century, as are many of the windows. The nave floor is home to a slab of black marble, so worn that its inscription has disappeared, but which is reputed to be the tomb of Robert Pierrepont, 1st Earl of Kingston-upon-Hull, and killed during the English Civil War in 1643. The church was restored in 1667, 1831-32, 1892 and 1907, while in 1950 up to fifty skeletons were found buried in three tiers under the nave, when workmen were applying a concrete raft to help deal with mining subsidence. The skeletons were re-buried near the old west door of the church. They are thought to have been young men killed during the Anarchy period of the 12th century when King Stephen was on the throne. NB: See page 20 for a photo of the church, which was built on the site of the early 12th century Cuckney Castle.

Norton Historic Trivia: Carucates and Cuckeneys

Before the Norman Conquest of 1066, neighbouring Cuckney was home to an old knight called Gamelbere, and who held two carucates of land on the condition that he shoe the king's palfrey whenever he visited the area. Gamelbere died without heirs, and Henry I later gave the land to Richard, son of Joce de Flemangh who, in turn, had a son called Thomas de Cuckeney. It was de Cuckeney who built Cuckney Castle and founded Welbeck Abbey (see pages 20 and 29 for more on both). By marriage the lands of de Flemangh passed to the Fauconberg family, but eventually worked their way into the domain of Welbeck Abbey by 1329.

Norton Quirk Alert: A Cunning Plan

Following the Norman Conquest of 1066, the chief part of the Norton parish was held by none other than Hugh Fitz Baldric! Meanwhile, Norton may only be a small village, lacking in sugar substitute but it is home to nearly 30 Grade II listed houses!

NAME (STATUS):	**NUTHALL** (Village)
POPULATION:	6,311
DISTRICT:	Broxtowe
EARLIEST RECORD:	*Nutehale*, 1086 (Domesday Book); *Nuchala*, 1195; *Niewehale*, 1197
MEANING:	Nook of land where nut-trees grow
DERIVATION:	From the Old English words *hnutu* (nut-tree) and *halh* (nook or corner of land)
FAMOUS RESIDENTS:	**Anne Askew** (1520-1546), Protestant martyr

Nuthall Pub: The Nuthall Inn

The Three Ponds is one of five pubs in Nuthall, and along with The Lark's Nest is located in "Old" Nuthall – this being the part of the village on the northern side of the A610 along the B600 heading towards Kimberley. As for "New" Nuthall, this sits the other side of the A610 and includes the late 20th century Mornington Crescent Estate. The latter includes The Old Moor Lodge, while at the eastern end of the parish where Nuthall borders Broxtowe Country Park is the Millers Barn and The Nuthall Inn, with the latter boasting strikingly different, but attractive facades, to the front and rear.

The Nuthall Inn from the front ...

... and from the rear.

Nuthall Church: St Patrick's

The parish church of St Patrick probably dates from around 1100. At that time, the manor of Nuthall belonged to the de Patrice family, but whether they took their name from the church or vice-versa is not known; certainly St Patrick is unusual in England, this being one of only five so-named medieval churches. A certain Galfrid de St Patrico then gave the patronage of the church to Lenton Priory on the latter's founding in 1103, although this was disputed by his grandson in 1200 who claimed it back – asserting that the grant had been obtained by undue influence when his grandfather had been on his deathbed.

The next manorial family were the Cokefields, who held the patronage of St Patrick's for another eight generations and were responsible for rebuilding and extending the church from a simple tower and nave ... before passing it onto the Ayscough (Askew) family who inherited the manor in 1469 and held it until 1612. As for medieval remains today, the lower part of the tower is early 13th century, as is the western doorway, while the heads depicted on the doorway stops are thought to be of King John and Queen Isabella. The church was heavily restored in 1838, though, including most of the tower.

Nuthall Historic Trivia: Anne Askew and Nuthall Temple

In the mid-16th century, Anne Askew's family owned Nuthall Manor. Married at 15, Anne's marriage ended in divorce, largely because of her Protestant beliefs, which eventually led her to London where she gave sermons and distributed Protestant literature – and became friends with the Protestant Catherine Parr, sixth wife of Henry VIII. Alas, she became unwittingly entangled in a court struggle between religious traditionalists and reformers, with the former looking to implicate the Queen. In 1545, Anne was arrested and accused as a heretic, but the Anglican clerics were unable to prove anything during a five-hour examination during which time Anne ably defended herself, and she was therefore released. However, she was then re-arrested in June 1546 by the Lord Mayor of London, and the Constable of the Tower of London was ordered to torture her in an attempt to force her to name others. She was originally shown the rack and asked if she would name those who believed as she did. Anne declined and was thus bound to the rack. Still she would not give up a name, and thus the handles of the rack were eventually turned so hard that

St Patrick's church, Nuthall.

Anne was drawn apart, her shoulders and hips pulled from their sockets and her elbows and knees dislocated. Nevertheless, Anne still refused to give names, and so she was returned to her cell, only to be burnt at the stake at Smithfield, on 16 July 1546, aged just 26. Once again, her suffering was beyond imagination. She was carried to execution in a chair as she could not walk and every movement caused her severe pain. She was then dragged from the chair to the stake which had a small seat attached to it and there she was bound. But because of her non-cooperation, she was burned alive slowly rather than being strangled first or burned quickly. Those who saw her execution were awestruck by her bravery, and reported that she did not scream until the flames reached her chest.

Gate pier from the now-demolished Nuthall Temple and which dates from 1754.

Two centuries on, and Nuthall Temple was built between 1754 and 1757. It was one of four houses built in the UK said to have been inspired by Antonio Palladio's Villa Rotonda in Vicenza, and is today described as one of England's "lost houses". Designed by the architect Thomas Wright for Sir Charles Sedley, it was formed of a square building topped by a dome and entered via a temple-like portico. The temple passed through generations of the Sedley family and then on to the Holden family in 1819, but in the 1920s the Holdens faced high death duties and so sold the estate to a demolition firm. In July 1929 the west wing was set alight and the weakened structure was then pulled down wall by wall. The ruined shell remained until 1966 when this was also pulled down in order to make way for the extension of the M1 motorway. The site of the former house is now under one of the slip roads at Junction 26!

Nuthall Quirky Trivia: Nuthall Temple's Twin

It was mentioned above that Nuthall Temple was one of four estate houses in England modelled on Palladio's Villa Rotonda. One of the others was Chiswick House in West London and, somewhat complementing the Shire-Ode insinuation, it was let out in the late 19th century as a lunatic asylum!

The Old Rectory, Nuthall.

Inset: *Illustration of Nuthall Temple by James Beardmore, 2014, based on early 20th century photographs.*

NAME (STATUS):	**OLD BASFORD** (Suburb)
POPULATION:	16,207 (Basford ward)
DISTRICT:	City of Nottingham
EARLIEST RECORD:	
MEANING AND DERIVATION:	Either "ford belonging to a man called 'Bassa', deriving from the Old English personal name, *Bassa*, plus the Old English word *ford*, or "the lower ford" deriving from the Old French words *le bas ford*. The "Old" affix was assigned in order to distinguish it from adjoining New Basford.

Old Basford Pub: The Fox and Crown

The Fox and Crown, Old Basford, with a mural painted alongside showing a fox, a crown and Robin Hood, Maid Marian and Friar Tuck, with Nottingham Castle in the background.

The White Swan, Old Basford.

Old Basford is home to a number of pubs of which the most handsome is probably the White Swan, although it is the Fox and Crown which offers the most trivia. The pub is located where early 18th century records position an inn, a gaol and a bowling green, with the Fox and Crown seemingly synonymous with the bowling green (or perhaps a pub called the Bowling Green), as both names occur at different times on old documents referring to the same site. Furthermore, an old record at nearby St Leodegarius Church states that the Fox and Crown is reputedly haunted by a gentleman wearing a tricorn hat – perhaps a town crier – although if that is the case, the gentleman is uncharacteristically silent! As for the pub name, the Fox and Crown is quite unusual; there are many named the Fox and Hounds on the one hand, or the Rose and Crown on the other, but rarely the Fox and Crown – although it seems to be predominantly a Nottinghamshire thing with further pubs of the same name at Newark and Sutton-in-Ashfield, while another existed on Alfred Street in Nottingham until 1953.

Old Basford Church: St Leodegarius

St Leodegarius' church, Old Basford.

One of only four churches in England called St Leodegarius, the church is Grade II listed and has a chancel which dates back to the 1180s – although it is thought that there are Saxon stones hidden in the chancel walls. The previous Norman church possessed a typical Norman arch between nave and Norman tower, but this version of the church was rebuilt in around 1200 with new nave arcades. The south arcade was then added in c.1250 and the south aisle and porch around 1340 along with a Lady Chapel, while the nave walls were raised in the late 14th century and a clerestory added. An unusual feature, the Pax or kissing stone was also in use from c.1250 – and which is now fixed in the south doorway. However the church was heavily restored and parts rebuilt by Arthur Wilson between 1858 and 1859. Unfortunately, just before it re-opened, the tower collapsed and the church was further rebuilt, this time by Thomas Allom; records don't explain why Arthur Wilson wasn't re-hired! Nevertheless, the new tower was re-built in Early English style and crowned with eight tall pinnacles. Other alterations carried out between 1859 and 1860 led to a sharply pitched roof, along with a new north aisle, north porch and clerestory. However, a fire ruined the chancel once more in 1900 and it had to be repaired yet again, while fire beset the church again in 1974 – although this time, it was down to some mindless vandal who set fire to the organ and organ screen. The churchyard is also home to a Grade II listed 17th century chest-tomb.

Old Basford Historic Trivia: Peverel Gaol and Shipstones Ales

Some historians suggest that Old Basford is the precise location of Barnsdale, Robin Hood's home; certainly, Sherwood Forest did once extend as far south as the Basford area of Nottingham, so you never know! The chances are that, if he'd ever been caught, Robin would have ended up in Old Basford's Peverel Gaol, an institution founded by William Peverel, alleged illegitimate son of William the Conqueror and owner of 170 Nottinghamshire towns and villages as well as Nottingham Castle. That said, Peverel Gaol was actually a Court of Pleas for the recovery of small debts and for damages in case of trespass with its jurisdiction extending over the entirety of Peverel's Nottinghamshire manors.

Peverel Gaol then turns up again in the 18th century for a piece of historic trivia that takes us back to the Fox and Crown and this alleged bowling green that occupied the same site. The best evidence comes from a Will and Inventory, dated 1707. It belonged to Innkeeper James Pearson, who also appears to have been a butcher and a gaoler, too – the gaol being Peverel Gaol. But Pearson is also said to have kept a bowling green which was "waited upon" by the prisoners – thereby suggesting that their confinement was about as rigorous as those confined at Lenton's White Hart (see page 111) – and which also, intriguingly, had an area that doubled up as the Peverel Prison, and which also had a bowling green ... and which also let out their prisoners to act as waiters! Now you might be forgiven for thinking that there's a bit of a common theme here – i.e. pubs doubling up as gaols and trebling up as bowling greens. But actually, despite the three mile difference between Old Basford and Lenton, they are actually the same institution. For in 1791, the Old Basford gaoler, John Sands, had allowed all of the prisoners to escape because he was no longer able to feed them and because if any of them died of starvation, he was likely to be tried as a murderer. As a result, the Court of Peverel was moved to Lenton, alongside the White Hart – although it was eventually abolished in 1849 by an Act of Parliament.

As a brief aside, the former villages of both Lenton and Old Basford were absorbed into Nottingham in 1877. By this stage, coal mining had become a focus of the Old Basford area, with a 666ft deep mine having been sunk at Cinderhill in 1841 by the Duke of Newcastle. Given the depth of the mine and the super-

OLD BASFORD BREWING: PAST AND PRESENT

The Basford Maltings, once home to a thriving brewery industry in Old Basford, but now converted into modern student accommodation owned by Nottingham Trent University.
Inset (right): *Across the road from the Basford Maltings is this impressive 19th century building, once the home of Prince of Wales Brewery. However, since 1919, it has been home to Murphy & Son Ltd, who still manufactures brewing supplies and equipment here today.*

stitions of the age, one wonders if miners were reluctant to descend to such depths!

Finally, we have already covered the demise of long-established brewing companies in the Arnold, Kimberley and Mansfield sections. Alas, the same sad story can be applied to Old Basford, as it was also home to three breweries over the years, of which the most famous was Shipstones. Founded in 1852 and owning 550 licensed premises by 1939, the brewery was purchased by Greenall's of Warrington in 1978. But despite becoming the main shirt sponsor of Nottingham Forest in 1987, with shirts graced by such legends as Messrs Pearce, Clough and Webb, Greenall's announced in 1990 that they were ending all beer production and becoming a retailer-only company. Production at Shipstones Brewery thus ended in early 1991 after 139 years.

One brewery-related business that has survived in Old Basford, though, is Murphy & Son Ltd, and who still manufacture brewing supplies and equipment today. The firm was founded in 1887 by Albert John Murphy and by the early 1900s the company was developing leading edge liquor treatments along with cask lining material. Also a founder member of the Brewer's Guild, the firm moved to their current impressive premises on Alpine Street in 1919, and which became a Grade II listed site in 1986. The 1920s and 1930s saw the company expand into chemicals, preservatives and yeast foods while the late 20th century saw the company go from strength to strength when local brewing industries were folding around them.

Old Basford Quirk Alert: A Cruel Duel

Remarkably, we are now going to return to the Fox and Crown for a *third* time. This is because in 1806, the pub was the scene of a quarrel between 17 year-old Lieutenant Browne of the 83rd Regiment, and Ensign Butler of the 36th, and which ended up being settled by a duel. Sadly, Lieutenant Browne was fatally wounded in the duel after which his body was removed to St Leodegarius Church in Old Basford, and later interred at St Mary's churchyard in Nottingham. Interestingly, the coroner's jury returned a verdict of wilful murder against Butler and his seconds, all of whom absconded.

The Nottingham Tram system passes right through Old Basford, with the tram station in the background.

A great idea in action outside the Old Basford Primary & Nursery School, designed to make drivers think twice about speeding.

NAME (STATUS):	**OLDCOTES** (Village)
POPULATION:	684 (Styrrup with Oldcotes parish)
DISTRICT:	Bassetlaw
EARLIEST RECORD:	*Aldcotes*, 1804; *Oldcoats*, 1809; *Oldcotes*, 1840
MEANING	Place at the old cottages
DERIVATION:	From the Old English words *ald* (old) and *cot* (cottage, hut or shelter)

Oldcotes Pub and Church: King William IV and St Mark's

The King William IV is the only pub in Oldcotes and is situated at the crossroads of the A60 and the A634. Diagonally opposite is St Mark's church. This Grade II listed building is relatively recent, having been built of brick and timber in 1900 by the local architect Charles Hodgson Fowler. Today, the brickwork has been rendered pristine white, lending the church the appearance of a very attractive Tudor-built edifice; in fact, with its tall brick chimney which rises from the clay tile roof on the north side of the building, at first glance it resembles a large family home more than a church! The only slight giveaways are the bell in a turret on the west gable, with pyramidal cap and cross, and the one diamond-shaped stained glass window at the apex of the east gable. However, internally, the church consists of a nave, two steps up to the chancel, a north-west porch and a north-east vestry.

Oldcotes Historic Trivia: Roman Villas and Hermeston Hall

The earliest evidence of settlement at Oldcotes is courtesy of a Roman villa that was discovered under the church, and on what was a recognised Roman road. However, Oldcotes doesn't appear on John Speed's 1610 map of Nottinghamshire or his later map of 1646. Furthermore, the place isn't deemed significant enough to appear on 18th century maps either. However, it does appear on Charles Smith's map of 1804, but still sporting its Old English derivation of *Aldcotes*. The first occurrence of the modern name *Oldcotes* appears on Archibald Fullarton's map of 1840 – although spellings

St Mark's church, Oldcotes.

King William IV, Oldcotes.

of *Old Coats* and *Oldcoats* appear on later 19th century maps.

At the southern end of Oldcotes is Hermeston Hall, and which is situated on the site of a previous 12th century manor house built for the Cress family who lived there until 1408. In the 16th century, Bess of Hardwick was known to have connections with the property, but from the mid-17th century, it fell into decline despite being under the ownership of the Mellish family from 1765. However, today's hall was built in 1848 by Edward Challoner, a timber importer from Old Swan, Liverpool, while Challoner's daughter, Catherine, added another two wings.

Wayside Water Gardens is located in Oldcotes and specialises in pond supplies, water lilies and other pond plants, as well as tropical fish and "outdoor" fish such as Koi Carp.

Oldcotes Quirk Alert: Most Haunted

Hermeston Hall is also famous for its paranormal activity and reported ghostly goings-on. Most famous of the many spectres is a woman with red hair and black Elizabethan clothing resembling Bess of Hardwick, and who is said to haunt the grounds, while ghostly Roman soldiers have allegedly been spotted marching along the driveway. Inside the house, the Bishop's Room is thought to be haunted by a lady in white and an evil bishop, while a malevolent spirit is thought to haunt the attic. Other phantoms include Victorian children and servants who tend to stick to the corridors and the dining room, whilst the latter along with the billiard room has been the location of low voices, the smell of tobacco and a sense of being watched. Then there is the ghost of a little boy playing the piano, a child's handprint on the window in the Chinese room, and the sound of screaming children. Needless to say, therefore, that the hall *has* been investigated by paranormal investigators who have caught unexplained orbs and red mists on camera and experienced unusually high EMF readings, while the television programme, *Most Haunted*, also visited the hall naming it "The Ghost House".

Hermeston Hall, Oldcotes – the location of an episode of Most Haunted!

NAME (STATUS):	**PLUMTREE** (Village)
POPULATION:	246
DISTRICT:	Rushcliffe
EARLIEST RECORD:	*Pluntre*, 1086 (Domesday Book)
MEANING:	Place at the plum-tree
DERIVATION:	From the Old English word *plūm-trēow* (plum-tree)
FAMOUS RESIDENTS:	**Edward Hagarty Parry** (1855-1931), footballer and captain of Old Carthusians when they won the FA Cup in 1881, is buried in the graveyard of St Mary the Virgin, Plumtree

Plumtree Church: St Mary the Virgin

It is thought that the church of St Mary the Virgin at Plumtree dates back to the 9th century, making parts of it the oldest in the county. However, the current church was heavily restored in the 19th century between 1873 and 1874 by George Frederick Bodley and Thomas Garner. In 1889, its 1686 clock was also replaced, while the Norman tower was rebuilt in 1906 by P.H. Currey. This latter rebuild was when the Saxon work was discovered, with the pulling down of the north wall revealing that the Norman tower had been built up against an earlier Saxon wall, with its herringbone course of stones constructed with a more durable mortar than its later Norman replacement. Add the aforementioned rebuilds to the fact that the chancel had already been restored once before in the 15th century, that the gallery was enlarged in 1818, and that some of the 19th century work was further restored in the 1980s, and this perhaps explains why the building is only Grade II listed today. Other than the Saxon remains, the other oldest element is the Norman arch between nave and tower, the 13th century tower arcading and the ancient sedilia and piscina, while the nave is also 13th century and the clerestory late 15th. Finally, inside the church is a painting known as "The Descent from the Cross", and which is a replica of the same painting by Rubens that graces Antwerp Cathedral; it was presented to the church in the 19th century by a former rector, the Reverend William Burnside.

Built in 1843 on the site of a former coaching inn known as The Plough, the Griffin Inn is Plumtree's only pub.

Plumtree Historic Trivia: Plumtres and Perkinses

The prominent Nottingham-associated Plumtree family are thought to originate from the *village* of Plumtree, and are probably descended from the medieval Plumtre family – one of whom was cited in a lawsuit during the reign of Edward I. However, the manor of Plumtree was actually held in medieval times and for several centuries after that by the Hastings family, thanks to holding the office of Chief Steward to the Crown. Meanwhile, Plumtree Cricket Club dates from around 1815 and still has a traditional village cricket ground located at the western end of the village. Then there is the award-winning Perkins Restaurant and

St Mary the Virgin church, Plumtree.

Carriage Hall, Plumtree.

Plumtree Cricket Club in action. The club was founded in around 1815.

their clever utilisation of the former Plumtree railway station building, which sits alongside an events venue known as Carriage Hall. The railway station was a victim of the Beeching Axe in the early 1960s, and stood empty until Tony and Wendy Perkins bought it off British Rail in 1982 and initially converted it into Perkins' Bistro which went onto become renowned as one of Nottinghamshire's leading restaurants.

The crossroads in Plumtree.

The former Plumtree railway station and now Perkins Restaurant.

Plumtree Quirk Alert: Ignorance and Old Trent Bridge

Back in the early reign of Charles I, two men, two women and two children were charged with religious ignorance by the rector of Plumtree. They were also charged with refusal to attend church! It would appear that the charges didn't result in any action, though; merely a warning and therefore suggesting that the offenders eventually saw the error of their ways. Meanwhile, some of the stonework on the north side of the nave of St Mary the Virgin, includes stone taken from the Old Trent Bridge and was incorporated during the restoration work carried out in 1873.

NAME (STATUS):	**RAINWORTH** (Village)
POPULATION:	7,693
DISTRICT:	Newark and Sherwood; Mansfield
EARLIEST RECORD:	*Reynwath* 1268
MEANING:	Either "clean ford or boundary ford", or "Regehere's ford"
DERIVATION:	From the Old Scandinavian words *hreinn* or *rein* (clean or boundary) and *vath* (ford), or from the Old English personal name, *Regehere*, plus *vath*

Rainworth Geographic Trivia: Divided Loyalties

Rainworth is highly unusual in that it is split between two districts: Newark and Sherwood to the east and Mansfield to the west, with the border located near to the bridge over Rainworth Water on Southwell Road East. The census of 2011 revealed that the population for the civil parish of Rainworth in Newark and Sherwood was 6,315, while the Mansfield portion of Rainworth was counted at 1,378. Of the two, the Newark and Sherwood part of Rainworth is a parish in its own right while the Mansfield part is unparished and part of the Ransom Wood Ward.

Rainworth Pub: The Archer

The Archer is located at the southern end of the village, and The Lurcher is at the eastern edge. Meanwhile in the centre, the former Robin Hood Inn has been converted into a Tesco store, leaving no trace of the former pub logo or the Mansfield Bitter logo that used to grace its frontage.

Rainworth Church: St Simon and St Jude

The parish church of Rainworth is St Simon and St Jude, so-named because it opened on the 28th October – the festival day of St Simon and St Jude. The year was 1939, so the church opened in somewhat sombre circumstances, a month after the start of World War II, although the foundation stone was laid in slightly happier times on the 23 July 1938. This relatively new church replaced a wooden predecessor, itself not that old having been constructed in 1890. The architect of the new brick-built church was the Nottingham architect C. E. Howitt, and consists of an organ chamber and choir and clergy vestries on the north side, a small chapel and bell turret on the south side, and a porch in the south west corner. The western end of the church is dominated by a large window, while an upper room was built into the west end of the roof as the new parish hall in 1973. As for the eastern end of the church, this accommodates a large cross rather than an east window.

Rainworth Historic Trivia: Ancient Battles and Recent Coal

The Rainworth place-name meaning and derivation above, offers two theories, and the most historically interesting of the two is that the name derives from Regehere's Ford. It is thought that the sheltered location and access to clean water at what is now called Rainworth Water, meant that the area was often used by travellers for overnight stops, including the Romans who passed this way between Mansfield, Newark and Lincoln (*Lindum*) and set up a camp here. As already mentioned in the *Eaton* section, it is thought that the village of Eaton pinpoints the site of the famous Battle of the River Idle in 616, fought between the East Angles under Rædwald and the Northumbrians under Æthelfrith. But another proposed site of the battle is near to what is now known as Rainworth Bogs off Pit Lane, with Regehere, who was thought to be Rædwald's son, having been killed here in battle; allegedly from that day onwards the area became known as Regehere`s Wath – with *wath* being the Old

The Archer, Rainworth.

St Simon and St Jude's church, Rainworth.

English word for a ford or crossing point over a river – and similar to the later Old Scandinavian *vath*, meaning the same thing.

Moving forward to 1190, and this was the year that Rainworth Lodge was first built. It is thought that a certain forester called Rufus Clarke lived there in 1212 and regularly accompanied King John on his hunts in Sherwood Forest. A later Rainworth Lodge was the home of the famous 19th century ornithologist Joseph Whitaker, after whom the village's secondary school is named.

By the 16th century, recorded dwellings in Rainworth included Three Thorn Hollow Farm, the original Robin Hood Inn (then named the Sherwood Inn), and the Toll House – which was subsequently nicknamed The Inkpot due to its angled design.

Moving forward to 1911, and two mineshafts were sunk at Rufford Colliery. Alas, it was only two years further on before the mine suffered its first and worst disaster, when 14 men were killed in an accident. Of course, as the pit prospered, so the population of Rainworth began to grow, and new housing sprung up, first on Southwell Road and which became known as White City due to the houses being white-washed half way up on the instruction of the Mayor of Mansfield, as he feared that the bare brickwork would offend passing dignitaries! These houses were followed by more along Kirklington Road with the Colliery providing housing for around 400 families. The village's first school, Heathlands, was also built in 1914, followed by Python Hill School in 1924, while the Colliery also provided shops, a village green, and leisure facilities such as a football ground and lido, along with the Miners Welfare. Alas, Rainworth Colliery was closed in 1993, thus suffering the same fate as most other Nottinghamshire pits in the late 20th century.

Rainworth Quirk Alert: The Black Panther and the Tree of Knowledge

The Black Panther in question isn't the usual "stray cat escaped from a zoo" story, but notorious serial killer Donald Neilson. The police got an unexpected break in December 1975, when two officers were in a Panda car in the Rainworth area, and spotted a man with a holdall who averted his face as he passed the car. As a matter of routine, they went to question him – at which point Neilson produced a sawn-off shotgun from the holdall. He forced one officer into the back of the panda car, and jammed his gun under the armpit of the driver, ordering him to drive to Blidworth. Later evidence revealed that as they were driving along Southwell Road in Rainworth, Neilson asked if they had any rope. It was at this point that the driver reached a junction in the road. Turning the steering wheel violently one way then the other, he asked "which way?" causing the gunman to look at the road ahead. With Neilson's attention distracted, the policeman in the back pushed the gun forwards and the driver stamped on the brake. The panda car screeched to a halt outside the Junction Chip Shop in Rainworth. The gun went off, grazing one policeman's hand while the other dived out of the car and sought help from the chippie – at which point, two men ran from the queue and helped overpower Neilson; in fact, the locals attacked him so severely that in the end the police had to protect him! They then handcuffed Neilson to some handy iron railings and called for backup – before discovering two Panther hoods on him, and thus realising that they'd just caught Britain's most wanted man!

In 1879 an elm tree was planted on the village green in front of the Robin Hood Inn. Because it became a favourite place for people to meet and talk, it eventually earned the moniker of "The Tree of Knowledge"; certainly, the miners would meet there to discuss union matters. Alas, by 1962, the tree was held up with iron bars and as it was deemed to be dangerous, it was cut down. However, the remaining stump began to grow again, but by the 1970s, it became a bone of contention at Parish Council Meetings; a road improvement scheme had been proposed by the County Council meaning that the tree had to be cut down again as it was deemed to be a hazard to traffic. This was vehemently opposed by conservationists, but their argument was shot down in flames when a tree surgeon confirmed that the tree had Dutch Elm Disease. The tree was therefore cut down and removed … but many locals believed that the Dutch Elm Disease story was simply a ploy by the Council to get their own way!

The Junction Chip Shop where notorious serial killer Donald Neilson was overpowered by both police and public in December 1975.

The River Ryton at Scofton

Name (Status):	**RYTON** (River)
District:	Bassetlaw
Length:	21 miles
Source:	Lindrick Common
Source Elevation:	200ft
Mouth:	River Idle, Bawtry
Mouth Elevation:	9.8ft
Meaning:	Probably farmstead on the River Rye
Derivation:	From the Celtic river-name, probably meaning "stream", plus the Old English word *tūn* (farmstead) – although a document from 958 actually refers to the Ryton as the River Blithe!

River Ryton Geographic Trivia: From Lindrick Common to the River Idle

The source of the River Ryton is just over the border in South Yorkshire, at the western edge of Lindrick Common, and is formed by the confluence of the Anston Brook from the west and Pudding Dyke from the south. After flowing variously eastwards and southwards, it crosses the Nottinghamshire border near to Shireoaks, where the former pit village hosts both the Ryton and the Chesterfield Canal. It is also near to here that the Ryton passes underneath the Sheffield to Lincoln railway line and through a three-arched aqueduct below the Chesterfield Canal. It then loops around the former mining village of Rhodesia (named after G. Preston Rhodes, long-time chairman of nearby Shireoaks Colliery), before passing underneath the A57 to arrive on the western edge of Worksop. However, the course of the Ryton through Worksop is largely man-made, having been diverted in places in the 19th century, and then culverted as it passes under a shopping complex and the shops of Bridge Street. Towards the south-east of Worksop, the Ryton passes once again under the Chesterfield Canal through a three-arched aqueduct, after which the river and canal run in parallel until they pass through separate arches of a nine-arched viaduct which once again carries the Sheffield to Lincoln railway line. Both water courses then pass through the estate of Osberton Hall and the village of Scofton in a north-easterly direction, before turning north to the west of Ranby at Chequer Bridge. Shortly after here, the Ryton heads off in a north-westerly direction and the Chesterfield Canal carries on eastwards to Retford.

No, you're not hallucinating. This is Rhodesia, a mile west of Worksop!

The River Ryton eventually flows past Bilby and then under the B6045 at Hodsock Red Bridge, beyond which an early 19th-century Grade II listed twin-arched bridge carries the drive of Hodsock Priory over the river. Passing to the east of Hodsock and then to the west of Blyth, the Ryton passes under the A634, with this Grade I listed bridge consisting of three arches. It was built for William Mellish of Blyth Hall around 1770 and probably by the architect and bridge designer John Carr of York. Despite being nearly 250 years old, it is actually called Blyth New Bridge, to distinguish it from Blyth Old Bridge which carries the same road over Oldcotes Dyke, a little further to the west. As for Oldcotes Dyke, this watercourse flows eastwards from Roche Abbey and joins the Ryton half a mile north-east of Blyth New Bridge. From

The River Ryton flows under the Grade I listed Blyth New Bridge, which takes the A634 over the river just to the west of Blyth.

Hodsock Red Bridge, with its three red brick-built arches, takes the B6045 over the River Ryton near to Hodsock.

this point to the River Idle, drainage of the surrounding flood plain is managed by the Rivers Idle and Ryton Internal Drainage Board courtesy of a network of drainage channels. In the meantime, though, the Ryton passes under the A1 before meandering around Serlby and Scrooby. To the north of Scrooby, the river passes under the A638 Great North Road, the road into Scrooby village and the East Coast Main Line railway. The river used to flow through Scrooby, and powered an 18th-century corn mill, but milling stopped in 1939, and the river was diverted in the 1960s to follow its present course further to the north. Beyond the railway, flood banks have been raised on both sides of the Ryton until it finally flows into the River Idle a mile south-east of Bawtry.

The River Ryton between Scofton and Ranby.

The River Ryton from Mill Lane, Scrooby.

River Ryton Historic Trivia: More Mills and Some Stolen Goods

Like the Maun in Mansfield and the Idle in Retford, the River Ryton was used for centuries to power mills in Worksop. Three water mills were mentioned in a survey carried out in 1636, including the Priory Mill and the Bracebridge Mill, while by 1826, a new water mill known as Beard's Mill existed, named after its owner, Joseph Beard. The latter mill survived until 1985 when it was demolished to make way for the Worksop bypass. Meanwhile, the Priory Mill survived into the 19th century, and a large lake called the Canch was formed in 1820, by constructing a dam across the leat (millstream) which fed it. The Priory Mill eventually ceased milling in 1876, but the buildings continued to be utilised by William Bramer and Sons for their chair-making business until the buildings suffered from a disastrous fire in 1912.

As well as being culverted in Worksop, the Ryton's general flow has been deliberately altered in places, too. It originally flowed much nearer to Castle Hill, perhaps forming part of the former castle's defences, but was then diverted in 1842 into a channel further north when the 4th Duke of Newcastle constructed Newcastle Street as part of the town's development. As for those culverted portions of Worksop, these were surveyed in 2007 and a number of interesting items were found, including five tons of debris, half a ton of steel and some stolen goods!

Ryton Quirk Alert: A Millpond Never Forgets

The millpond belonging to Worksop's Beard Mill saw plenty of unusual activity in its time. It was certainly used as a skating rink in winter, and for fishing at other times of the year, but it was also used at varying times for the launching of a lifeboat ... and for the bathing of elephants when travelling circuses visited the town!

Ryton Environmental Trivia: Aquifers and Trout

The water quality of the Ryton is classed as moderate, thanks to a considerable proportion of the total flow being supplied by the processed water from sewage treatment works. This means that the river supports significant populations of fish and is hence a regular location for organised angling. As for the geology of the river, it is underlain by a water-bearing porous rock structure called the Magnesian Limestone aquifer; the Triassic Sherwood Sandstone aquifer is another porous rock layer which comes into play towards the eastern reaches of the river. Where these aquifers reach the surface, they often supply water to the river system, but can also take water from it. As for feeders to the Ryton, these include the Anston Brook, the Pudding Dyke, the Bondhay Dyke, and to a lesser extent the Broadbridge Dyke, with the latter having a significant amount diverted in order to form the reservoirs at Pebley and Harthill which, in turn, supply the Chesterfield Canal. As well as the outflows from various sewage treatment works, excess flow from the canal at Manton also tops up the river. As for the General Quality Assessment rating for the Ryton in terms of water quality, that is rated as a "B" for the Upper Ryton (on a scale of A to F), while Oldcotes Dyke registers a "C". Wild brown trout therefore thrive as far downstream as Worksop, while some trout and various types of cyprinids inhabit the water below Worksop.

NAME (STATUS):	**SCOFTON** (Village)
POPULATION:	c.30
DISTRICT:	Bassetlaw
EARLIEST RECORD:	*Scotebi*, 1086 (Domesday Book)
MEANING:	Farmstead or settlement of the Scots
DERIVATION:	From the Old Scandinavian words *Skoti* (Scot) and *bý* (farmstead, village or settlement); the Anglo-Saxon *tūn* was clearly reinstated at a later date

Scofton Geographic Trivia: Access by Ford

Scofton is a tiny, private village that is located about three miles east of Worksop. It is located on the Osberton Estate, and is therefore not easily accessible by road; indeed, those roads that do access the village do so by ford over the River Ryton, although the main approach does sport a bridge, too! As well as the fords that lend access to Scofton, there are also a number of others across the Ryton on the 4,000 acre Osberton Estate, such as those at Bilby and Hodsock. Besides the church, Scofton also contains the kitchen gardens of Osberton Hall, together with part of the pleasure grounds, the head keeper's residence, the schools, and a number of cottages, while the Chesterfield Canal also passes just to the south of the village.

Scofton Church: St John the Evangelist

The main feature of the village is the parish church of St John the Evangelist which was built in 1833 by architect Ambrose Poynter as a family church for the landowning Foljambe family who owned and ran the estate from Osberton Hall. The church was specifically built as a private chapel by heartbroken George Savile Foljambe as a memorial to his wife, Harriet, who died giving birth to their son. The church architecture reflects the then popular Norman Revival style, including a three-stage Normanesque tower with a west doorway over which were sculpted standard Norman mouldings. Interestingly, a church is recorded on the Osberton Estate as long ago as the Domesday Book of 1086, although it is unclear whether this church lay on the site of the present building at Scofton or elsewhere on the estate; in turn, the church was built on, or near, to the site of the long-since demolished Scofton Hall, which had been the manor house on Scofton Manor to the north of Osberton Manor. St John the Evangelist was created a parish in 1876, while nearly a century later in 1970, it was restored and sympathetically modernised internally, while the churchyard was also re-landscaped.

Scofton Historic Trivia: Jessop, Banks and Sutton

Geographically, Scofton is separated from Osberton by the River Ryton. In the 16th and 17th centuries, both were owned by the Jessops, a family who hailed from Broomhall in Sheffield. One of the Jessops who resided at Scofton was Wortley Jessop; this we know thanks to his will, written in 1615, and which was proved before the Steward of the Manor of Mansfield. Alas, Wortley died before his father, having been lost at sea following a crossing to Ireland in 1617. After the Jessops, Scofton came into possession of Joseph Banks, an eminent Sheffield attorney, and agent to the Dukes of Norfolk, Leeds, and Newcastle. Banks soon acquired a large fortune, while he also sat in one parliament for Grimsby, and in another for Totnes. As well as Scofton, the Banks family also owned a large property at Reevesby Abbey, in Lincolnshire. A later Sir Joseph Banks (1695-1741) became the long-time president of the Royal Society and his son, William Banks, was another M.P. He was also the father of Sir Joseph Banks (1743-1820), the eminent botanist who took part in Captain James Cook's first great voyage and after

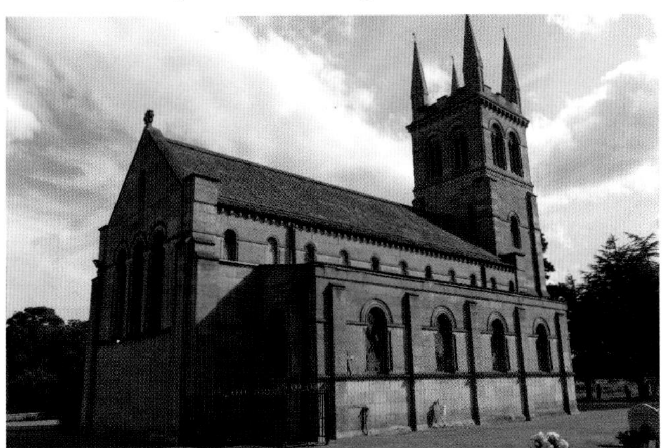

St John the Evangelist church, Scofton, seen from the north-east and the south-west.

whom the Banks Islands in modern-day Vanuatu is named as well as the Banks Peninsula in New Zealand, the Banks Strait between Tasmania and the Furneaux Islands, and Banks Island in Northwest Territories, Canada. Back to Scofton, though, and the Banks family passed ownership onto the Sutton family, when the estate was purchased by Brigadier Richard Sutton – although due to a delay in the acquisition, and being an officer in command of a number of troops, he promptly dispatched them to take and occupy the Hall! Eventually Major-General Sutton (as he was to become), died in August, 1737, and was succeeded by his eldest son Robert, whose grandson, Robert William Evelyn Sutton sold the estate to the Foljambes.

Finally, Scofton was also once close to RAF Worksop, which was also known as Scofton Airfield. It was opened in 1943 as a bomber airfield but was never used for its intended purpose. However, it did accommodate 54 Vickers Wellingtons and 4 Hurricanes from nearby RAF Finningley – and which is now Doncaster (Robin Hood) airport. It was home to RAF No. 18 Operational Training Unit between 1943 and 1945, and various other units after that, culminating in RAF Squadron No 616 between 1955 and 1957. The squadron was disbanded in March 1957 and the airfield became redundant. Today, there is little remaining of the former airfield and it is mostly used for farming!

Scofton Quirk Alert: Moving to the Other Side and Fancy Dress

Where canal towpaths were concerned, it was obviously convenient when they stayed on one side of a canal. However, one example of a towpath changing sides is the Chesterfield Canal on its approach to Osberton Hall from the south-west. Here, it initially runs alongside the north side of the canal, but the resident Foljambes objected to boatmen passing too close to their residence, and hence a few yards before Osberton Hall comes into view, the towpath is moved to the south side of the canal. As for the towpath today, it is part of the Cuckoo Way, which runs alongside the Chesterfield Canal for 46 miles from Chesterfield to West Stockwith.

Finally, Scofton is home to an annual dog show which attracts hundreds of dogs each year – some of whom come along with their owners, too! Held at Osberton Mill, the show runs both pedigree and novelty classes, with the latter including an obstacle course ... and fancy dress.

The ford on the approach to Scofton – although vehicles tend to take the bridge, just visible on the left of the photograph!

Scofton Village Hall.

The Chesterfield Canal, a few yards south of Scofton.

Osberton Lock on the Chesterfield Canal, at the southern tip of Scofton.

NAME (STATUS):	**SCROOBY** (Village)
POPULATION:	315
DISTRICT:	Bassetlaw
EARLIEST RECORD:	*Scroppenthorpe*, 958; *Scrobi*, 1086 (Domesday Book)
MEANING:	Farmstead of a man called Skropi
DERIVATION:	From the Old Scandinavian personal name, *Skropi*, plus initially the Old Scandinavian word *thorp* (secondary settlement, dependent outlying farmstead or hamlet), and then later the Old Scandinavian word *bý* (farmstead, village or settlement)
FAMOUS RESIDENTS:	**William Brewster** (1566-1644), elder of the Pilgrim Fathers

Scrooby Pub: The Pilgrim Fathers

The pub known as The Pilgrim Fathers lies just off the A638 at Scrooby, and is named after the pioneer settlers of the same name who sailed for North America on the *Mayflower* in 1620 and became founders of the Plymouth colony in New England. It is particularly pertinent to the village of Scrooby, because one of their elders was William Brewster, probably born around 1567 in the village to a father who lived at Scrooby Manor and from 1575 held the position of Bailiff of the Archbishop of York's estates (at Scrooby) and Master of the Queen's Posts. William Brewster Jr. went on to study at Cambridge, and around 1583 entered the service of William Davison, Secretary of State to Queen Elizabeth I, and her representative in the Netherlands in 1585. However, around 1588 Brewster seems to have arrived back in Scrooby, where he assisted his father until the latter's death in 1590, after which Brewster eventually succeeded him as Master of the Queen's Posts, as well as bailiff and receiver at Scrooby. Then in 1606 Brewster appears to have become a member of the Gainsborough Separatist Church – an organisation of devout Christians who did not support some of the fundamental principles of the Established Church, such as a hierarchy of archbishops and bishops and the wearing of clerical vestments. When their leader, John Smyth, was obliged to depart for Holland (Separatists were not popular with either Church or State), Brewster's Scrooby Manor House became the secret meeting place for the group, and he became their new leader. However, discovery was inevitable, and as a result, on 30 September 1607 Brewster resigned his position as bailiff and postmaster at Scrooby and became outlawed for his Separatist views. After a period of imprisonment at Boston with other leading members of the Scrooby Church, Brewster eventually reached Amsterdam in 1608 and re-joined John Smyth's church. In the following year Brewster left Amsterdam with other members of the Scrooby Church and settled in Leyden, ultimately ending up on the *Mayflower* in 1620. Of course, this makes William Brewster the ancestor of thousands of Americans and accounts for why so many visit the village each year on ancestry-themed holidays – effectively making Scrooby a place of pilgrimage!

The Pilgrim Fathers, Scrooby, named after the famous North American settlers of 1620. One of their leaders/elders was William Brewster of Scrooby.

St Wilfrid's church, Scrooby, noted for its octagonal spire.

As for the pub, a date-stone on the gable bears the date 1771, suggesting that the inn was built to cater for travellers on the 1766 turnpike road. It was originally known as The Saracens Head, but was changed to its present name in 1969.

Scrooby Church: St Wilfrid's

The Grade II listed St Wilfrid's church was built in the 14th and 15th centuries, although there are references to a church in Scrooby as far back as 1177-81, and which was a Chapel-of-Ease to Sutton. Two hundred years later, in 1380, the predecessor church was destroyed and the current one rebuilt in the Perpendicular Gothic style that was so popular between 1350 and 1530 – although the current incarnation was heavily restored in both 1830 and 1864, the latter by C. J. Neale. The church is noted for its octagonal spire which rises from a square, magnesium limestone-built tower. However, the steeple top is actually a replacement, with two halves of the original steeple top accommodated in two graveyard walls. The replacement may date from 1817 or from 1831 when the steeple was damaged by lightning. The angles of the tower's upper stage are also chamfered, while four tall crocketed pinnacles adorn the tower's crenelated parapet. Unusually, a west door in the tower is missing – a feature also absent from several other local churches – while the stone roof on the south porch is also an unusual feature, albeit once again found in other Nottinghamshire churches, too.

Inside the church the arches and octagonal piers are contemporary with the exterior structure, and the chancel arch is also Early English Gothic in style – although the latter was actually rebuilt as part of the 1864 restoration. The three bells are older though, dating from 1611, 1649 and 1787, respectively, while the west window and that in the tower are almost certainly 1380 originals; the east window is 15th century. As for the church pews and the ancient church font, they were sold to America in 1891 – this due to the connections to the Pilgrim Fathers; as already stated above, Scrooby harboured a Separatist Puritan group in the early 17th century, led by William Brewster who was originally a ruling elder who worshipped in Scrooby Church. Indeed, some of the 16th century benches in the chancel were retained in 1891, one of which is still known as Brewster's Pew.

Scrooby Historic Trivia: Scrooby Manor House and the Pilgrim Fathers Revisited

A 1997 excavation at Scrooby Top turned up Romano-British pottery, coins and jewellery from the first to the third centuries. However, the first *recorded* history of Scrooby (as *Scroppenthorpe*), comes from 958, when King Edgar granted the large estates of Scrooby and Sutton, each of which contained several villages, to Oscytel, Archbishop of York – and the Archbishops continued to exert a major influence over the estate until the 17th century.

Until 1766, Scrooby was actually on the Great North Road and thus became a resting place for numerous famous people, including King Henry VIII, Queen Elizabeth I and Cardinal Wolsey. Indeed, Wolsey also stayed at Scrooby Manor House throughout September 1530, after his fall from favour – a house which still belonged to the Archbishops of York at that time. The earliest reference to a building on the site, though, comes from 1207, when King John ordered wine to be sent there for the use of his half-brother – who also happened to be the Archbishop; King John himself visited in 1212. The eldest daughter of Henry VII, Margaret, also stayed at Scrooby in 1503 on her way to Scotland to become the second wife of James IV, while it was also at around this time that the earliest brick buildings were built, fragments of which can still be seen incorporated into Manor Farm. Then in around 1538, Henry VIIIs historian, John Leland, visited

Low Road, Scrooby. Inset: *The timber-framed Old Vicarage is the only house left in Scrooby that dates from the Pilgrim Fathers era.*

Scrooby and described the manor house as "a great manor place, standing within a moat, built in two courts". King Henry VIII himself then stayed at Scrooby overnight and held Privy Council here in 1541.

At the end of the 16th century, Scrooby Manor House was occupied by the aforementioned Brewsters, father and son of whom were the Archbishop's bailiff, and royal post-master – and thus responsible for the safe accommodation of Crown messengers journeying along the main road from London to Scotland. Of course, William Brewster Jr went on to form a Separatist Church in Scrooby before becoming a leading member of the Pilgrim Fathers. But one element we haven't touched on so far, is the manner of Brewster and his followers' departure for Holland. Outlawed for their Separatist views, the first attempt at a departure for the more religiously tolerant Netherlands took place during the winter of 1607-8. The Scrooby Church members arrived in Boston where they had arranged their passage, only to find that the ship's master had betrayed them to the authorities. A number of them were imprisoned at Boston for a month before being sent home. However, the group had more success in the spring of 1608, with departure this time arranged via a Dutch ship from a deserted point on the Lincolnshire side of the Humber. The women and children made their way secretly by the river to the assigned place, whilst the menfolk walked overland. Strangely, the men boarded first, but spotting the approach of a large number of armed men, the Dutch captain panicked and set sail, leaving the women and children to be taken into custody in full sight of their anguished menfolk. After fourteen stormy days at sea, the men reached Holland. Thankfully, the women and children were just seen as an embarrassment to the authorities, and were passed from one magistrate to another until they were eventually allowed to leave for Holland to join their husbands. The Scrooby Church were then able to re-join the members of John Smyth's Gainsborough Church in Amsterdam, but division set in again, and the Scrooby Church re-established themselves as an independent church in Leydon in 1609. However, they still never felt that they fitted into the community there and so, ultimately, the majority of them set sail for the New World on *Mayflower* in 1620.

As for Scrooby Manor House, most of it was demolished in around 1636 along with its outbuildings on the order of Charles I, although by c.1750, part of a surviving wing of the manor house was renovated as a farmhouse for the Archbishop's tenant, and still survives today. Meanwhile, like the church pews and church font, the village stocks were also sold to America in the late 19th century, too!

Finally, just north of Scrooby, where the A638 meets the A614, is Gibbet Hill Lane. The road is so-named as it marks the location of the post-execution display of a certain John Spencer – not a snooker player, but a card player, as it happens! Spencer had been playing cards into the early hours of 3rd July 1779 with Scrooby's toll-bar keeper, William Yeadon, and his elderly mother. However, Spencer returned to the toll house later that night and brutally killed them both with a hedge stake, with robbery his main intention. Unfortunately for him, a group of travellers caught him in the act of dragging one body across the road towards the River Ryton, and he was arrested shortly afterwards by a search party. He was executed following a trial at Nottingham Assizes, and his body returned to the scene of his crime to be hung from a gibbet cage on what is now known as Gibbet Hill, with the hedge stake placed in his right hand. Astonishingly, the gibbet cage and its gruesome contents survived until 1846, when it finally collapsed!

The local pub sign depicting the Pilgrim Fathers embarking upon their long voyage to America on Mayflower *in 1620.*

Scrooby Quirk Alert: A Military Stink, A Tower of Trees and What's in a Name?

Following on from the gibbet cage story, a few weeks after its erection a group of soldiers were escorting a deserter when their sergeant fired at and hit the corpse. This caused such an overwhelming and lingering stench that the sergeant was court-martialled and demoted to private!

Up until 2010, the top of the tower of St Wilfrid's Church was a bizarre sight, with trees having taken root on all four sides, and clearly visible from below. Along with other plants and weeds, the trees were growing on the parapet where the square tower supports the octagonal spire. However, on the 26th June 2010, a small team of locals scaled the internal ladders of St Wilfrid's and removed the trees and foliage that had taken root in the stonework.

Finally, the aforementioned Pilgrim Father, William Brewster of Scrooby, had five children with his wife, Mary. Their first-born, Jonathan, born in 1593, clearly had a regular name. Their second child, a daughter called Patience fared slightly worse … but infinitely better than the last three children, a daughter and two sons called Fear Brewster, Love Brewster and Wrestling Brewster, respectively … the first two of whom sound like slogans, and the third of whom was perhaps destined to become a large father!

NAME (STATUS):	**SHERWOOD FOREST** (Forest)
DISTRICT:	Newark and Sherwood; Mansfield; Bassetlaw; Gedling
EARLIEST RECORD:	*Scirwuda*, 955
MEANING:	Wood belonging to the shire
DERIVATION:	From the Old English words *scīr* (shire) and *wudu* (wood or forest)
MODERN SIZE:	Today's Nature Reserve is 423.2 ha (a mere 1.7 square miles)
MEDIEVAL SIZE:	Some say a quarter of Nottinghamshire, which would be c.200 square miles, but 100,000 acres (156 square miles) is more regularly touted, and thus nearer to a fifth of the county

Sherwood Forest Geographic Trivia: Not What It Was

Sherwood Forest was once reputed to cover a quarter of Nottinghamshire, but today's focal point for the forest, Sherwood Forest National Nature Reserve, covers a mere 1.7 square miles – and even that was only doubled in size as recently as 2007 when Natural England officially incorporated the Budby South Forest. At the heart of the nature reserve is the Sherwood Forest Visitor Centre which can be found on the back doorstep of the village of Edwinstowe. Happily, some portions of the forest still retain a number of very old oaks – in fact, some of the oldest in Europe – while other golden oldies can be found in the area known as the Dukeries to the south of Worksop, so-called because it used to contain five ducal residences in close proximity to one another. Sherwood Forest is also home to the source of the River Idle which, in turn, is formed from the confluence of several other Sherwood-based watercourses.

Sherwood Forest: The Major Oak

Sherwood Forest is home to the famous Major Oak which weighs an estimated 23 tons, has a girth of 33 feet (10 metres) and its branches spread to over 92 feet (28 metres). There are a number of theories as to why it became so large and oddly shaped, the main one being that several trees fused together when they were

The Major Oak, Sherwood Forest. The plaque alongside it suggests that it may be as old as 1,150 years. Inset: *Perhaps we can call this one the Minor Oak? Certainly, it is an oak sapling that is located 100 yards or so from its more illustrious elder ... although is calling an oak an elder politically incorrect?*

saplings. Another suggests that the tree was pollarded, a system of tree management that enabled foresters to grow more than one crop of timber from a single tree, and which caused the trunk to grow large and thick.

Of course, the Major Oak's main claim to fame is that, according to local folklore, the tree was Robin Hood's principal hideout. The oak tree is certainly between 800 and 1,150 years old and, since the Victorian era, its large, ageing limbs have been partially supported by an elaborate scaffolding system. Presumably with its mortality in mind, a local company took cuttings from the Major Oak in February 1998 and began cultivating clones of the famous tree with the intention of sending saplings to be planted in major cities around the world. Then in 2003, a plantation in Dorset planted 260 saplings grown from Major Oak acorns, in a semi-scientific, semi-tourist-related project; the former recording photographic evidence, variation in size and leafing of the saplings, comparison of DNA, etc., and the latter delivering an eventual public amenity and tourist attraction.

As for the name of the tree, it was described in detail by Major Hayman Rooke (1723-1806) in 1790, and thereafter became known as the Major Oak. As for Major Rooke, he had become an antiquary after retiring from the army, and was a pioneer archaeologist in Nottinghamshire, unearthing major Roman finds at Mansfield Woodhouse and frequently contributing to archaeological journals, as well as writing in detail about his beloved Sherwood Forest.

Finally, the Major Oak was also featured on the 2005 BBC TV programme *Seven Natural Wonders* as one of the natural wonders of the Midlands, while in a 2002 survey, it was voted "Britain's favourite tree".

Sherwood Forest Tourism Trivia: Festivals and Fire-Eaters

Sherwood Forest attracts around 500,000 tourists annually, including many from other countries drawn by the world-famous legend of Robin Hood and his Merry Men. Each summer, the Sherwood Forest Visitor Centre at Edwinstowe hosts the annual, week-long Robin Hood Festival, which re-creates a medieval atmosphere and features all of the major characters from the Robin Hood legend. The week's entertainment includes jousters and strolling players, all dressed in medieval attire, while in its medieval encampment you will find jesters, medieval musicians, alchemists, fire eaters … and rat catchers!

Throughout the year, visitors are also attracted to the Sherwood Forest Art and Craft Centre, which is situated in the former Coach House and Stables of Edwinstowe Hall in the heart of the forest. The centre contains art studios and a cafe, and hosts special events, including craft demonstrations and exhibitions. Meanwhile, a couple of miles south of Edwinstowe is Sherwood Pines, another visitor centre, this time run by the Forestry Commission and offering walking, cycling, mountain biking and the mandatory Go Ape!

Sherwood Forest Historic Trivia: Kings, Hunting and Heritage

Today's Sherwood Forest is a remnant of an older and much larger royal hunting forest. Indeed, bordering the Forest of East Derbyshire to the west, the two forests covered a vast wooded area that stretched from the Trent to the Derwent – although it wasn't all woodlands; it was also comprised of open sandy heath and rough grassland. Meanwhile, it also contained three royal deer parks, at Nottingham Castle, at Bestwood and at Pittance Park, just south-west of Rufford Abbey. Of course, by this stage, Sherwood Forest was also a royal hunting forest, too, and was popular with many kings, particularly King John and Edward I, and the ruins of King John's hunting lodge can still be found near the village of Kings Clipstone. Severe forest laws were also imposed at this time by agisters, foresters, verderers and rangers, who were all employed by the Crown. It was also at this time that the Great North Way from London to York ran straight through Sherwood Forest, and travellers were often robbed here by outlaws – and hence certain famous legends! Still going strong in 1609, this year records 21,000 oaks in the area known as Birklands and 28,900 in Bilhaugh, both located just north of Edwinstowe.

Sherwood Forest supported several industries, such as charcoal burning and the stripping of oak bark to use in tanning leather, while it also became home to a

Statues of Robin Hood and Little John at the Sherwood Forest Visitor Centre.

Statues of Maid Marian and Robin Hood in Edwinstowe.

King John's Hunting Lodge, near Kings Clipstone.
Inset: *St Mary's church, Edwinstowe, where Robin Hood was rumoured to have married Maid Marian.*

number of monastic orders with large estates such as the abbeys at Newstead, Rufford, Thurgarton and Welbeck. Most of these suffered during Henry VIII's 1536 Dissolution of the Monasteries, and their land gradually found its way into private country house estates, with Thoresby and Wollaton added to the aforementioned and the estates collectively earning the title of the Dukeries. The forest continued to court royal interest, though, with James I a big fan of hunting in Sherwood – although his son, Charles I, was the last king to hunt there. However, by 1830, the last of the Crown's lands in Sherwood were sold, these being the aforementioned Bilhaugh and Birklands.

The location known as Birklands was designated as a Site of Special Scientific Interest (SSSI) in 1954, its selection based upon the fact that it represented the part of old Sherwood Forest still best maintaining its historical character and wildlife interest. Then 15 years later in 1969, the Sherwood Forest Country Park was born, initially only an 87 acre lease from the Thoresby Estate. During the next few years the site was developed to include footpaths, car parking facilities, a park ranger service, and a new Visitor Centre which opened in May 1976. By 1978, the park totalled 448 acres, and had been designated as a Grade I site for its ancient woodland and heathland in a Nature Conservation Review a year earlier, and then re-notified as an SSSI under the 1981 Wildlife and Countryside Act. In 2002, Sherwood was then designated as a National Nature Reserve (NNR), thanks to being home to over 1,000 ancient oaks, a unique mix of old wood and heathland, and providing shelter to some of Europe's rarest invertebrates.

Finally, Thynghowe, an important Danelaw meeting place where people came to resolve disputes and settle issues, was rediscovered in 2005-06 by local history enthusiasts amidst the old oaks of Birklands. Experts believe it may also yield clues as to the boundary of the ancient Anglo Saxon kingdoms of Mercia and Northumbria.

A statue of Robin Hood in Sherwood Forest.

Sherwood Forest Quirk Alert: A Corny Acorny Story

Earlier it was mentioned that in 1998, the Major Oak had been cloned with the intention of sending its saplings around the world. It was also around this time that a Mansfield resident was cautioned by the Nottinghamshire Police for selling alleged Major Oak acorns to unsuspecting Americans via a *branch* of an Internet-based mail-order company. The scam appeared to be legitimised by a certificate of authenticity, and it was months before any of the recipients *twigged*. Then, having taken a *leaf* out of the Mansfield resident's book, another news story broke on 1st October 2002 about someone illegally selling acorns from the Major Oak on an Internet-based auction website. The *seed* of the idea had clearly *stemmed* from the 1998 scam, but this time, although the police were able to narrow the scam down to a five mile section of the A46 *trunk* road, they were ultimately unable to get to the *root* of this particular crime. A local newspaper described the victims who had fallen for such a scam as *barking*, and thus felt little remorse at taking the *sap* out of them!

NAME (STATUS):	**THORNEY** (Village)
POPULATION:	248
DISTRICT:	Newark and Sherwood
EARLIEST RECORD:	*Torneshaie*, 1086 (Domesday Book)
MEANING:	Thorn-tree enclosure
DERIVATION:	From the Old English words *thorn* (thorn-tree) and *haga* (hedged enclosure)

Thorney Church: St Helen's

St Helen's church is a Grade II listed church that was built in 1850 by L. N. Cottingham, and who was rather cuttingly said to be "better known for his writing than his buildings". Pevsner certainly seems to agree, describing Thorney's church as "sumptuous ham-fisted Norman exterior, with west façade." Arthur Mee's Nottinghamshire volume of *The King's England* is more diplomatic, stating that its huge blocks of stone need "the mellowing touch", and that "we may imagine that the builders sought to make it a pictorial encyclopaedia of church ornamentation in Norman England". But anyway, for the record, it consists of a nave, chancel, vestry, and west turret with two hemispherical bells, while the carving both inside and outside is, as Mee describes, a pictorial Norman encyclopaedia! This is most in evidence on the west façade that Pevsner mentions. The Norman-style doorway alone has differently carved pillars, while its round arch accommodates almost every manner of Norman moulding, including cable, rope-work, dragon heads, heads of humans and animals, along with a hood with zigzag lines and wheels ending in crowned heads! Then above the doorway are three lancet windows and above that a wheel-window. However, if you look up, it is the stringcourse that grabs your attention with rings and chip carving, and which is terminated at each corner with a projecting dragon's head with a curled tongue; there are 17 in all around the stringcourse. Finally, that west façade is topped off by a striking bell turret which is matched by another elaborate turret that rises above the junction of nave and chancel.

Of course, the 1850 version of St Helen's replaced an earlier church and which was described by Throsby in 1797 as having "a low brick tower with two bells, a nave and side aisle". A number of ruins remain, including two 15th century arcades that were reconstructed in the churchyard, and a number of fragments of carved stones.

Remains of the original St Helen's church.

Thorney Historic (and Quirky) Trivia: Repeat Caravanning Anglers

Not exactly ancient history, but the quiet and secluded Lakeside Touring Caravan Park was created at Thorney in the 20th century and is a flat, landscaped grass site located in 15 acres of private land with wooded and open areas. The site contains two well-stocked lakes *(top right)* full of carp, tench, bream, chub, roach and rudd. Apparently, these are easily caught using traditional methods and with ideal bait such as bread, paste, maggots, sweetcorn … and luncheon meat! Those poor fish, though; probably caught dozens of time a year, and probably by the same people, too. There's a funny sketch in there somewhere. Something along the lines of the fish, as it's hauled out of the lake for the fifth time that day, catching the eye-line of the angler, cocking its head to one side and saying, "Seriously?"

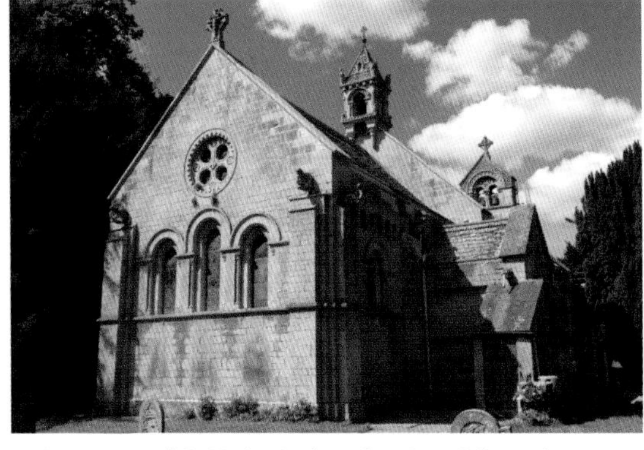

The 1850 version of St Helen's church, viewed from the east.

Name (Status):	**THRUMPTON** (Village, Suburb)
Population:	165 (Village); c.200 (Suburb)
District:	Rushcliffe (Village); Bassetlaw (Suburb)
Earliest Record:	*Turmodestun*, 1086 (Domesday Book); relates to the village, only
Meaning:	Farmstead or village of a man called Thormóthr
Derivation:	From the Old Scandinavian personal name *Thormóthr*, plus the Old English word *tūn* (farmstead).
Famous Residents:	**Miranda Seymour** (b.1948), literary critic, author and biographer

Thrumpton Geographical Trivia: Pugh, Pugh!

So, those of you who know your 1970s' children's TV *might* be on the same wavelength! Anyway, unusual though the place-name is, there are actually *two* Thrumpton's in Nottinghamshire, while the inclusion of the place-name in the Shire-Ode was a play on words based on the Trumpton series of the 1970s … which always started with the drill-call for the firemen of the imaginary village of Trumpton … starting with Pugh, Pugh – one for each Nottinghamshire Thrumpton, perhaps? OK, fair enough; *no one* is on this wavelength … so suffice to say, that there is a very pretty village called Thrumpton down in south-west Nottinghamshire alongside the River Trent, and there is also an area of south-east Retford called Thrumpton as well – almost diametrically opposite in the north-east of the county. I wonder if Barney McGrew still lives there…

The Elms Hotel, Thrumpton, Retford.

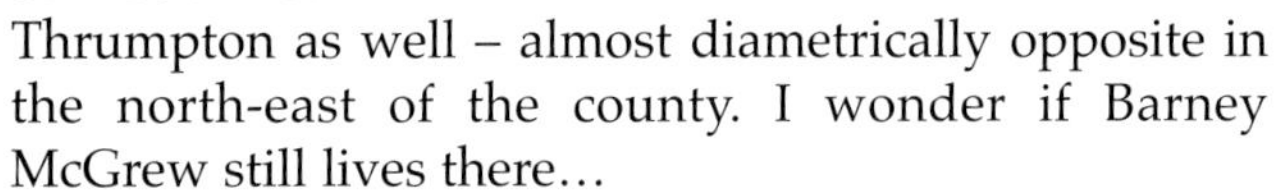

Thrumpton Pub: Elms Hotel

The Elms Hotel is located in the Bassetlaw Thrumpton (the Rushcliffe Thrumpton doesn't have a pub). It is located on the A638, or London Road as it is known in Retford, and is set so far back from the road in its own grounds that it looks more like a manor house than a pub.

Thrumpton Church: All Saints

The Grade II listed All Saints' church dates from the 13th century, but was restored in 1871. In 1870 restoration work to the church was carried out for Lucy, Lady Byron by the acclaimed Victorian architect G E Street. The chancel was rebuilt and the nave restored but the tower remained unaltered. In 2004 the tower was subject to significant repair and restoration work.

Thrumpton Historic Trivia: Thrumpton Hall

Many of the gabled brick houses in the village were built between 1700 and 1745 by John Emerton (1685-1745) of Thrumpton Hall. However, the village is dominated by the earlier Thrumpton Hall itself, with the main part of the Hall dating from the early 17th century, and built by the Pigot family in rose-coloured brick. That said, the Hall also incorporates substantial parts of an older 16th century house which was occupied by the Roman Catholic Powdrill family. However, the Powdrills were evicted following the failed Babington Plot of 1586 – a plot to assassinate Queen Elizabeth I and put Mary Queen of Scots onto the English throne, and which was concocted by a group led by Sir Anthony Babington of Dethick in Derbyshire, and who was also owner of Thrumpton's neighbouring Kingston on Soar estate. Thrumpton Hall subsequently came into the possession of the Pigot family in 1605, and the

All Saints' church, Thrumpton, Rushcliffe.

Houses and post box along Church Lane, Thrumpton, Rushcliffe.

hall was altered and improved by Gervase Pigot in the 1660s in an attempt to turn it into a spectacular show-piece. He removed much of the old interior, in order to create a magnificent cantilever staircase carved in wood from the estate, and an exquisite double-cube reception room overlooking his formal garden. However, ambition ruined the Pigots, and in 1685, the house was taken over by their lawyer, a Mr Emerton, to whom the Pigots had been unable to keep up mortgage payments. Further alterations were made in the late 18th century by John Wescomb Emerton (owner from 1745 to 1823) and around 1830 by John Emerton Wescomb (owner from 1823 to 1838). This latter Emerton – said to be the most handsome man in Nottinghamshire – spent £70,000 on house and land transformation, including the creation of a beautiful lake in front of the house. The pavilion which now stands to the west of the house, looks towards John Emerton's lake; beyond it, lies the celebrated 350 acre park which he and his descendants landscaped and planted with rare specimen trees, including several magnificent Lebanon cedars.

In 1838, Thrumpton Hall was inherited by John Emerton's 16 year old niece, Lucy, whose marriage to George Byron, the 8th Baron Byron in 1843, brought the Hall under the ownership of the famous Byrons. The Byrons then owned Thrumpton Hall for around a hundred years, and *the* Lord Byron's daughter (*the* being the 6th Baron and famous poet), Ada Lovelace, was known to have regularly visited her relations at the Hall from her mother's home at Kirkby Mallory. Meanwhile, Frederick Byron, 10th Baron Byron, owned Thrumpton Hall from 1917 to 1949. However, although the 10th Baron Byron married Lady Anna FitzRoy – she being a direct descendant of King Charles II – they didn't produce any heirs. The manor was therefore inherited by George Fitzroy Seymour in 1949, the son of Lady Anna's sister. So when George died in 1994, the Hall was inherited by his daughter, Miranda Seymour, who also happens to be a celebrated literary critic, author and biographer. Her biographies include the lives of Ottoline Morrell, Mary Shelley, Robert Graves (about whom she also wrote a novel, *The Telling* and a radio play, *Sea Music*) and a group portrait of Henry James during his later years (*A Ring of Conspirators*). Then in 2004, Miranda published a highly acclaimed book about Hellé Nice, a French Grand Prix racing driver from the 1930s. Her next book, in 2008, was all about her Thrumpton home and was entitled *In My Father's House: Elegy for an Obsessive Love* and which was also published in the US as *Thrumpton Hall*. The book won the 2008 Pen Ackerley Prize for Memoir of the Year. Bringing her literary achievements up-to-date, 2013 saw the publishing of *Noble Endeavours: Stories from England; Stories from Germany*, which is all about the life of a charismatic 1930s film star called Virginia Cherrill.

Thrumpton Quirk Alert: Squarson Byron

We've already mentioned that the Byrons owned Thrumpton Hall for around a hundred years, and one of them, Frederick Byron, 10th Baron Byron, was Lord of the Manor from 1917 to 1949. However, he had also become the local vicar of All Saints' church in 1914 … which means that three years later when he inherited the Hall, he became a member of that rare club known as "squarsons" – on account of the fact that he was both squire and parson at the same time!

The entrance to Thrumpton Hall at Thrumpton, Rushcliffe. Inset: *Manor Farm, Thrumpton, Rushcliffe.*

Direction to the River Trent at Collingham

NAME (STATUS): **TRENT** (River)
NOTTS DISTRICT(S): Rushcliffe, City of Nottingham, Gedling, Newark and Sherwood, Bassetlaw
FULL LENGTH: 185 miles
SOURCE: Biddulph Moor, Staffordshire
SOURCE ELEVATION: 902ft
MOUTH: Trent Falls, Humber Estuary, Lincolnshire
MOUTH ELEVATION: 0ft
MEANING: Unknown, but possibly "strongly flooding" or perhaps "the trespasser", meaning liable to flood the land.
DERIVATION: The derivation is certainly Celtic. A theory is that it is taken from a contraction of two Celtic words, *tros* and *hynt*, meaning "over" and "way", respectively. A more likely explanation is that it was considered to be a river that could be crossed principally by means of fords, courtesy of a number of place-names along the Trent bearing the name *rid*, and thus possibly derived from the Welsh word *rhyd*, meaning "ford". Yet another offering is that the name derives from the Romano-British *Trisantona*, meaning "great feminine thoroughfare". Finally, Izaak Walton claims in his 1653 classic *The Compleat Angler* that the Trent is named after the thirty types of fish found in it!

River Trent Geographic Trivia: From Thrumpton to Heckdyke

Having been sourced many miles away near Biddulph Moor on the Staffordshire moorlands, the River Trent enters Nottinghamshire from Derbyshire immediately after Trent Lock, where the Trent is joined by the Erewash Canal from the north and the River Soar from the south. The Trent then forms the border between Derbyshire and Nottinghamshire for around three miles, passing Thrumpton and Barton in Fabis on the Nottinghamshire side, after which it moves fully into Nottinghamshire, passing to the east of the nature reserve at Attenborough and then past Beeston. It then enters the City of Nottingham via Clifton and then Wilford, where it is joined by the River Leen, after which it enters its most photographed section around the Victoria Embankment where it flows to the north of West Bridgford before passing under Trent Bridge near the cricket ground of the same name, and beside Nottingham Forest's City Ground.

The Trent then exits Nottingham in an easterly direction beyond Colwick, passing alongside the National Watersport Centre at Holme Pierrepont before taking another north-easterly turn at Radcliffe on Trent. It then passes alongside Stoke Bardolph and Burton Joyce before reaching Gunthorpe with its bridge, lock and weir. Still heading north-east, Toot Hill and the Trent Hills pass on the eastern side before the Trent does a loop back on itself at Fiskerton, briefly heading south-east before looping round to the north-east again and towards Farndon. To the north of Farndon, beside the Staythorpe Power Station the river splits, with one arm passing Averham and Kelham, and the other arm, which is navigable, being joined by the River Devon before passing through the market town of Newark-on-Trent and beneath the town's castle walls. The two arms then re-join at Crankley Point to the north of Newark, before splitting the villages of North Muskham and Holme after which it reaches Cromwell and Cromwell Weir, below which the Trent finally becomes tidal.

The now tidal river, meanders across a wide flood-plain, at the edge of which are located riverside villages, first Carlton-on-Trent, then Sutton on Trent, then Low and High Marnham on the west bank, and Besthorpe, Girton, South and North Clifton on the east bank. Immediately north of North Clifton, the Trent then begins a run of around 15 miles where it marks the border between Nottinghamshire and Lincolnshire, while a mile into the run, the Trent reaches the only toll bridge along its course at Dunham on Trent. Downstream of Dunham the river passes Church Laneham and then does some major meandering, doubling back on itself twice before reaching Torksey, where it meets the Foss Dyke Navigation Canal which connects the Trent to Lincoln and the River Witham. A little further north, the Trent passes Littleborough, site of the former Roman town of *Segelocum*, where the Roman road known as Till Bridge Lane once crossed the river.

Now you may not have been counting, but the Trent by this stage has passed alongside around a dozen of the Shire Ode places, and in its last few miles in Nottinghamshire, it flows within a mile or so of Coates, Bole and Beckingham, too, the latter of which faces the Lincolnshire town of Gainsborough on the eastern bank, which has its own Trent Bridge. Downstream of Gainsborough, the Trent marks the last few miles of the Nottinghamshire border, passing Walkerith and West and East Stockwith which is also where the River Idle joins the Trent. The last village in Nottinghamshire that the Trent passes is Heckdyke, after which it flows solely into Lincolnshire, ultimately arriving at Trent Falls

The River Trent at Nottingham.

The River Trent at Newark.

where it joins the River Ouse to form the River Humber which then flows into the North Sea.

As for the Trent's catchment area – also known as the Trent Basin – unsurprisingly, this covers all of Nottinghamshire as well as pretty much all of Derbyshire, Staffordshire, Leicestershire and the West Midlands, plus parts of Lincolnshire, Rutland, South Yorkshire and Warwickshire. Its terrain therefore runs from one extreme – i.e. the Derbyshire uplands of the High Peak – to the other extreme – i.e. the fenlands of Lincolnshire and northern Nottinghamshire, as well as pretty much everything else in between. The Trent Basin also includes many large urban areas with the majority lying in the upper reaches of either the Trent itself – as is the case with Stoke – or its tributaries, such as Birmingham (upper reaches of the Tame) and Leicester (upper reaches of the Soar). The result, though, is a considerable amount of "urban runoff", thus leading to deterioration of the water quality of the Trent.

As a lowland river, the Trent is vulnerable to long periods of rainfall, leading to a water-logged catchment, and with so many feeder systems, Nottingham is vulnerable sitting as it does a considerable way down the Trent's course. Widespread flooding occurred in Nottingham in February 1977, when heavy rain produced a peak flow of nearly 1,000 cubic metres per second, and again in November 2000 when similar conditions applied. During the latter period, I was working in Beeston and at lunch-times, I used to go running alongside the Beeston Canal, and which is separated from the Trent by around half a mile of meadows, sports fields and the occasional building. I cannot ever remember an equivalent visual impact to the one I got when approaching the canal one lunchtime in November 2000. We become naturally accustomed to expecting a scene of normality – a sea of green fields in this particular case. But although I was aware there had been some "extensive flooding", nothing prepared me for this shocking sight. Basically, the entire half-mile stretch, from the Beeston Canal to the Trent, was under water. And not a small amount either. Only the top of the sports centre was visible, as were just the very tops of full-sized football goalposts, while whole caravans had completely disappeared!

River Trent: Different Courses

Around 1.7 million years ago during the Pleistocene epoch, the source of the River Trent was somewhere in the Welsh hills. It still made its way generally eastwards to Nottingham, but once east of Nottingham, instead of heading in a north-easterly direction to Newark and then north to the Humber, it flowed eastwards through the Vale of Belvoir to cut a gap through the limestone ridge at Ancaster, now known as the Ancaster Gap. From here it flowed to the coast and out into the North Sea. However, around 130,000 years ago a mass of stagnant ice left in the Vale of Belvoir caused the river to divert north along the old Lincoln River, and this time through the Lincoln Gap. Then in a subsequent glaciation around 70,000 BC, what is today known as the lower Trent basin was home to vast areas of water known as Glacial Lake Humber. The "lake" was kept in check by a glacier, and when this retreated, the Trent adopted its current, northern-bound course – making it fairly unusual amongst English rivers, the majority of which flow in the other three directions courtesy of the country having mainly west, south and east coasts!

River Trent Historic Trivia: Floods, Ferries and Fords

Flooding caused by the Trent has been well-documented for centuries, and certainly since 1852, significant flood levels have been carved into a bridge abutment next to Trent Bridge in Nottingham. Flood marks have also been added to it from its medieval predecessor bridge, so we know that the river rose to a height of 80.5ft in February 1795, to 80ft in October 1875, to 79.7ft in March 1947 and to 79.6ft in November 1852, while the aforementioned flood of 2000 only rose to 78.1ft; that said, the average height is 68ft! Clearly the largest of these floods was the 1795 one, known as the Candlemas Flood. It was caused by a harsh winter followed by a rapid thaw which triggered the record-breaking flood which either badly damaged or washed away every bridge in Nottinghamshire. In Nottingham,

The River Trent at Cromwell Lock. The weir shown here marks the point where the Trent ceases to be tidal, while the lock system to the right allows boats to continue downstream.

River Trent flood levels recorded on the church wall at Collingham.

residents of Narrow Marsh were trapped by the flood-waters in their first floor rooms, while 72 sheep drowned at Wilford and ten cows were lost in Bridgford. However, one of the earliest recorded floods along the Trent occurred much earlier in 1141, and was caused by a large snow-melt following heavy rainfall. This caused a breach in the outer flood-bank at Spalford, and which only failed when flows were greater than 35,000 cubic feet/sec; the bank was also breached in 1403 and, significantly, 1795! Then, a little later in 1309, many bridges were recorded as being washed away or damaged by severe winter floods, including Nottingham's Hethbeth Bridge, while its replacement was also partially destroyed in 1683 by a flood that also took the medieval bridge at Newark.

As for the second largest recorded flood, in October 1875, six people were drowned in Wilford Road, Nottingham, following the overturning of a cart, while nearby houses were flooded to a depth of 6ft. In Newark the water was deep enough to allow people to row across the countryside to Kelham while the 1875 flood mark at Girton is only 4 inches lower than the 1795 mark, when the village was flooded to a depth of 3ft. Meanwhile, the 1947 flood saw the banks over-topped in Nottingham and large parts of the city inundated, along with surrounding areas at Long Eaton, Beeston and West Bridgford. This event led to the construction of flood defences in the 1950s to prevent major urban flooding in Nottingham, and they just about held for the November 2000 flood – although they have been subsequently improved, as it was a close call! However, further afield, undefended areas such as those at Gunthorpe and poor Girton again were badly affected.

The River Trent upstream and downstream at Dunham-on-Trent.

Prior to the mid-18th century there were only four bridges over the Trent downstream of the confluence with the River Tame: at Burton, Swarkestone, Nottingham and Newark. However, there were over thirty ferries that operated along its course as well as numerous fords, such as those at Bridgford, Littleborough and Wilford. The ford at Littleborough actually dated back to Roman times, and was discovered during the drought of 1933. It was dated to the time of Hadrian (117-138) and was constructed with paved flagstones, supported by substantial timber pilings. Of course, the fording points for all of these crossings only allowed passage across the river when water levels were low. At other times, ferries were used and as they were a source of income, most of them were recorded in the Domesday Book, such as that at Fiskerton, and which was still in operation in the middle of the 20th century. The ferry boats used along the Trent ranged in size from small rowing boats all the way up to flat decked craft that could carry livestock, horses, carts or wagons. Over time, though, the delays incurred by ferry crossing led to a demand for bridges, such as those at Gunthorpe and at today's crossover points from Nottinghamshire to Lincolnshire on the A631 and A57, where the ferry was replaced by a toll bridge. By the end of the 19th century, many of these toll bridges had been bought out by the new county councils.

River Trent Quirk Alert: A Bit of a Bore and the North-South Divide

Along with the River Severn, the River Trent is the only other English river that exhibits a tidal bore. Known as the Trent Aegir, it takes its name from the Norse god of the ocean. And talking of Scandinavian's, the Aegir was also rumoured to be the scene of King Canute's legendary tide-turning feat. As for the bore itself, it can rise by up to five feet (1.5m) and so when a good spring tide meets the downstream flow of the river, the Aegir can easily reach the north-eastern boundary of Nottinghamshire, and it is regularly spotted at East and West Stockwith.

One commonly held belief is that the North-South divide of England runs roughly along the route of the A46. However, other schools of thought define the Trent as the boundary between Northern England and Southern England. For example the administration of Royal Forests was subject to a different Justice in Eyre (the highest magistrates in forest law) north and south of the river. Similarly, the jurisdiction of the medieval Council of the North (a northern administrative body originally set up in 1484 by Richard III) also started at the Trent. Then there were the former subdivisions of Oxford University, dividing folk up into a "Northern Nation" (English folk from north of the Trent plus the Scots) and a "Southern Nation" (English folk south of the Trent, the Welsh and the Irish). And on top of that, a bygone phrase "born north of the Trent", apparently used to be quite common in order to convey that someone came from the North of England! As for that medieval Council of the North, it is thought that Henry Hotspur, in order to seize more land in around 1593, actually investigated the possibility of diverting the Trent back onto its original, pre-glacial course, thus giving him the eastern portion of Nottinghamshire and most of Lincolnshire, too!

The marina at West Stockwith, where both the River Idle and the Chesterfield Canal join the River Trent, just before the Trent exits Nottinghamshire.

NAME (STATUS):	**TROWELL** (Village)
POPULATION:	2,378
DISTRICT:	Broxtowe
EARLIEST RECORD:	*Trowalle*, 1086 (Domesday Book)
MEANING:	Tree stream – perhaps referring to a tree-trunk used as a bridge
DERIVATION:	From the Old English words *trēow* (tree) and *wella* (spring or stream)

Trowell Geographic Trivia: Divided

Trowell is unusual in that it is bisected by the M1 with the Festival Inn, the church and the village hall lying to the north, and further houses and Trowell Garden Centre to the south. Trowell Service Station between junctions 25 and 26 of the M1 is also named after the village, and actually appeared in an episode of the second series of *Auf Wiedersehen, Pet*, where the characters discuss who they would be in *The Magnificent Seven*.

Trowell Pub: The Festival Inn

Trowell's only pub is The Festival Inn on Ilkeston Road. It was built in 1951 to commemorate Trowell's selection by Herbert Morrison, Deputy Prime Minister, as the "Festival Village" for the 1951 Festival of Britain (more on that shortly). Much of the pub's original character was lost when it underwent a major refurbishment in the mid-1990s. However, this refurbishment, along with a reputation for good live music, actually led to the pub becoming known as one of the most popular and profitable in the East Midlands.

The Festival Inn, Trowell.

Trowell Church: St Helen's

St Helen's church is Grade II listed and dates from the 13th century. However, there are references to an earlier Saxon church here in the *Annals of York Minster*, where it is stated that "*An application was made by the Lord of the Manor in Trowell, for a Church to be established, at the request of the people*". That permission was granted in 801, meaning that St Helen's has been the site of a church for at least 1200 years! As for the Saxon church, no traces remain today but it is thought that its foundations still exist under the present chancel – although that is extremely old, too, dating from 1180 and built in typical Early English style. But the Saxon church was certainly still around when Domesday Book was recorded in 1086, as it mentions a priest, six acres of meadow and "half a church" – although this latter reference is to the fact that Trowell's church was shared with the parish of Cossall; in fact, the Rectors of Trowell received half the tithes of Cossall until 1787.

Also contemporary with the 1180 chancel are the piscina (a small niche to hold a bowl of water where the priest washed his hands during communion), the credence (another small niche with a shelf to hold the communion bread and wine), and the sedilia (a group of three seats in which the clergy would sit during communion). The 14th century then saw the addition of the octagonal font, the porch, the nave and side aisles, and the arcade of three arches each side of the nave, while the clerestory was added in the 15th century along with the tower – the latter having been completed in 1480. As for the *outer* walls of the aisles, they are of interest since the square-headed windows are only found in parts of Nottinghamshire and Derbyshire.

Funded by Lord Middleton, St Helen's was restored in 1836 by Charles Hodgson Fowler, with further restoration carried out in 1890 including new roofs for

St Helen's church, Trowell, with the 1180-built chancel nearside.

An original footbridge over the Nottingham Canal (built 1793-95) at Trowell. The structure is now Grade II listed.

both chancel and nave. Further restoration commenced in 1956, focusing on replacing some of the outside face of the nave and the tower walls with Derbyshire gritstone. Finally, from 1480 to 1792 there were only three bells in the tower of St Helen's church, but in 1792 six bells were cast and fitted by Taylors of Loughborough. They must have done a good job, for 139 years later in 1931, Taylor's were selected to re-cast the bells!

Trowell Historic Trivia: A Second Mediety and The Festival of Britain

The patronage of Trowell Benefice was held by William Peverel from the time of the Norman Conquest until 1241, when the Convent of Sempringham took over. The Crown then took control from 1550 to 1588, after which the Willoughby family purchased the patronage. However, this patronage was known as the First Mediety – because from 1259, St Helen's church came under two patrons when the Brinsley family applied for a dispensation to hold an additional Benefice – and thus two patrons and two rectors. The Brinsley half became known as the Second Mediety and was eventually purchased by the Hacker family in 1602. The First Mediety remained with the Willoughby family until 1724 when Lord Middleton became Patron, with the two halves eventually re-united in 1787 when a later Lord Middleton became Patron of the whole church.

As already stated in the *Trowell Pub* section, Herbert Morrison, Deputy Prime Minister, selected Trowell as the "Festival Village" for the 1951 Festival of Britain – allegedly as a typical example of British rural life. However, his "research" was purely based on the fact that Trowell was located close to the geographical centre of England. Of course, the reality was that Trowell was not of the quintessentially English chocolate-box design that he might have hoped for. Indeed, without a village green, with all three pubs closed and overshadowed by the belching chimneys and slag heaps of Stanton ironworks to the west of the village, the big man had somewhat gaffed, and thus found himself fielding hostile questions in the House of Commons. An archetypal politician, though, Morrison responded with the pitch that Trowell was *"the type of English village where the old rural life is passing away and where an industrial community has been superimposed"*, and that it was *"chosen merely as an example of modern social problems in a village"*, and that its selection would *"encourage places which are not conventionally beautiful ... to have a go at improving their amenities"*.

An obelisk commemorating Trowell's selection in 1951 as the Festival Village as part of The Festival of Britain. In the background is Trowell Parish Hall where the impetus for this book was given a significant boost in 2009!

Trowell Quirk Alert: Merrie England and Arnold's Daughter!

Returning for a third time to Trowell being Britain's "Festival Village" in 1951, the inhabitants celebrated their selection with several events. These included a cricket match played in Victorian dress, awards for the best back and front gardens, a performance of Sir Edward German's comic opera *Merrie England* ... and cleaning the church clock!

Trowell, however, will always be special to me. For it was around five years ago that I entered an "international" competition run by the Trowell and District Writers (one of the winners was from Canada, I'll have you know), with a certain composition called *Arnold's Daughter*. There are four categories each year for Best Article, Best Short Story and Best Poem, while the most original piece goes onto win the Vambria Walters Memorial Trophy. Happily, *Arnold's Daughter* won the Vambria award, a success which gave me the impetus to develop the concept of a Shire-Ode and ultimately the *Unusual and Quirky* series. The evening was also a very humbling experience, too. The Trowell and District Writers is run by the loveliest family who, naturally, had a number of entries into the other event of the night – a Stand and Deliver poetry competition. By far the best for me was by Arthur Walters, a dapper gentleman wearing a nice bow tie, and who read out a beautiful poem in memory of his wife – who happened to be Vambria Walters, the former leader of the writing group. It was deeply touching to watch Arthur just about made it through his delivery, and then wipe his tears away with his handkerchief. Thank you so much, Trowell Writers.

The Trowell & District Writers award winners, 2009. That's me on the front row holding the Vambria Walters Memorial Trophy, while second right, middle row, is Arthur Walters who earlier in the evening delivered a moving poem to his late wife, Vambria.

Photograph by Peter Jordan.

NAME (STATUS):	**UPTON** (Village *2)
POPULATION:	425 (Upton [Newark]); 253 (Headon cum Upton [Bassetlaw])
DISTRICT:	Newark and Sherwood; Bassetlaw
MEANING:	Higher farmstead or village
DERIVATION:	From the Old English words *upp* (higher up) and *tūn* (enclosure, farmstead, village, manor or estate)
FAMOUS RESIDENTS:	**James Tennant** (1808-1881), Professor of Mineralogy at King's College London, and mineralogist to Queen Victoria

The Cross Keys, Upton (Newark) – the only pub in the two Nottinghamshire Uptons!

St Peter and St Paul's church, Upton (Newark).

Upton Geographical Trivia: Two's Upton!

From herein, the two Uptons in Nottinghamshire will be referred to as Upton (Newark) and Upton (Bassetlaw) – although the church at the latter which is shared with its neighbouring village of Headon is known as St Peter's of Headon cum Upton! Location-wise, though, Upton (Newark) is situated around two miles east of Southwell, while Upton (Bassetlaw) is located around four miles to the south-east of Retford.

Upton Church: St Peter and St Paul; St Peter's

The church of St Peter and St Paul at Upton (Newark) is a Grade I listed building which possesses a substantial 15th century Perpendicular tower that is crowned by eight pinnacles clustered around a central pinnacle, earning the feature the moniker of the Nine Disciples. The tower is also rare in that it is home to a priest's room with a fireplace while, externally, it has holes for doves, making it one of very few tower dovecotes in the country. Inside, the nave arcades, the chancel arch and the small arch between the aisle and transept are all 13th century, while the six foot chest that is adorned with iron bands and stars with tiny roses and trefoils is thought to be contemporary with them. The church was restored in 1820, 1867 and finally in 1893 by local architect Charles Hodgson Fowler. See the *Headon* section for more on St Peter's church.

Upton Historic Trivia: Upton Hall

Upton Hall was built in 1828 in Upton (Newark) on the site of a former manor house, by Nottinghamshire banker Thomas Wright (1773-1845). Later, in 1895, the hall was purchased by John Warwick, a brewer of the Newark-based firm Warwick & Richardson, and he added a ballroom, a billiards room, and six additional bedrooms. In 1936 the property was bought by Sir Albert Ball, Lord Mayor of Nottingham, and the father of the famous World War I pilot Captain Albert Ball (see *Lenton* section for more on him), although Albert Ball Senior never actually lived there. Nevertheless, by 1952, the hall had been declared a listed building, but it was another 20 years before it was acquired by its current owners, the British Horological Institute, who promptly made it their headquarters and it has remained so ever since. The hall now includes a library and a museum, as well as a substantial collection of antique long-case clocks, owned by the institute.

Upton Hall, built in 1828, and now home to the British Horological Society.

The centre of Headon cum Upton.

Village emblem in Headon cum Upton.

Upton Quirk Alert: Loud and Clear

In the church of St Peter and St Paul, are some fragments of two earthen jars. Apparently, in centuries gone by, these were used to help amplify the voice of the vicar during his sermon, and were thus amongst the first ever loudspeakers used!

Sculpture outside the British Horological Society's HQ at Upton Hall, in Upton (Newark).

Bibliography

Books

John Beckett, *A Centenary History of Nottingham* (Phillimore & Co. Ltd, 2006)
David Kaye, *A History of Nottinghamshire* (Phillimore & Co. Ltd, 1987)
Arthur Mee, *The King's England: Nottinghamshire* (Hodder & Stoughton, 1970)
A.D. Mills, *Oxford Dictionary of British Place Names* (Oxford University Press, 1991)

Pamphlets and Guides

Chesterfield Canal Visitor Guide, Chesterfield Canal Trust
Creswell Crags Guide
Newark Civil War Trail, Sherwood District Council
Newstead Abbey, Nottingham City Council
Nottingham Castle, Nottingham City Council
Rufford Abbey Country Park, Nottinghamshire County Council
Scrooby Village Guide
Sherwood Forest Visitor Centre, Nottinghamshire County Council

Key Websites

http://www.airfieldinformationexchange.org
http://www.alcazarbrewery.co.uk
http://www.bbc.co.uk/archive/mining/6927.shtml
http://www.blackburn-house.co.uk/history
http://www.blackpigborder.co.uk
http://www.britishlistedbuildings.co.uk
http://www.bunnyvillage.org.uk
http://www.colstonbassetthistory.org.uk
http://www.experiencenottinghamshire.com
http://www.felleypriory.co.uk
http://forrest-feeds.co.uk
http://www.gothamhistory.org.uk
http://gothamvillage.org.uk
http://www.highfieldsgroup.co.uk
http://www.hucknalltorkardhistory.co.uk
http://www.information-britain.co.uk
http://www.lentontimes.co.uk
http://www.ljacksonandco.com
http://www.microflight.co.uk
http://www.murphyandson.co.uk
http://www.nottingham.ac.uk
http://www.nottinghampost.com
http://www.nottinghamshirewildlife.org
http://www.nottsheritagegateway.org.uk
http://nottshistoricchurchtrust.org.uk
http://www.nottshistory.org.uk
http://www.perkins-family.co.uk
http://rainworthvillage.webs.com
http://www.rattlejagmorris.org.uk
http://www.robinhood.org.uk
http://www.scrooby.net
http://www.southwellchurches.nottingham.ac.uk
http://www.stapleford-notts.co.uk
http://www.thrumpton.org.uk
http://www.vinasdolls.co.uk
http://www.waysidewatergardens.co.uk
http://en.wikipedia.org